MW00611131

The Witch's Feast

A Kitchen Grimoire

The Witch's feast
A Kitchen Grimoire

MELISSA JAYNE MADARA

NOURISH

EAT WELL, LIVE WELL

To my mother, my grandest support, whose love of storytelling is why I write.
To Paul, my love, my satyr, my best friend.
To my beloved, hardworking assistants, Damien and Lucy.
And to all of my good friends at The Waffle House.

The Witch's Feast
Melissa Jayne Madara

First published in the UK and USA in 2021 by
Nourish, an imprint of Watkins Media Limited
Unit 11, Shepperton House, 83–93 Shepperton Road
London N1 3DF

enquiries@nourishbooks.com

Copyright © Watkins Media Limited 2021
Text and recipes copyright © Melissa Madara 2021
Photography copyright © Frances F. Denny 2021
Illustrations: shutterstock.com 2021

The right of Melissa Jayne Madara to be identified
as the Author of this text has been asserted in
accordance with the Copyright, Designs and Patents
Act of 1988.

All rights reserved. No part of this book may be
reproduced in any form or by any electronic or
mechanical means, including information storage
and retrieval systems, without permission in writing
from the publisher, except by a reviewer who may
quote brief passages in a review.

Managing Editor: Ella Chappell
Editor: Rebecca Woods
Proofreader: Sarah Epton
Art Director: Glen Wilkins
Senior Designer: Karen Smith
Production: Uzma Taj
Commissioned photography: Frances F. Denny
Prop Stylist: Brita Olsen

A CIP record for this book is available from the
British Library

ISBN: 978-1-84899-403-4 (Hardback)
ISBN: 978-1-84899-407-2 (eBook)

10 9 8 7 6 5 4 3 2 1

Typeset in Amador, Aleo and Gotham
Printed in China

Publisher's note
While every care has been taken in compiling the recipes for this book, Watkins Media Limited, or any other persons who have been involved in working on this publication, cannot accept responsibility for any errors or omissions, inadvertent or not, that may be found in the recipes or text, nor for any problems that may arise as a result of preparing one of these recipes. If you are pregnant or breastfeeding or have any special dietary requirements or medical conditions, it is advisable to consult a medical professional before following any of the recipes contained in this book. Some activities in this book, for example those involving burning incense or cutting tools, may be dangerous if instructions are not followed precisely. Always follow manufacturer's instructions when using tools. Wild foods such as berries can be poisonous, so eat only what you can identify as safe. When foraging, it is likely that you will be trying food that you have never eaten before. Therefore, and especially if you are prone to allergies, try just a little first, as you would with any food. The material contained in this book is set out in good faith for general guidance and no liability can be accepted for loss or expense incurred in relying on the information given. In particular this book is not intended to replace expert medical advice. This book is for informational purposes only and is for your own personal use and guidance. It is not intended to diagnose, treat, or act as a substitute for professional medical advice. Watkins Media Limited, or any other persons involved in working on this publication, cannot accept responsibility for any injury, illness or damages that result from participating in the activities in this book.

Notes on the recipes
Unless otherwise stated:
Use medium fruit and vegetables
Use medium (US large) organic or free-range eggs
Use fresh herbs, spices and chillies
Use granulated sugar (Americans can use ordinary granulated sugar when caster sugar is specified)
Do not mix metric, imperial and US cup measurements:
   1 tsp = 5ml 1 tbsp = 15ml 1 cup = 240ml

nourishbooks.com

Contents

©Frances F. Denny

ABOUT THE AUTHOR

Melissa Jayne Madara is a witch, herbalist, chef and storyteller. They are a co-owner at Catland Books, Brooklyn's favorite little witch shop, where they serve as an educator and curator of Catland's courtyard garden. Melissa is also the editrix of *Venefica Magazine*, an arts and occult journal based in NYC. Their work as a witch has been featured in the *New York Times*, *Vice*, *Broadly*, *Teen Vogue* and *Refinery 29*, and their writing on magic has been published in *Fiddler's Green Peculiar Parish Magazine* and *Susie Magazine*.

As an occultist, Melissa's practice is largely concerned with the ancient religions of Eastern Europe and the Mediterranean coast, divination, herbal magic, and work with poisonous plants. Their research deals primarily in plant folklore, mythology, and historical formularies, with a particular interest paid to culinary recipes and fragrance. As an herbalist, their work with incense, perfume and tinctures can be found under Melissa's apothecary brand, Moon Cult Herbs. Melissa's culinary work began in traditional French pastry, but they are best known for hosting ritual dinners and full moon feasts at Catland Books and beyond.

Playing with Fire

ood, like magic, was an art I taught myself. It was something I fell into heart first, drawn deeper into its depths by a yearning to understand that which lured me in – the compelling force of aroma and flavour, both seductive and immediate in the way they grab the attention. I've always had a keen interest in chemistry and science as methods for understanding the invisible world – the unseen, microscopic machinations of reality, which are hidden from all experience and yet influence every aspect of our entire lives. From the very beginning, cooking captivated me in this way, offering an opportunity for tactile engagement with the mysteries of chemical flux and the transformative power of fire – avenues of exploration which are too often denied to young femmes like myself. But more than the metamorphic possibility of transforming ingredients into delicious dishes, it was the playful and somatic nature of cooking that placed my early practice on the powerful, liminal ground between science, magic and art. Cooking became my artistic medium of choice, as a creative practice wherein food and feast became things experienced with both the hands and the heart, visibly and invisibly, taking place both inside and outside the body. In many ways, this wandering, exploratory trajectory of my work in the kitchen and my work as a witch are both marked by that same, nonlinear journey of feeling and creating, guided always by intuition, curiosity and a sensual engagement with the world.

And it can certainly be said, with a little poetic licence, that the two disciplines of magic and cooking share some things in common. Both practices possess an air of secrecy, never revealing their techniques too readily, and requiring great practice to fully understand. Both are deeply seductive, calling the adept deeper and deeper, and tempting the wise with a bottomless well of possible knowledge and experience. Both require study, practice, diligence, faith and a willingness to experiment – offering pathways to either greatness or disaster. But most of all, both cooking and magic require an understanding of subtle worlds and nonverbal communication – a symbolic language that exists beneath the conscious mind. You read the chocolate or the sauce for opportune moments the same way you read a scrying bowl, and you learn to communicate with chemistry the way you communicate with spirits in the same mysterious, nonverbal fashion. In this way, these disciplines probe the occulted world – the one which is felt rather than thought, and guided by the unknowable machinations of the senses and soul.

While history can certainly attest to this mystical link between magic and food, there is often considerable overlap between discussions of culinary witchcraft and apothecary science, such that there is little room to consider kitchen magic in itself. There is, of course, much to be said about the way food and herbs can influence the body in miraculous ways, and so much has already been written on this perspective of kitchen witchcraft. Here, in a herbalist's view of kitchen magic, the practitioner is a healer-by-food, positioned as both magician and doctor – somewhere between faith and science, where magic truly lies. However, we find that when we remove herbal healing and green witchcraft from contemporary discussions of culinary magic, a blankness emerges. Unlike other magical traditions, and even non-religious practices like breathwork and trance, kitchen witchcraft lacks an overt heritage to draw from, with no traditional tools or frameworks readily apparent. This is not surprising, as the vein of kitchen magic lies so close to the mundane world, where its history is often obscured by the forgotten everydayness of domestic duty. Nevertheless, there do exist some fine and exquisite threads of culinary magic woven throughout history, beginning in the far ancient past and stretching forward to the present. Perhaps, through deliberately tracing these scraps and tatters, we can come to know the shape and form of this important work.

For these reasons, *The Witch's Feast* was created not to provide a complete praxis of kitchen magic or witchcraft in general, but to investigate what the nature of this work might be. Certainly other texts abound which can instruct on the philosophical and spiritual frameworks necessary for practising magic in existing traditions. However, this experimental tome, which charts a delicate path through still-ambiguous waters, is intended as one perspective or application along the crooked path, and one method by which we may begin to consider kitchen witchcraft in itself. It extends an invitation to play with fire, both figuratively and literally, and through this playful investigation explore what power and potency kitchen witchcraft may offer us today.

With regard to the perspective of *The Witch's Feast*, it is only natural that this text take the shape of my personal practice, beliefs and research. My work as a witch is greatly informed by the praxis of chaos magic, but my research is mostly into ancient religions along the Mediterranean Sea (where my ancestral Croatia is located), along with plant folklore, mythology and herbalism. Because of the nature of my personal work, you will find that this book focuses heavily on the history and magic of European traditions. Certainly, this narrow angle cannot represent magic at large, especially when you consider witchcraft as a global experience. It is, however, my personal area of interest and research from which I am prepared to share what I know.

For readers approaching magic and witchcraft for the first time through *The Witch's Feast*, you may examine within these pages a number of different tools and techniques which gesture toward the various ideas of what witchcraft is or could be. It is one portal through which to view a complex and dynamic whole, which rebels against definition by its very nature. For witches who arrive at this text seeking to expand their practice into the kitchen, you should find the following chapters relatable and customizable to all paths, traditions and perspectives. While the precise nature and customs of kitchen magic remain elusive, this book presents an areligious framework, and it's your beliefs and devotional relationships that will inform how these tools are integrated into practice.

Before we begin, there are a few useful tools and techniques which will help the reader take full advantage of all that *The*

Witch's Feast has to offer. These skills are not necessary to cook through this book, but will be instrumental in fully exploring rituals ahead. Armed with these simple tips and instructions, the wise may proceed safely and confidently into the unknown world that is kitchen witchcraft.

Foraging

As this is a magical cookbook, you will find that some of the ingredients we will be working with require us to stray slightly from the beaten path. Herbs and wild foods will feature prominently within these pages, and in some cases you may choose to forage for your ingredients in order to find them fresh. Despite being an important source of food for our ancestors, this practice of foraging is a lost art today, as humans further and further evict themselves from the natural world. However, with a little education and understanding, this can be yet another tool under your belt to bring magic and abundance into your kitchen witchcraft practice. With that said, here are three tips that I use to forage more safely within my neighbourhood:

1 ALWAYS USE THREE POINTS OF IDENTIFICATION

When you first learn to identify plants, it can be really exciting to start making positive identifications in the field. However, plants are crafty little shapeshifters and can sometimes look very similar to their toxic, poisonous cousins. For this reason and so many others, it's important to use at least three known facts about the plant you're searching for to make a positive identification. Being able to recognize a trademark leaf shape, flower colour or fragrance often does the trick. We can also consider the plant's native bioregion, natural growing season or even plant type

(tree, shrub, cactus, taproot, etc) as useful ways to make our ID. This method helps us stay safe when we forage, and keeps us mindful of what details distinguish edible plants from their dangerous doppelgangers. Never, ever ingest any plants that you are even slightly unsure of. And consult other herbalists or foragers in your area for more detailed information on what botanical allies grow near you.

2 ALWAYS FORAGE A SAFE DISTANCE FROM HUMAN ACTIVITY

Unfortunately, human interactions with the natural world are not always positive. Humans have a bad habit of leaving our garbage around in nature – sometimes in ways that are very hard to detect. In the case of soil toxicity – caused by land development, industrial runoff, rain pollution, pesticides and car exhaust – extremely fine but toxic particles can become absorbed into the bodies of plants – among them lead, cadmium, arsenic and asbestos. When eaten by humans, these plants can transfer their poisons and heavy metals to us. To stay mindful of this ecological impact, it is important as a general rule to harvest your plants at least 15 metres (50 feet) away from any man-made structure, especially buildings, roads, train tracks or places where humans walk their pets. For this reason, protected wild lands, such as state and national parks or private wilderness, are perfect places to begin your foraging practice, as they are far removed from most human sources of toxicity. If you prefer to stay close to home but are concerned about the soil in your neighbourhood, local universities will sometimes offer to test it for you to determine whether or not these areas are safe for foraging.

3 NEVER HARVEST MORE THAN A QUARTER OF WHAT YOU SEE

When you're out in nature, it's so important to be mindful of our effect upon the landscape, and to remember that we are likely not the only creatures to use this space. As foraging has become more and more trendy, we see places that were once overrun with wild foods become vacant lots where plants have been severely over-harvested. This creates problems not only for the humans who lose their access to the plants, but also the animals and natural cycles which relied upon their presence. As such, it's important to always leave the vast majority of what we find in nature, so that the birds, squirrels, foxes and chipmunks can have their due share as well. This bit of mindfulness will protect the land we harvest from, and ensure future harvests as well.

Hopefully, these simple tips will provide a useful framework for going forth and foraging in your local environment. If you have never foraged or learned to identify the plants in your bioregion, consider this your invitation to explore! This kind of intimate, inter-reliant relationship with our local flora is useful not only to the chef, but to the witch as well. If you choose to venture into the wild, you may find that some of the common herbs mentioned in this book, like mugwort, rose hips or dandelion, can be found just outside your front door.

Magical inks

The practice of hand-blending your own magical ink is a tradition that extends deep into the ancient world, where certain herbs like myrrh and saffron were used as pigments specifically for ritual work. Making these inks at home can be extremely simple, even if you're not necessarily crafty. In magic, making your own ink has a twofold benefit: you can infuse your inks with botanical allies that are useful to your work, and you can ensure that your inks are nontoxic and safe to ingest. This latter point is especially important in kitchen witchcraft, as several recipes in the coming chapters will mention sigils, inscribed leaves or other markings that are meant to interact with our food. Having a fully customizable, food-safe alternative to store-bought inks and markers is an essential step in moving forward through this book.

To make your own magical inks at home, you will need high-proof neutral grain alcohol (150 proof or higher) and powdered arabic gum. You will also need to select the nontoxic, botanical pigments of your choice, which will be used to infuse your ink with colour. For black or deep red inks, consider myrrh, alkanet, beetroot, black tea or black walnut hulls. For yellow or orange inks, try saffron, goldenrod, ivy stems, barberry, eucalyptus or paprika. For blue or green inks, reach for butterfly pea, cornflower, indigo, chamomile or coneflower. These can be steeped fresh or dry into your alcohol until all of the pigment is infused. You will want the infusion to be much darker and bolder than the ink should appear on paper. Feel free to test the pigment on a strip of paper after one week and continue the infusion or add more plant material if you'd like to go bolder. When your infusion is perfect, remove a small 30ml (1fl oz) quantity of the liquid, strain it and add small scoops of powdered arabic gum, stirring until fully dissolved. Continue adding more powder until the ink reaches a workable viscosity, where it can be carried by a quill or paintbrush. Store your inks in an opaque, airtight vessel to prevent evaporation, and use whenever necessary, in kitchen magic or elsewhere.

Incense

Several entries in the coming chapters will, in addition to recipe ingredients, include brief lists of herbs for making a fumigation or incense blend. If you've never made your own incense before, this is an exciting, sensuous practice that can be easily prepared at home. These hand-blended fumigations will differ significantly from store-bought incense sticks and will require the use of a small charcoal to burn. These charcoals can typically be found at most new age or spiritual supply shops, or anywhere that resin incense is sold.

To make your fumigation, begin by selecting your botanical ingredients. Here, we will be using incense resin (frankincense, myrrh, etc), as well as dried flowers, leaves, roots, barks and any other fragrant plant material you like. I like to select at least one resin, one delicate herb (flowers, leaves, stamens) and one dense herb (roots, barks, seeds) for each of my blends. Measuring by weight, your blend should contain 70 per cent resin, 20 per cent dense herbs and 10 per cent delicate herbs. For a 30g (1oz) batch, this would be 21g resin, 6g dense herbs, and 3g delicate herbs. I know this ratio may sound very skewed, but resin is much heavier and denser than the other ingredients and is also the most important component in making sure the incense burns properly. For example, if dry herbs are placed on a burning coal, they will singe and char very quickly, releasing an acrid, burnt-smelling smoke. When resin is added, which melts at the touch of heat, the charring process slows, allowing the blend to smoulder instead of burning and release a long-lasting, fragrant smoke. For those without a kitchen scale at home, conversion tables found online can help you convert grams or ounces to tablespoons – just be sure to search for each ingredient individually, as they all have different weights.

Once each ingredient is measured, they can be ground using a mortar and pestle or spice grinder. I prefer to keep my blends at a coarse grind, like freshly cracked pepper, so that they burn a bit more slowly. In a mixing bowl, combine your herbs first, then add a small quantity of plain carrier oil (grapeseed or coconut oils are perfect here) until the mixture is the consistency of wet sand and just barely moist – about 1–2 tablespoons of oil for 240ml (8fl oz/1 cup) volume of incense mix. Then, add your ground resin, stirring until the entire blend is evenly mixed. If you'd like to add any essential oils, you may do so here, but their fragrance does not burn well on charcoal and quickly loses strength. You may choose to finish your mix here and your incense can be stored in an airtight jar for 1 month to fully cure before using (trust me, the fragrance will be worth the wait!). For a more traditional finish, add powdered arabic gum, 10 per cent by weight, along with a few tablespoons of water, which can be mixed with the incense to form a dry dough. This dough can be rolled into 1cm (½in) incense "pearls", which will dry at room temperature for 2 weeks and then are ready to use. These pearls are incredibly attractive and make it easy to store your incense in perfect, individual portions for every ritual.

As with any fumigation, it's best to burn these outdoors or in a room with windows open and good ventilation. Consider the examples on the opposite page or try your hand at some of the fumigations given alongside recipes within this book.

Full Moon Incense

100g (3½oz) frankincense resin
30g (1oz) orris root
15g (½oz) dried clary sage
2 camphor crystals (optional)
½ teaspoon powdered pearl (optional)

New Moon Incense

100g (3½oz) myrrh resin
30g (1oz) poppy seeds
15g (½oz) dried mugwort
½ teaspoon dried mushroom (optional)
½ teaspoon Irish moss (optional)

Feast of the Ancestors

Traditional feasts, recipes and rituals of witches past

Feast of the Ancestors

rchaeologists estimate that humans began to feast together about 12,000 years ago, just around the end of the Stone Age. Still a few thousand years before the dawn of agriculture, humans were not yet linked to one another in complex societies or trade relationships. Yet as global populations swelled and humans began to encounter one another more frequently, the advantages of working together with one's neighbours began to transform early societies. Humans found it was more advantageous to hunt wild game in large groups, increasing the frequency of successful hunts and creating surpluses of nutritionally dense food. These surpluses transformed early societies, raising healthier people who lived longer and cementing the bonds between them which made such collaborations possible.

These groups of individuals, bound together by their agreement to share the work of food production, formed the basis for early societies – especially as humans began to take up the agricultural tools of the Neolithic age. The demands of planting and harvest schedules, as well as the work of cooking and preserving food, created even more incentive for early humans to stick together. However, these complex processes relied upon considerable cooperation between humans, and began to bring up questions of collective action in these early communities: how do you convince a group of loosely banded individuals to come together and work toward their collective goals? As it turns out, food and feast were likely significant motivators.

During this time, humans began to demonstrate mastery over the natural world in other regards as well – fermenting fruits into wine, grinding wild grains to make bread, and perfecting preservation techniques in order to stockpile food for the future. Humans, who had only been eating wild foods as hunter-gatherers until this point, were transformed physically and culturally by this new surplus of food, and organized these first societies around the work of cooking and sharing together. This trend toward communal sharing provided a twofold benefit to early societies – it helped to control the food supply and also created a medium for social engagement. For example, an archaeological excavation in 2010 uncovered the remains of a grand funerary feast in northern Israel, estimated to be from 10,000 BCE, making it one of the earliest examples of organized feasting among humans. At this site, researchers uncovered the remains of 75 tortoises and three wild cattle – evidence of an abundant feast which would have fed up to 35 people, likely representing weeks of preparation and the work of several hunters. This great effort speaks not only to the elegant organization of these early societies, but also to the kinship between these people, who undertook the task of preparing this great funeral for the sake of sharing their collective grief. And so while this trend toward the consolidation of work demonstrates the organization of early human communities, it is in their ritualized feasting where we can see the pinnacle of their advancement, existing as expressions of both their great intellect and love.

But if food and feast are central rituals of the human experience, they run parallel to another of humanity's oldest traditions

– storytelling. These early feast tables were not just a place to share resources, but also to share stories, and through story, to reframe the human identity as it began to assimilate into the collective. What did it mean to be a human being within a society and to share one's life so intimately with others? Around these early feast tables, that collective identity began to coalesce, and feasting became one of the primary modalities of social connection and communal responsibility. These early societies began to hold regular feasts to celebrate religious holidays, the funerals of beloved elders, and other events of great collective import around which the community revolved. These feasts became expressions of civility and human identity, held as part of the narrative of who we are, what we value and what it meant to be alive in these first societies.

As the story of our collective identity took shape, we began to tell similar stories about our gods and goddesses as well. In the religions of these early societies, humans began to depict their deities engaged in cosmic feasts, joining their human worshippers in a shared love of luxurious meals and special-occasion parties. In Sumerian religion, the gods drank oceans of beer and were offered entire sacrificial feasts in the belief that they ate as humans did. In ancient Greece, the Olympians dined on nectar and ambrosia, carried to their holy feast table on the backs of doves. In ancient Egypt, the goddess Hathor could be placated with feasting and drunkenness, revelling in the same ecstatic decadence as her devotees. In sharing the ritual of feast with their divinities, these ancient humans created a new story, one which separated themselves from the rest of the animals to join the gods as "the ones who feast". These primary rituals thus informed the cosmology of early peoples, allowing them to step out of the wandering existence of the Stone Age and take their place at the feast table in a new world of civility and community which was, in every sense, wholly human.

It is important to examine these early origins of feasting and gathering, because they present us with the image of the grand feast as one of humanity's oldest rituals, responsible for binding us together in the first human civilizations. Every great work of human collaboration since – monuments, governments, empires and cities – can be attributed to these early gatherings, where humans connected with one another over the shared goal of survival. When we consider what remnants of these feasts are left for us to examine – prehistoric feast tables, piles of bones and layers of soot on cave floors that detail decades of gathering and sharing around fires – we realize how little has changed about these early feast rituals, despite how different our societies look today. Drawn together by those same ancient motivations, this ritual persists as modern people continue to reap the benefits of shared food production and gather in feast as their ancestors did. From this simple ritual, which many of us take for granted as a part of our daily lives, the echoes of the early human past call out to us with a message that feels familiar even now – "We ate and we survived. We ate and we lived."

In the following pages, we will explore a history of the ritual feast, through recipes that consider various expressions of feasting throughout the ages. Because our book takes the perspective of the witch, these recipes will focus on feasts of high spiritual importance – dishes which mark religious holidays, employ magical symbols and represent moments when the mystical intersects with the material world, with the feast table acting as the magic circle and nexus between these spheres. This is not to say that the following chapter presents a cohesive body of "kitchen witchcraft" – if such a thing exists, it does so in very fine threads woven through larger traditions, often hidden too close to the mundane to be considered magical work outright. While some of those threads will be examined here, our task is to consider these recipes as part of a larger question: what does this lineage of ritual feasting have to say about the relationship between food and magic, and what can these ancestor-chefs of our distant past tell us about kitchen witchcraft?

The Feast of the Ancestors begins in the most distant past, examining recipes from the earliest human civilizations. We begin, as all humanity did, in ancient Mesopotamia, the cradle of the first human cities, where the Babylonian culinary tablets were produced almost 4,000 years ago. These tablets, which constitute the oldest human cookbook, reveal a landscape of flavour and texture foreign to the modern palate. These recipes feature mostly roasts and stews, favouring one-pot, family-style meals that cook slowly, developing rich flavours from humble ingredients, like leeks, pigeons and wild herbs. In this chapter, a faithful reproduction of one of these recipes connects the present to the past, revealing a mysterious, yet tangible aspect of what it meant to be alive in ancient Babylon at the dawn of human civilization.

Next, we look ahead some 2,000 years to the culinary traditions of ancient Rome, where we encounter one of the most distinctive and ostentatious feasting cultures humanity has ever known. The Roman Empire is often regarded as the peak of western civilization in the ancient world, and their feast tables were considered to be the fullest expression of their civility. Here, simple dishes and family-style meals are replaced with exotic ingredients and complex course processions, favouring feasts which highlight the aesthetics of the dining experience. Guests at these feasts were not merely satisfied with being fed, but expected to be wowed and challenged, with the host vying to deliver the most elaborate and provocative feasts of all. While the recipes in this segment are not wholly traditional to ancient Roman cuisine, they are inspired by this flair for the dramatic and present a meditation on the decadence and sensuality of these ancient pagan feasts.

In contrast to the Babylonian recipe, the Roman feast presents an inversion of earlier feasting practices, where the feast is no longer an opportunity to build community, but instead is used by the upper classes to reinforce social stratification and competition. However, when considered side by side, these two sets of recipes provide a similar value to modern chef-witches in that they act as portals to the feast cultures of our culinary ancestors – a sort of edible time-travel to the distant past. These recipes reveal a great deal about the role of the ritual feast within these early permutations and provide useful meditations for us as we trace the lineage of feast-as-ritual from the ancient world into the future.

This chapter continues with a discussion of five specific holiday feasts, featuring a selection of recipes that spans the European continent, from spiritual traditions both living and dead. If there is a place where we may hope to find those numinous threads of an existing "kitchen witchcraft" tradition, it is in these devotional meals, where we can consider the applications of culinary magic in action. These recipes operate almost entirely within the vehicle of sacrifice and were used to affect various ends, from supplicating deities, to allegorically representing the change of seasons, to ensuring practical survival for the year ahead. From the ancient Greek tradition, we examine a particularly fascinating recipe for sacrificial offering cakes, or pharmakos cakes, as well as traditional meals for two important religious holidays – the feast of Fornacalia and Hekate's Deipnon. These are accompanied by selections from two other spiritual traditions, both still very much alive and widely practised today. From Scotland, we receive the Michaelmas struan, a mixed-cereal bread baked as a bid for

protection on the Catholic feast of St Michael the Archangel. Finally, we head west to Russia and encounter the crepes of Maslenitsa, the "butter lady" or "butter witch", who is burned in effigy at her spring festival to herald winter's wane.

Considered as one body of work, this selection of recipes demonstrates one possible avenue of investigation for "traditional" culinary magic, where the ritual of feast allows us to break bread with gods, and even secure their blessings through our sacrificial culinary efforts. This kind of magic is reminiscent of those early depictions of cosmic dining, suggesting that the ritual of feast is valuable to gods and men alike. The threads of this ancient belief echo up from the past into modern interpretations of witchcraft – particularly as animistic notions of "feeding" our intangible allies. Thus the sharing of sustenance becomes a vehicle for communion between the mundane and supermundane, with the feast table creating a liminal, temporary space for the two worlds to engage.

From here, the Feast of the Ancestors continues by looking at three specific recipes from occult authors, whose work is useful to consider as part of a discussion of what constitutes "kitchen witchcraft". While these recipes are not necessarily magical ones, they represent the role of food in the lives of three accomplished occultists, whose work both in and out of the kitchen is still relevant to practitioners today. This segment considers works from the 11th century astrological grimoire the *Picatrix*, as well as St Hildegard von Bingen and Aleister Crowley. These three documents come from vastly different worlds: the *Picatrix* is attributed to Maslama ibn Ahmad al-Majriti, an Andalusian astrologer, chemist and mathematician; St Hildegard was a visionary polymath and Benedictine abbess in 12th-century Germany; and Aleister Crowley was an incredibly prominent ceremonial magician from *fin-de-siècle* England, most famous for founding the Thelemic tradition. However, this unique selection of their writings gives us a rare view into the mundane lives of these influential practitioners, and calls us to consider the role of food and feast rituals within the context of their other, more mystical, works.

Finally, two more recipes are offered within this chapter, which represent extrapolations of some traditional feast folklore, interpreted through a modern witchcraft lens. For this, we trace two mysterious traditions – the use of the SATOR word square and the practice of the Silent Supper – both of which arise from murky, dubious origins and appear in a variety of permutations throughout history. These ghostly threads of folklore feel almost incomplete, in that not enough is known about the origins of either to give concrete instructions for their use or application.

However, these recipes fasten to the tatters of what is known and use this limit as a jumping-off point for further exploration, leaping into the void between tradition and experimentation. It is in this spirit that our first chapter concludes, raising many more questions about the origin and tradition of kitchen witchcraft than it answers.

Our ancestors are not just those that we can name or whose blood we share in our veins. As chefs and kitchen witches, we share a tutelary lineage with cooks throughout the ages, all called to our vocation by a shared passion for food and feast. It feels right, then, to begin our feast of the ancestors by seeking out the root of this tradition and travelling backward in time to explore the feast tables of the ancient world.

While the research and writing here cannot provide a formal or organized tradition for us to follow, it does present us with a glimpse of what kitchen witchcraft could be. The goal of this chapter is not to instruct, but to generate curiosity about the facets of history which hint at a hidden lineage of occulted culinary arts, bridging the gap between the spiritual and the mundane with one of humanity's oldest rituals. If no such tradition readily exists today, then it is the role of modern witches to tread into the valley between the known and the unknown and discern the shape of this magic for ourselves. As you navigate the following pages, consider the lives of witches and mystics long gone who continue to communicate with us through these recipes, and let their work inform your practice as you venture out from the edge of tradition and into the magical unknown.

☰ Roast Chicken with Babylonian Spices ☰

In the early 20th century, a profound discovery shed new light on culinary traditions from the oldest civilizations. Several clay tablets were found, inscribed in Akkadian with recipes, dated to the Old Babylonian period, from around 1700 BCE. The tablets, first translated in 1995 and housed at Yale University, are humanity's oldest written recipes. They offer a glimpse at the food of the ancient world, and prove that the ancient Mesopotamians possessed a mastery of culinary arts more complex than we imagined.

This is a reconstruction of recipe two of tablet 8958 ("*amursânu* pigeon with broth"), inspired by the work of culinary historian Laura Kelley. There have been many adaptations of the recipes. This contribution uses traditional ingredients of the region and stays true to the procedure, with some creativity to fill the gaps. Ancient cooking methods may feel exotic, so move carefully through the steps, as some may not be intuitive. The result should be an exploration of the flavours and textures created by our culinary ancestors, left to us 3,700 years ago. This recipe was intended for pigeon, but I have adapted it for chicken. If you prefer a smaller bird, substitute the chicken with a pigeon or game hen and halve the other ingredients.

Serves 4
Prep time: 20 minutes
Cook time: 60 minutes

FOR THE CHICKEN

* A whole chicken, salted inside and out, giblets reserved
* 2 tablespoons butter
* 1 tablespoon coriander seeds
* 1 teaspoon cumin seeds
* 1 teaspoon fennel seeds
* 60g (2oz) rocket (arugula), chopped
* A pinch of ground asafoetida
* 1 cinnamon stick
* 2 tablespoons dried mint
* 455ml (16fl oz/2 cups) chicken stock
* 120ml (4fl oz/½ cup) pomegranate or red wine vinegar, plus 3 tablespoons for rubbing
* 4 large cloves garlic
* 1 small leek, washed and chopped
* ½ yellow onion, cubed in 2.5cm (½ in) pieces
* 125g (4½ oz) whole-fat Greek yogurt
* 4 tablespoons semolina
* Salt and black pepper

FOR THE SPICE RUB

* 60g (2oz) fresh mint leaves
* 60g (2oz) fresh sage leaves
* 1 teaspoon olive oil

1 Preheat your oven to 200°C/400°F/Gas 6. Begin by butterflying your chicken, removing the backbone and cracking the breastbone so the bird lies flat on its back.

2 Heat your butter in a large saucepan over a high flame and sear the giblets. Add your seeds, toasting them, followed by your rocket, asafoetida, cinnamon and dried mint. Cook for a minute until fragrant. Add the stock to the pan to deglaze, then add the vinegar. Bring to a boil, then add your chicken. Add a little more water if necessary to submerge the bird totally, then return to boil for 5 minutes.

3 In a mortar and pestle or food processor, mash your garlic, leek and onion together until finely chopped but not puréed. Stir into your yogurt and set aside.

4 Reduce to a gentle simmer and remove the giblets from the broth. Temper your yogurt mixture into the broth by stirring a few tablespoons of hot broth into the yogurt, then adding the mixture to the pot. Keep the pot at a gentle simmer for 15 minutes, stirring occasionally and monitoring the heat to keep the yogurt from splitting.

5 Remove your chicken from the pot, pat dry, and allow to cool. Keep the broth at a simmer, stirring frequently, cooking uncovered so it can reduce. Whisk in the semolina to thicken and keep the heat low. Season with salt and pepper to taste. When the sauce is thickened, remove from the heat.

6 In the mortar and pestle or food processor, make the herb rub by grinding your fresh mint and sage with the oil and 1 tablespoon water, seasoning with salt. Place your chicken breast-side-up in a roasting pan and rub generously with the 3 tablespoons vinegar, and then with the herb mixture. Roast for 10 minutes, then rotate your pan and finish by roasting for another 10–15 minutes, or until the chicken is cooked through.

7 Allow the chicken to rest for 5 minutes, then serve with the sauce and simple whole grains. As you eat, explore the surprising flavours and textures that differ from the modern palate. Offer thanks for this unique knowledge from the past and consider how lucky we are to receive this gift from its mysterious Mesopotamian author.

Pharmakos Cakes

In classical antiquity, purgative rites of cleansing held significant weight. If malady should enter the community – disease, pestilence, violence, abnormality – the response took the form of an appeal to the gods, through sacrifice. While the ancient Greeks are well known for their use of animals in sacrifice, this sacrificial purification is reputed to have included humans offered as scapegoats for the malady at hand, called the *pharmakos*, a word that means "scapegoat". While it is debated whether or not these human sacrifices were literal or symbolic, the poet Hipponax describes the *pharmakos* rite in his writings from the late 6th century BCE.

In his writing, Hipponax suggests that the *pharmakos* ritual was carried out to placate the wrath of the gods, and to purify a city after the gods' holy anger brought forth famine, pestilence or plague. In the ritual, an outcast from the community – criminals, people with disabilities or, according to Hipponax, even those who were just exceptionally ugly – was selected to be publicly humiliated and burned in sacrifice. This sacrifice transferred the ills of the city into the one accursed individual, who embodied all that was wrong or ill within the community. The sacrifice would be placed upon the pyre holding figs, barley cakes and cheese as offerings, and burned upon the wood of wild trees before their ashers were scattered to the winds and to the sea.

This fate is brutal, but was thankfully believed to be an uncommon, perhaps even mythical, practice. Sacrificial animals were expensive and difficult to come by in the ancient world – even more so for human sacrifices. Thus, many ancient Greeks created sacrificial animals in representation, in the form of cakes shaped as the offering. These *pharmakos* cakes are bloodless alternatives, containing ingredients that were highly prized – wine-soaked figs, rich cheese, sweet honey.

While there are many sacrificial cake recipes from the ancient world, ours draws upon the style of the *phthois* cakes, a type that would have been offered and eaten in the temples of Apollo, Artemis, Hekate, Selene, Demeter and Kronos (Saturn). Consider these as an addition to your sacrificial and cleansing rites, particularly for those in Hellenic traditions, or any time when a bloodless sacrifice is appropriate.

Makes 12 cakes
Prep time: 20 minutes, plus 30 minutes chilling
Cook time: 40 minutes

* 60g (2oz/½ cup) dried figs, diced
* 120ml (4fl oz/½ cup) white wine
* 312g (11oz/2½ cups) wholewheat, spelt or barley flour, plus extra for dusting
* 3 tablespoons granulated sugar, plus extra for sprinkling
* 8 tablespoons unsalted butter, cut into 5mm (¼in) cubes and frozen
* 55g (2oz) soft goat's cheese, chilled and crumbled
* 1 teaspoon salt
* 120ml (4fl oz/½ cup) double (heavy) cream, chilled, plus extra for brushing
* 8 tablespoons honey
* Black pepper

I Preheat your oven to 190°C/375°F/Gas 5 and line a baking sheet with baking parchment. In a small bowl, soak the chopped dried figs in the white wine.

2 In a large bowl, combine the flour and sugar. Using a pastry cutter or your hands, work the frozen butter into the flour mixture until it resembles wet sand and fingers pressed into the mixture leave an imprint.

3 Drain your figs well, reserving the wine, and gently toss these into your flour mixture, along with your chilled goat's cheese cubes, the salt, and some black pepper to taste.

4 In a separate bowl, whisk together the cream and honey, then slowly pour these into the flour mixture, working just until a firm dough forms. Wrap the dough in clingfilm (plastic wrap) and allow to rest in the refrigerator for at least 30 minutes.

5 On a floured surface, roll out your dough to a 1.5cm (½in) thickness. Using a floured cookie cutter, either circular or in the shape of your sacrificial animal, cut out your cakes and place them onto the prepared baking sheet. Brush these gently with cream and sprinkle them with sugar.

6 Bake for 35–40 minutes, or until the cakes are golden and come away easily from the parchment, feeling fully dry to the touch underneath.

Recreating a Pagan Feast

Recreating a Pagan Feast

Many historians and philosophers have meditated on the pagan feasts of the Roman Empire. From surviving writings, it's clear that these events were spectacles of indulgence and debauchery, full of customs and traditions that would make modern diners cringe. These endless, extravagant banquets lasted hours and epitomized the wastefulness and love of high glamour that characterized the Roman ruling class. Dishes were elaborate and pungent, with most Roman cooking favouring a fusion of sweet and savoury flavours. Romans also placed emphasis on aesthetics, and thus planned their dishes to be both delicious and visually engaging. Game meats, fermented fish guts and even exotic curiosities like parrot tongue stew created potent aromas in dining halls, where guests reclined on sofas during dinner and were encouraged to vomit between courses to create room for more. These events were seen as the ultimate expression of civility, culture and *joie de vivre*, even if they were only reserved for the elite. In fact, feasts were used as status symbols among the higher classes, with hosts competing against one another to deliver ever more extravagant, shocking and awe-inspiring experiences to their guests.

Because they conjure such marvellous images, these banquets have been a source of fascination and intrigue since the fall of the Roman Empire. Luckily, many Roman writers have left us detailed accounts of these banquets, and even surviving recipes to draw from in planning our own pagan feasts. Of the recipes in this offering, the most traditional will be the *moretum* – a simple but flavourful spread of fresh cheese and herbs to be eaten with salad and unleavened bread. This would have been served in the *gustatio*, the appetizer course of a Roman banquet, though traditional feasts in Ancient Rome would have begun with eggs before all else. The other recipes in this feast draw on the popular ingredients and flavour profiles of ancient Roman cuisine, exploring some unique pairings that should still inspire awe at feast tables today. To make your own banquet even more authentic, serve your meal in repose, drinking wine mixed with water to stave off drunkenness, and savour each bite slowly over good conversation as the evening stretches on. When you have lost track of the time and feasted your senses to fullness, you'll be dining like a true ancient Roman.

Serves 4

Prep time: 40 minutes, plus overnight marinating and 4 hours chilling

Cook time: 1 hour

FOR THE MORETUM AND HERB SALAD

* 3 tablespoons chopped fresh parsley
* 3 tablespoons chopped fresh mint
* 2 tablespoons chopped fresh coriander (cilantro)
* 2 tablespoons chopped fresh savory
* 1 tablespoon fresh thyme leaves
* 1 teaspoon chopped fresh rue (optional)
* 3 chives, finely chopped
* 4 tablespoons olive oil, plus more for drizzling

* 225g (8oz/1 cup) fresh ricotta cheese
* Zest and juice of ½ lemon
* Salt and pepper
* Pita breads, to serve

FOR THE LAMB

* A 2.25kg (5lb) lamb loin
* 1 tablespoon olive oil
* 4 cloves garlic, minced
* 240ml (8fl oz/1 cup) whole milk
* 85g (3oz/⅓ cup) honey, plus 2 tablespoons to glaze
* 1 tablespoon ground cumin
* 3 tablespoons butter
* 3–4 sprigs rosemary
* Juice of 1 lemon
* A handful of thyme sprigs, stems removed

FOR THE CHEESECAKE

* 4–5 fresh fig leaves, scrubbed clean
* Olive oil, for greasing
* 115g (4oz/¾ cup) chopped dried figs
* 115g (4oz/heaped ¾ cup) raw walnuts
* 450g (1lb/2 cups) cream cheese, softened at room temperature
* 450g (1lb/2 cups) mascarpone cheese, softened at room temperature
* 250g (9oz/2¼ cups) granulated sugar
* 1 tablespoon pure vanilla extract
* 4 large eggs, at room temperature
* Salt

1 Begin a day early, by preparing your lamb. Your joint should be washed and patted dry, then trussed with butcher's twine. To truss, tie the twine crosswise around the joint every 2cm (1in) for the length of the loin. Prepare the marinade by heating your olive oil in a pan over a medium heat. Add your minced garlic and sauté until fragrant and soft. Remove from the heat and set aside. In a small saucepan, warm your milk over a low heat until the edges of the pan begin to bubble slightly. Whisk in your honey until dissolved, then add your cumin and sautéed garlic. Remove from the heat and allow to cool. Place your lamb loin in a large bowl or deep pan and cover completely with the marinade. Allow to marinate in the refrigerator overnight.

2 The following morning, prepare your cheesecake. This dish is best prepared hours in advance, as the cheesecake needs to set in the refrigerator for at least 3 hours before serving. Preheat your oven to 180°C/350°F/ Gas 4. On the stovetop, bring a large pot of water to a boil and prepare a bowl of ice water nearby. One at a time, blanch your fig leaves in the boiling water for 5 seconds, then plunge them into the ice water. This will make them pliable. Drain the leaves and pat them dry completely. Set aside.

3 Prepare a 23cm (9in) springform pan by lightly coating the bottom and sides with olive oil. Line the pan with your dry, blanched fig leaves, ensuring they come 1cm (½in) over the edges of the pan, and tuck them into place. In a food processor, blend your chopped

figs and walnuts until the nuts are coarsely ground. Press the fig mixture into the pan, on top of the fig leaves, creating a 5mm (¼in) crust over the entire base of the pan and halfway up the walls. Bake the leaves and crust for 10–15 minutes until just beginning to set, then remove from the oven and cool completely.

4 On the stovetop, bring 2 litres (2 quarts) of water to a boil. In your oven, set a casserole dish that is at least 5cm (2in) deep and wide enough to fit the cheesecake pan, and allow the empty pan to warm inside the oven.

5 In a large bowl, stir your softened cheeses and sugar together with a rubber spatula. Add your vanilla and, one at a time, your room temperature eggs. Take care not to whip the mixture too hard, as any air incorporated now could cause your cheesecake to crack in the oven. Season with salt to taste and spoon the mixture into your prepared pan.

6 Carefully, place your cheesecake into the hot casserole dish and pour the prepared boiling water into the casserole dish so that it comes at least halfway up the sides of the cheesecake pan. Many amateur bakers skip this crucial step, but a water bath is essential for a finished cheesecake that is creamy, set and free of surface cracks. Bake for 50 minutes, or until just the very centre of the cheesecake has a slight wobble, but the rest is set. Carefully remove the cheesecake from the water bath and allow to cool fully before placing in the refrigerator for at least four hours to set completely. It is worthwhile to note here that, while the fig leaves lend an irreplaceable flavour to this dish, they have an undesirable flavour and texture on their own and should be removed before eating.

7 Next, prepare your moretum. This was traditionally done in a mortar and pestle, but a food processor will also work just fine. By either method, grind your fresh herbs to a fine mince along with 3 tablespoons of the olive oil and some salt and pepper. Add your cheese, and pulse until evenly blended. Set this aside in the refrigerator.

8 Closer to serving time, begin cooking the lamb by preheating your oven to 180°C/350°F/Gas 4. Heat your butter over high heat in a cast-iron or oven-safe skillet. Remove the loin from the marinade, season with salt and pepper, and tuck your rosemary sprigs into the twine along the top of the loin. Using tongs, sear the meat evenly in the hot pan on all sides. Place the hot pan in the oven and roast for 1 hour.

9 In a small dish, stir together the 2 tablespoons honey and the lemon juice. Remove the lamb from the oven and turn the heat up to 200°C/400°F/Gas 6. Brush the loin with the honey mixture, reserving any leftover glaze, and return it to the oven for 10-20 more minutes, or until the internal temperature reads 57°C/135°F for medium doneness. Remove the pan from the oven and rest the meat on a chopping (cutting) board for 10 minutes. In the meantime, return the pan to the stovetop over medium heat and add 120ml (4fl oz/½ cup) water to deglaze. Simmer the sauce for 2 minutes until slightly thickened, then add the remaining lemon and honey glaze.

10 At serving time, remove the twine and rosemary from your lamb, slice, sprinkle the lamb with thyme and serve with your sauce.

11 Spread your moretum in a shallow dish and top with your salad, drizzling liberally with olive oil before serving. Serve these with pita bread and good wine, and save room for your cheesecake at *mensae secundae*, the dessert course.

Fornacalia Focaccia

In Ovid's *Fasti*, a monolithic poem detailing the Roman calendar, he provides one of the few pieces of lore that remain from the ancient feast of Fornacalia:

> The earth of old was tilled by men unlearned: war's hardships wearied their active frames. More glory was to be won by the sword than by the curved plough; the neglected farm yielded its master but a small return. Yet spelt the ancients sowed, and spelt they reaped; of the cut spelt they offered the first-fruits to Ceres. Taught by experience they toasted the spelt on the fire, and many losses they incurred through their own fault. For at one time they would sweep up the black ashes instead of spelt, and at another time the fire caught the huts themselves. So they made the oven into a goddess of that name (Fornax); delighted with her, the farmers prayed that she would temper the heat to the grains committed to her charge.[1]

And so Fornax was honoured in spring at Fornacalia, the feast of bakers. She is a personification of the oven as alchemical flask, and sole priestess of its powers of transformation. She is also described as one who can temper the power of fire, safely containing it within the home at her altar, the hearth. Her feast at Fornacalia was a moveable feast in the Roman calendar, lasting from February 10th to the 17th, with each Roman district performing their rites on a different, predetermined date. This was no marginal feast and every citizen was expected to make offerings during the weeklong celebration. However, with citizens often in confusion about their region's designated offering dates, many would wait until the last available day in the season to perform their rites, leading to the holiday's alternate name, the Feast of Fools.

Although few details are known about the specifics of these rites, we do know that offerings of bread and toasted grains were delivered to Fornax to bless the harvest and the ovens, ensuring a productive and safe year ahead. We can also imagine that an incense of frankincense mixed with flax, wheat chaff or straw would be a suitable offering for the goddess alongside her portion of toasted grains, as incense would have been offered as well in Ancient Greece. While Ovid's passage suggests applications for both the setting of intentions and protective magic on this date, the primary purpose of this feast is to ensure Fornax receives her due, lest the fires of her holy hearth work against the baker's designs. For home bakers who desire a year of unburnt loaves, this springtime festival is not to be missed!

Makes 1 loaf
Prep time: 50 minutes, plus 2½ hours proving
Cook time: 35 minutes

- 250g (9oz/1½ cups) whole wheat berries (or 250g/9oz/1¾ cups wholewheat flour)
- 1 head of garlic
- 4 tablespoons extra virgin olive oil, plus extra for greasing
- 1 teaspoon sugar
- 2 teaspoons active dry yeast
- 350ml (12fl oz/1½ cups) warm water
- 250g (9oz/1¾ cups plus 2 tablespoons) plain (all-purpose) flour
- 1 tablespoon sea salt

- 85g (3oz/scant 1 cup) pitted Kalamata olives
- 4–5 grape or cherry tomatoes, halved
- A bunch of chives
- A small handful of rosemary sprigs
- Edible flowers
- Large-crystal garnishing salt

I Begin by toasting and grinding your wheat berries. While this procedure adds a cumbersome step to an otherwise simple bread recipe, it is one of the few elements of traditional Roman Fornacalia that can be historically authenticated. I also find that freshly toasted wheat lends a depth of flavour to this bread that cannot be found elsewhere, and celebrates the humble wheat berry by unlocking its sweeter, more caramel notes. For this, you will need a spice grinder or heavy-duty blender, as analogue technologies like the mortar and pestle will be insufficient in grinding our wheat to a fine powder. (For those who wish to skip this step, use wholewheat flour instead.)

2 Preheat your oven to 180°C/350°F/Gas 4 and spread your wheat berries in a single layer on a baking sheet lined with baking parchment. When the oven is sufficiently warm, light a single beeswax candle on the stove top. Offer incense, and speak a greeting to Fornax. There are no traditional verses or epithets preserved for her, so taking poetic licence is appropriate here. Toast your wheat berries for 8–10 minutes, stirring occasionally, or until fragrant and lightly browned. Allow to cool, then grind your flour as finely as you can and set aside.

3 When the berries have been toasted, halve your head of garlic crosswise and place it on a sheet of kitchen foil. Drizzle both halves with olive oil, then seal the foil and roast until the garlic is golden and soft, about 20–30 minutes. Remove from the oven and allow to cool, then carefully remove the cloves and set aside.

4 In the bowl of a stand mixer or in a large mixing bowl, mix your sugar and yeast. Add your water, which should be as warm as an almost-too-hot bath, about 43°C/110°F. Allow to stand for 5 minutes, or until the mixture is frothy and bubbling. Add your flours, salt and 2 tablespoons of your olive oil and mix using the paddle attachment or a wooden spoon until just combined. Switch to the dough hook or your hands and knead the dough for 8–10 minutes, or until it is smooth and passes the windowpane test. Grease a large bowl with olive oil and place your dough into the bowl, covering with a tea (dish) towel and allowing to prove for 90–120 minutes in a warm place until the dough has doubled in size. I recommend taking a photo of the dough before proving, so you can accurately check how much it has risen before proceeding.

5 When the dough has doubled in size, preheat your oven to 220°C/425°F/Gas 7 and set a baking sheet in the middle of your oven as it warms.

6 On a counter, turn your dough out onto a sheet of baking parchment the size of your baking sheet. Roll or press out your dough onto the parchment, spreading the dough as close to the edges of the parchment as you can. Allow the dough to rise on the parchment for 30 more minutes, then drizzle the dough with the remaining olive oil and dimple the surface thoroughly with your fingertips. Decorate the bread with your olives, tomatoes, roasted garlic, herbs and edible flowers, poking them into the soft dough. Garnish with large-crystal salt.

7 Carefully remove your hot baking sheet from the oven and slide the dough-covered parchment on top. Return the tray to the oven and bake for 20–25 minutes, or until the bread is deeply golden. Remove from the tray and cool on a baking rack for 10 minutes before serving. The first slice from this loaf should be burned in offering to Fornax, along with any remaining incense, in exchange for her blessing on all that we wish to grow in the coming year.

Hekate's Deipnon:
Roasted garlic and leek quiche

Perhaps among the most feared and revered of the Greco-Roman pantheon, Hekate is the triple-formed goddess of crossroads, witchcraft, nighttime and spirits of the dead. She is a lunar divinity and psychopomp, most remembered for her success in guiding the young goddess Persephone in her return from Hades. The Deipnon is the most sacred of her ancient feasts, occurring each new moon, on the night before the *noumenia*, the return of the waxing moon in the night sky.

During these feasts, the goddess received offerings of raw eggs, cakes, leeks, garlic and honey at her shrines, or *hekataia*, which stood before the homes of her devoted at the place

where the path to the front door meets the street and forms a three-way crossroads. These gifts were sent to the curb along with the sweepings and trash from the household, as part of a ritual purification of the home and its inhabitants. While it was well understood that these street-side offerings were often taken by the poor, this too was seen as a gift of charity in the goddess' name. To this point, Aristophanes writes in the 4th to 5th century BCE:

Ask Hekate whether it is better to be rich or starving; she will tell you that the rich send her a meal every month, and that the poor make it disappear before it is even served. [2]

Serves 6–8

Prep time: 40 minutes

Cook time: 1½ hours

FOR THE PASTRY

* 150g (5½oz/1 cup plus 2 tablespoons) plain (all-purpose) flour
* 1 teaspoon sugar
* 1 teaspoon salt
* 85g (3oz/⅓ cup plus 2 teaspoons) unsalted butter, cut into 1cm (½in) pieces
* 1 tablespoon vegetable oil
* 3 tablespoons water

FOR THE FILLING

* 3 whole heads of garlic
* 2 tablespoons olive oil
* 4 large eggs
* 175ml (6oz/scant ¾ cup) double (heavy) cream
* 175g (6oz/heaped ¾ cup) crème fraîche
* 175g (6oz/1½ cups) grated pecorino cheese
* 2 tablespoons fresh dill, finely chopped
* ½ leek, halved lengthwise, finely sliced
* Salt and pepper

1 Before dusk on the new moon, begin by making your tart shell. Preheat your oven to 180°C/350°F/Gas 4 and mix together your flour, sugar and salt in a large bowl. In a saucepan, heat your butter until it bubbles and begins to brown, then add your oil to the pan. Pour the hot butter mixture and the water into the flour and stir to combine with a wooden spoon. Using your fingers, press the dough into a 23cm (9in) tart dish, working it across the bottom and up the sides to an even 5mm (¼in) thickness. Prick all over the bottom of the tart shell with a fork, then bake the crust for 10 minutes, or until just set. Set aside and allow to cool, but keep your oven on at 180°C/350°F/Gas 4.

2 For the filling, slice your heads of garlic in half horizontally, place on a sheet of kitchen foil and drizzle with the olive oil. Seal the garlic in the foil and bake for 30 minutes, or until the garlic is soft and deep golden-brown. Set aside.

3 Next, beat your eggs until homogenous, then whisk in the cream, crème fraîche and pecorino cheese. Carefully peel your roasted garlic, keeping the pieces whole if possible. Stir the roasted garlic, dill and finely sliced leek into your filling, and season with salt and pepper. Pour the filling into your tart shell. Bake the quiche for 35–40 minutes, or until the custard is just set in the centre.

4 To perform a version of the *deipnon* yourself, begin by thoroughly sweeping your home, working toward the front door. Burn myrrh, Hekate's sacred resin, and carry it through each room of your home. Carry a slice of this quiche, along with raw garlic, eggs, leeks, honeycomb and the sweepings from your home, to a three-way crossroads where you will not be observed. When you arrive, set down your offerings, and read the following invocation from the Greco-Egyptian Magical Papyri (PGM), a book of magical formulae from late antiquity, three times aloud: *ASKEI KATASKEI ERON OREON IOR MEGA SAMNYER BAUI PHOBANTIA SEMNE ("I summon forth the cloak of midnight, may all spirits bow to the flame.")* Stand and turn toward home, but do not look back over your shoulder, even if you should hear footsteps or the sound of barking dogs.

Maslenitsa:
Straw-infused crepes for the butter lady

As March begins and spring returns, the festival of Maslenitsa, the Butter Lady, returns to Eastern Europe. Sometimes called Cheesefare Week, Maslenitsa takes place on the last week before Lent, during which meat is forbidden to Orthodox Christians, but other animal products – cheese, eggs and dairy – are still encouraged. As such, this festival is a celebration of these ingredients, showcased in the traditional festival fare of crepes, or *bliny*, filled with cheeses, fruits, sour cream or caviar.

Despite being one of the oldest surviving Slavic holidays, Maslenitsa was not observed during the Soviet years in Eastern Europe, but has seen a resurgence in the last few decades. It is believed to be a remnant of forgotten pagan festivals, with the effigy of the Maslenitsa representing Marzanna (otherwise Morana or Mara), the Slavic goddess of springtime, death and rebirth. As a testament to these origins, celebrants observe a curious custom on the first day of the festival by fashioning a woman out of straw and naming her Maslenitsa. She is dressed in hag's clothes, given pancakes to hold in her hands, and paraded through the town as the first crepes of the week are offered in sacrifice to the hungry. At the end of the week, the effigy of the butter witch will be burned in public ceremony, as a symbolic end to winter.

While many witches may not observe Christian customs, our recipe is inspired by these older, more mysterious threads which run through the Maslenitsa festival. In homage to the butter lady, these crepes are filled with hay-infused ricotta, which is "dressed" in stewed cherries and delicate crepes. You may choose to reserve one or two of these crepes (especially the misshapen ones!) to burn in sacrifice at your own springtime rites, Lenten or otherwise.

Serves 4

Prep time: 20 minutes, plus chilling
Cook time: 30 minutes

FOR THE BATTER
* 2 eggs
* 3 tablespoons sugar
* ½ teaspoon salt
* 750ml (26fl oz/3¼ cups) milk, warmed
* 120ml (4fl oz/½ cup) double (heavy) cream
* 200g (7oz/1½ cups) plain (all-purpose) flour
* ¼ teaspoon baking powder
* 75g (2½oz/5 tablespoons) butter, melted but not hot, or vegetable oil

FOR THE FILLING
* 450g (1lb) fresh cherries, washed and pitted
* Juice of ½ lemon
* 115g (4oz/heaped ½ cup) sugar
* 120ml (4fl oz/½ cup) double (heavy) cream, chilled
* 4 tablespoons fresh hay or dried oat straw
* 1 teaspoon dried chamomile
* 115g (4oz/½ cup) full-fat ricotta cheese
* 2 tablespoons rum or brandy
* 2 tablespoons cornflour (cornstarch)
* 1 teaspoon vanilla extract
* Icing (confectioner's) sugar, for dusting

I Begin by making your fillings. In a medium saucepan, combine your cherries, lemon juice, half of the sugar and 120ml (4fl oz/½ cup) water. Bring to a boil, then turn down to a low heat and simmer until thick and bubbly, stirring occasionally. Pour into a bowl and set aside.

2 In another saucepan over medium heat, warm your cream with the hay or oat straw and chamomile. Bring to a gentle simmer, then remove from the heat. Allow the cream to infuse for 10 minutes, then strain and chill. In a mixing bowl, stir together your ricotta cheese, rum or brandy, cornflour, vanilla, and the remaining half of the sugar. When the infused cream is cold, whip in a stand mixer until stiff peaks form. Fold the cream into your ricotta mixture. Cover and chill both fillings.

3 Next, make your crepe batter. Add your eggs to a blender and purée until smooth. Add your sugar and salt, followed by the milk and cream. Mix together your flour and baking powder, then with the blender on a low speed, add it into your egg mixture. When incorporated, set your batter aside and heat a large skillet over medium heat. Brush the pan evenly with melted butter or vegetable oil, then use a ladle to pour a small amount of batter (about 5–6 tablespoons) into the centre of the pan. Working quickly, tilt the pan to spread out the batter, until it forms a thin, even circle. Cook for about 30 seconds, or until the edges of the crepe are golden and the centre is bubbling, then use a long offset spatula to flip the crepe and cook on the other side.

4 The first crepes will always come out messy, but the process gets easier as you go. If you were to construct your own Butter Lady out of straw, these would be the pancakes you would place in her hand. Cool your crepes in a stack, laying one evenly atop the other on a serving plate.

5 Bring out and uncover your fillings. Fold your crepes in half, fill them, and then fold them in half once more. Dust with icing sugar and serve.

Celtic Struan for Michaelmas

The Michaelmas struan is a Scottish tradition that celebrates the end of harvest season. It is a blessed bread, containing a mix of grains to represent the fruits of the field. Wheat flour, whole grain rice, oats and polenta are sweetened with honey and buttermilk to yield a soft, cake-like bread that is fluffy and aromatic.

The Michaelmas struan is one of the few culinary rituals mentioned by name in the *Carmina Gadelica*, a collection of Scottish poetry and charms compiled in the late 19th century. Traditionally, this bread would have been baked by the eldest daughter of the family, under careful watch of her mother, and for good reason – struan loaves are considered ruined if they crack on top while baking, and cracked loaves are not eaten. In the text, a ritual blessing for the bread is given, in which the loaf is consecrated in the name of St Michael. The blessing reads:

Each meal beneath my roof, they will all be mixed together
In name of God the Son, who gave them growth.
Milk, eggs, and butter, the good produce of our own flock,
there shall be no dearth in our land, nor in our dwelling.
In the name of Michael of my love, who bequeathed to us the power,
With the blessing of the Lamb, and of his mother;
Humble us at thy footstool, be thine own sanctuary around us,
Ward from us spectre, sprite, oppression, and preserve us.
Consecrate the produce of our land, bestow prosperity and peace,
In the name of the Father the King, and of the three beloved apostles.
Dandelion, smooth garlic, foxglove, woad, and butterwort,
The three carle-doddies, and marigold.
Gray cailpeach plucked, the seven pronged seven times,
The mountain yew, ruddy heath, and madder.
I will put water on them all in precious name of the Son of God,
In name of Mary the generous, and of Patrick.
When we shall sit down to take our food
I will sprinkle in the name of God on the children.

– "THE BLESSING OF THE STRUAN",
CARMINA GADELICA VOL 1[3]

This bread is intended for a Michaelmas celebration (29 September), but suits any harvest celebration occurring in early fall, especially near the equinox. It is not a fussy loaf, but keep a close eye on it when it's in the oven to avoid a cracked top.

Makes 1 loaf
Prep time: 25 minutes,
plus 1 hour proving
Cook time: 45 minutes

* 900g (2lb/7 cups) strong white bread flour, plus extra for dusting
* 3 tablespoons dry yeast
* 100g (3½oz/½ cup) brown sugar
* 40g (1½oz/scant ½ cup) rolled oats
* 125g (4½oz) cooked brown rice
* 15g (½oz/2 tablespoons) wheat bran
* 85g (3oz/heaped ½ cup) polenta
* 2 tablespoons poppy seeds, plus extra to garnish
* 1 tablespoon salt
* 115g (4oz/7 tablespoons) honey
* 350ml (12fl oz/1½ cups) warm water
* 1 egg
* 185ml (6fl oz/¾ cup) buttermilk, warmed
* Oil, for greasing

I In a large mixing bowl, combine your flour, yeast, sugar, oats, rice, bran, polenta, poppy seeds and salt. In another, whisk together your honey, water, egg and buttermilk. Mix the wet and dry ingredients together with your hands, then turn the dough out onto a floured surface. Knead for 15 minutes, or until the dough is elastic and tacky, but not sticky. Place the dough into a large, greased bowl, cover with a tea (dish) towel and prove in a warm place for 1 hour, or until doubled in size.

2 When the dough has risen, preheat your oven to 180°C/350°F/Gas 4. Grease a 23x13cm (9x5in) bread pan and set aside. Turn the dough out onto a floured surface once more and shape the loaf by pinching the edges into the centre of the loaf, then flipping it over and shaping it with your hands into a long, even loaf to fit the pan. Transfer the dough to the bread pan and bake for 45 minutes, or until the bread is a dark gold colour. Cool fully before slicing. The first slice of the loaf should be reserved and buried sacrificially in your garden, front yard, or the fertile ground of a nearby park.

ORIGINAL ILLUSTRATIONS FROM THE CARMINA GADELICA VOL 1

Hummus to Heal a Broken Heart

When flipping through one of the greatest grimoires of the Islamic golden age, most people are probably not expecting to find a hummus recipe. And yet, tucked at the very end of the *Picatrix*, a book of astrological and talismanic magic attributed to Maslama ibn Ahmad al-Majriti in the 11th century, we find that the author casts his eyes down from heaven for a moment and presents us with just that – a hummus recipe, and not a particularly interesting one. The dish consists of chickpeas and olive oil, with no other seasonings or ingredients mentioned. But what's noteworthy about this recipe is not just the everydayness of it that makes it feel so out of place, but the even more terrestrial, mundane problem that the recipe promises to fix – sorrow and heartbreak.

In the text, the author instructs the adept to set a dish of chickpeas under the first rays of the moon at sundown, and allow them to absorb her virtues over the course of the night. At dawn, the practitioner should rise again, and anoint the chickpeas with olive oil before allowing them to soak in water for two hours. After this, the *Picatrix* simply instructs to cook the chickpeas and blend them into a hummus, and says: "From all those to whom you give these to eat, all sorrow, ill will, evil thoughts, and every kind of melancholy will depart, and their hearts will rejoice in the highest virtue, and they will become joyful and alert in all things." [4]

An ambitious promise for a two-ingredient recipe. And yet this deceptively simple outlier within the *Picatrix*'s pages gives us a surprisingly intimate view of magic in the 11th century. Magic here is not just reserved for gaining the compassion of kings or blighting crops (both of which are covered in the *Picatrix* as well) but for solving even the most common of human problems, with the humblest of ingredients.

While the reproduction of this recipe contains a few more ingredients than originally called for, the procedural steps are true to the *Picatrix* text. This is a simple and classic hummus, which can be dressed up by adding whatever flavours you prefer. Consider adding herbs or ingredients renowned for their uplifting, antidepressant qualities – nutmeg, orange zest or roasted red (bell) peppers, for example.

Serves 6–8
Prep time: 10 minutes, plus overnight moon bathing and 2 hours soaking
Cook time: 2 hours

* 115g (4oz/⅔ cup) dried chickpeas
* 4 tablespoons olive oil, plus extra for drizzling
* 1 tablespoon salt
* 55g (2oz/¼ cup) tahini
* Juice of 1 lemon
* Pinch of ground sumac
* Pita bread and/or crudités, to serve

I Begin this recipe on any night between the waxing half moon and the full moon, with the night before the full moon being the optimal choice. Place your dry chickpeas in a clean, white ceramic dish and place this outside or on a windowsill in view of the waxing moon. Before bed, take note of what time sunrise will be the following morning, as you should plan to rise at least 30 minutes before that time.

2 The following morning, when the sun has not yet risen, bring your chickpeas into your kitchen. You may choose to burn frankincense at this time, as the fragrance is a natural antidepressant and the smoke has purifying qualities as well, making it a suitable fumigation for this work. Anoint your chickpeas with 1 tablespoon of your olive oil, then place the chickpeas into a medium saucepan. Cover the chickpeas with 950ml (32fl oz/4 cups) water and allow to sit for 2 hours.

3 Place the pot of water and chickpeas over a high flame and bring to a boil. Turn the heat down to low and simmer the chickpeas for 1½–2 hours, or until tender and cooked through. Strain the chickpeas and allow to cool to room temperature.

4 Once cooled, place your chickpeas into the bowl of a food processor and add your salt, tahini and lemon juice. If using any additional flavours, add them here. Purée until smooth, then stream in the remaining 3 tablespoons olive oil. Transfer the hummus to a plate or shallow serving dish and spread evenly into a flat circle. Drizzle with extra olive oil, and dust with a pinch of ground sumac before serving alongside pita bread or crudités.

Hildegard von Bingen's Cookies of Joy

St Hildegard von Bingen is a curious character from occult history whose contributions to Christian mysticism and herbal medicine cannot be overstated. Born in 1098, she was an accomplished author and polymath who wrote plays and poetry, compiled botanical reference books, penned medical manuals, and was most famous for receiving detailed and insightful visions, which she illustrated and discussed extensively in her work. These visions informed her cosmology and approach to herbal medicine, in which human beings are viewed as a physical and spiritual microcosm of the universe at large. Through the power of *viriditas*, her concept of the "green", beneficial and healing potency of plants, she believed one could combat imbalance within the body's elements and humours, dispel illness and return to a state of harmony with the natural world.

Among her many remedies, she leaves us with a deceptively simple piece of advice within the pages of *Physica* regarding one of the most common household spices: nutmeg. St. Hildegard describes the warming spice as heart opening, and describes its use in clarifying one's judgement and deferring a pleasant disposition to those who consume it. She recommends using equal parts nutmeg and cinnamon, along with a dash of clove and whole wheat flour, to produce cakes which, if eaten often, promise to make one strong, happy, alert, and cheerful in all ways.

Almost 1,000 years later, we can scientifically verify St Hildegard's claims about these plants. Studies of nutmeg have proven its powerful abilities as an antidepressant, comparable to other medications on the market. It contains significant quantities of natural monoamine oxidase inhibitors (MAOIs), which improve mental clarity and help the brain retain crucial mood chemicals like serotonin and dopamine. These cookies use some of the humblest spices and yet, infused with the wisdom of St Hildegard's mystic visions, they are potent enough to nourish us today.

Yields 24 cookies

Prep time: 20 minutes, plus 30 minutes chilling

Cook time: 15 minutes

* 175g (6oz/¾ cup) unsalted butter
* 115g (4oz/heaped ½ cup) white sugar, plus extra to sprinkle
* 115g (4oz/heaped ½ cup) dark brown sugar
* 2 teaspoons ground cinnamon
* 2 teaspoons nutmeg, preferably fresh grated, plus extra to sprinkle
* ½ teaspoon ground cloves
* 1 large egg
* 225g (8oz/1¾ cups) wholewheat flour, plus extra for dusting
* 1 teaspoon baking powder
* A pinch of salt
* 2 tablespoons milk or non-dairy substitute

1 In a large mixing bowl, cream together the butter, sugars and spices. Beat in your egg until fully combined. In a separate bowl, sift together your flour, baking powder and salt. In several batches, add your flour slowly to your butter mixture, being careful not to overwork the dough. When it just comes together into a smooth ball, wrap the dough in baking parchment or clingfilm (plastic wrap) and refrigerate for at least 30 minutes.

2 Preheat your oven to 180°C/350°F/Gas 4 and line a baking sheet with baking parchment. Remove the dough from the refrigerator and unwrap. Place the dough between two sheets of lightly floured baking parchment and roll out to a 5mm (¼in) thickness. Using a round, 5cm (2in) cookie cutter, punch out cookies from the dough and place on the prepared baking sheet. Brush the cookies lightly with milk and sprinkle with extra grated nutmeg and sugar. Bake for 12–15 minutes, or until golden. Remove from the baking sheet and leave the cookies to cool on a wire rack.

leister Crowley's Glacier Rice

'estern occultism more revered
'he Beast 666, Aleister Crowley.
admire or critique his works, his
igs have significantly informed
the landscape of occultism today. Among his colourful
contributions to occult philosophy, Crowley left behind
a number of his culinary recipes as well. Though many
of his culinary works are frightful, and incorporate
bodily fluids, incenses and animal blood, his curry rice
or "Riz Aleister Crowley" is a surprisingly friendly and
mundane addition to Crowley's other works.

In his autobiography, Crowley recalls serving this
rice during a blizzard while climbing glaciers. Although
his original recipe contains no chillies, he describes
the spicy heat of his dish causing "strong men, inured
to every danger and hardship, [to] dash out of the
tent after one mouthful and wallow in the snow,
snapping at it like mad dogs." Nevertheless, Crowley

seems to consider this dish a wild success, saying of his
own recipe: "...it was very good as curry, and I should
endeavour to introduce it into London restaurants if
there were only a glacier. Perhaps, some day, after a
heavy snowfall."

Inspired by this unique piece of Crowley lore,
I've expanded upon his trademark recipe here,
suggesting a few of my own ingredients in addition.
While I don't mean to correct The Beast on his own
creation, the original text of his recipe leaves out
ingredient quantities, so there is some room for
creative interpretation. However, the procedure
detailed below is faithful to the original Riz Aleister
Crowley, and my additions are hopefully in keeping
with the original spirit of Master Therion's pilaf.
Stay true to the original or experiment with my
suggestions – do what thou wilt with this recipe,
as Crowley himself might suggest.

Serves 2
Prep time: 10 minutes
Cook time: 20 minutes

* 180g (6¼oz/1 cup) long grain
  white rice
* 3 pods of green cardamom
* 60g (2oz/4 tablespoons) butter
* ¼ teaspoon ground cloves
* ¼ teaspoon ground turmeric
* 30g (1oz/scant ½ cup) flaked
  (sliced) almonds
* 60g (2oz/scant ½ cup) sultanas
  (golden raisins)
* 30g (1oz/¼ cup) pistachios,
  finely chopped
* Salt and pepper

MY ADDITIONS (optional)

* 1 bay leaf
* 1 tablespoon Indian chilli powder
* 1 teaspoon curry powder
* 1 small handful of fresh coriander
  (cilantro) leaves, torn and roughly
  chopped

I Crowley instructs us to begin by
preparing the rice. Add 950ml
(32fl oz/4 cups) water to a
medium saucepan, and season
with salt and the bay leaf (if
using). Bring the water to a boil
and stir in your rice, then simmer,
covered, for 8 minutes, or until
a grain of rice crushed between
the index finger and thumb is
"easily crushed, but not sodden or
sloppy". Drain and rinse the rice
with cold water, then return the
rice to the empty saucepan. Heat
the pot again over a medium heat
and toss the rice with a wooden
spoon, "using a lifting motion,
never pressing down", drying it
gently until the rice is fluffy and
easily tossed.

2 In a separate pan, toast your
cardamom pods over medium
heat until fragrant. Add your
butter and, when melted, toss
in your dry spices. Sauté for 30
seconds, then add your almonds
and sultanas. Add the rice to the
pan and toss until thoroughly
mixed. Season with salt and
pepper, then stir in your chopped
coriander leaves (if using) and
pistachios until the green colours
make the dish "a Poem of Spring".

Sator Square Harvest Pie

The SATOR square is an ancient and enigmatic word puzzle, used as a charm of protection from various evils with its whirling arrangement of palindromes. It is sometimes believed that malevolent spirits are compelled to attempt puzzles and become distracted and trapped by the perfect repetitions of the square. While the earliest surviving SATOR squares are only from the 1st century AD, some scholars suggest the symbol has pre-Christian origins. Although there have been many attempts to translate and decode the mysteries of this symbol, little is known beyond its apotropaic use as a protective charm. Since the charm can be read the same backwards and forwards, some translations read the square as a *boustrophedon*, meant to be read left-to-right and right-to-left on alternating lines, which yields one possible translation: "As ye sow, so shall ye reap."

Despite its mysterious beginnings, this unique word square can be found in various places the world over – in ancient temples to the goddess Artemis, drawn inside medieval bibles, inscribed on Coptic tombs in Nubia. In France, the square was used in the middle ages as a protective charm for women in labour. In the hexerei of the Pennsylvania Germans, the SATOR square is employed against lightning, and fed to cows to stave off witchcraft. In South America, the square is often used against snake venom and animal bites. In one notable case from Lyon, the square was even inscribed on crusts of bread and eaten to recover from temporary insanity.

While there is no other traditional application for eating the SATOR square, its various uses tell us that its presence alone has the profound effect of warding off maledictions and troublesome spirits. As autumn is traditionally the time for setting wards and protections in advance of the coming winter, this symbol would be a welcome addition to the themes of a harvest feast. Here, artichokes and rosemary join the square in a rich harvest pot pie, lending their efficacy as allies for protection magic. Prepare this dish to accompany your own protection rituals and continue the varied, wandering legacy of this truly unique charm.

S	A	T	O	R
A	R	E	P	O
T	E	N	E	T
O	P	E	R	A
R	O	T	A	S

Serves 4

Prep time: 25 minutes,
plus 30 minutes chilling

Cook time: 1 hour 20 minutes

FOR THE CRUST

* 310g (11oz/2⅓ cups) plain
  (all-purpose) flour, plus extra
  for dusting
* ½ teaspoon sugar
* 1 teaspoon salt
* ½ teaspoon black pepper
* 225g (8oz/1 cup) unsalted butter,
  chilled and cut into 1cm (½in)
  cubes
* 6–8 tablespoons ice-cold water
* 1 egg, to glaze

FOR THE FILLING

* 1 medium onion, diced
* 1 large carrot, peeled and cubed
* 1 large sweet potato, peeled and
  cubed
* 400g (14oz) can artichoke hearts,
  drained and patted dry
* 4 tablespoons olive oil
* 2 cloves garlic, minced
* 60g (2oz/scant ½ cup) plain
  (all-purpose) flour
* 1 sprig rosemary, stems removed
  and finely chopped
* Pinch of ground cloves
* 120ml (4fl oz/½ cup) dry
  white wine
* 570ml (20fl oz/2½ cups) chicken
  stock (broth)
* 1 handful of kale, washed and torn,
  ribs removed
* Salt and pepper

I Preheat your oven to
180°C/350°F/Gas 4. Toss your
onion, carrot, sweet potato and
artichoke hearts in 2 tablespoons
of your olive oil and tip onto a
baking sheet in a single layer.
Season with salt and roast the
vegetables for 20 minutes, or
until browning at the edges.

2 While the vegetables roast,
prepare your pie crust by mixing
together your flour, sugar and
seasonings in a medium bowl.
Using your hands or a pastry
cutter, work the cold butter
into the flour until the mixture
resembles coarse, wet sand and
no clumps of butter remain. Add
in your ice water one tablespoon
at a time, slowly working until
the dough just comes together
in a smooth ball. Wrap the
dough tightly in clingfilm
(plastic wrap) and refrigerate
for 30 minutes.

3 Meanwhile, heat your remaining
2 tablespoons olive oil in a deep
saucepan and sauté your garlic
until fragrant – about 1 minute.
Add your flour, rosemary, and
ground cloves, then slowly add
your wine and chicken stock.
When the gravy is bubbly and
thick, add your roast vegetables
and kale. Season with salt and
pepper, then pour the filling into
your pie dish. Allow to cool to
room temperature.

4 When the dough is chilled and
the pie filling has cooled, remove
the crust from the refrigerator
and place it between two sheets
of floured parchment. Roll the
dough to a 5mm (¼in) thickness,
and transfer to the top of the
pie dish. Trim the excess dough
and set aside. Crimp the edges
of the crust and carve three vent
incisions near the centre of the
pie. Roll out your excess dough
and carve or punch out the
letters for the SATOR square,
illustrated on page 44.

5 Beat your egg and brush it over
the crust using a pastry brush.
Place the letters on top of the
pie, and then brush these with
egg wash as well. Bake for 35–
40 minutes, or until the crust is
golden and the filling is bubbly.

Silent Supper:
Stuffed cabbage with pork and chestnuts;
Olive oil and poppyseed cake;
Damiana and elderberry potion

The tradition of the silent supper, or "dumb supper", is a curious one, with various applications appearing across Europe and the United States. The tradition seems to have originated in the British Isles, but traces of silent supper lore were believed to have been carried across the Atlantic by Irish immigrants in the 1800s. During Hop-tu-Naa, the ancient Halloween festival from the Isle of Man, young girls could prepare "dumb cakes", crafted by multiple women in absolute silence, in the hopes that an apparition of their future love would appear at midnight to sample the bakes. In Appalachia, a similar love divination was observed, where a miniature feast was prepared in silence and set at midnight upon an incorrectly set table – with forks and knives swapped, chairs turned backward and dessert courses served first – in the hope that an apparition of one's future husband would later join the feast.

Despite these origins as a Halloween divination game, the tradition of the silent supper has seen revival in recent decades with a new emphasis on communication with spirits of the dead. These feasts are held in honour of the beloved dead, with one table setting reserved to welcome those who have passed. This empty seat should receive food and drink, with plates moved to ancestral altars once the feast is completed. This new interpretation of the silent supper is also completed on Halloween night, in absolute silence, and is viewed as an opportunity to meditate and "speak without tongues" to the spirits of the mighty dead. While it lacks historical precedent, these ancestral "dumb suppers" are a creative way to access and explore the potent liminality of the Hallowtide season, which does have a historical association with animating spirits of the dead.

This feast is inspired by the latter interpretation and serves up comforting, traditional foods in an effort to make ancestral spirits feel at home. These recipes feature seasonal ingredients of late fall and make use of two traditional Halloween foods – apples and chestnuts. However, for supplicating your own ancestral dead, you may wish to consider some traditional recipes from your heritage instead. This feast also features a gimlet-style cocktail, or potion, infused with elderberries and damiana to improve intuition and facilitate second sight. Whatever the purpose for your own silent supper – divination or communication with the dead – I hope you find inspiration from these historical traditions and explore them for yourself next Halloween night.

Serves 6–8
Prep time for full feast: 1 hour
Cook time for full feast: 90 minutes

FOR THE CABBAGE
* 1 large green cabbage
* 1 tablespoon butter
* 1 medium shallot, diced
* 3 cloves garlic, finely chopped
* 1 small apple (Jazz, Gala, McIntosh or similar), diced
* 175g (6oz/1 cup) whole chestnuts, cooked and chopped
* 60ml (2fl oz/¼ cup) dry white wine
* 185ml (6fl oz/¾ cup) chicken stock
* 450g (1lb) minced (ground) pork
* 3 sprigs thyme, stems removed
* Salt and pepper

FOR THE CAKE
* Butter, for greasing
* 200g (7oz/1½ cups) plain (all-purpose) flour, plus extra for dusting the pan
* 150ml (5⅓fl oz/⅔ cup) olive oil
* ½ teaspoon ground sage, plus 2 tablespoons for dusting
* 200g (7oz/1 cup) sugar
* 3 eggs
* ¼ teaspoon salt
* ¼ teaspoon baking powder
* 120ml (4fl oz/½ cup) buttermilk
* 225g (8oz/1½ cups) poppy seeds, plus 2 tablespoons for sprinkling
* 2 tablespoons sour cream
* 280g (10oz/2 cups) icing (confectioner's) sugar
* 2 tablespoons milk

FOR THE ELDERBERRY SYRUP
* 30g (1oz) dried elderberries
* 2 tablespoons dried damiana leaves
* 2 whole cloves
* 4cm (1½in) piece of fresh ginger, sliced
* 120ml (4fl oz/½ cup) agave syrup or honey

FOR THE POTION (per person)
* 75ml (2½fl oz) floral gin (such as Bombay Sapphire or similar)
* 15–20ml (½–¾fl oz) Elderberry Syrup (see above)
* 15ml (½fl oz) fresh lime juice
* Ice

1 Begin by preparing your elderberry syrup as this will need to chill fully before serving. In a medium saucepan, combine your elderberries, damiana leaves, cloves, ginger, agave syrup and 450ml (16fl oz/2 cups) water. Bring the pot to a boil over high heat, then reduce to low heat and simmer until the liquid has reduced to a syrup – you should have about 180ml (6fl oz/¾ cup). Pour the syrup into a plastic storage container and chill, unstrained, until the syrup is cold – about 1 hour. Strain and store in an airtight bottle in the refrigerator for up to 2 weeks.

2 Next, begin your cake. Preheat the oven to 180°C/350°F/Gas 4. Grease a bundt pan liberally with butter and dust evenly with a few tablespoons of extra flour, being sure to tap out any excess flour before proceeding. In the bowl of a stand mixer, mix together your olive oil, ½ teaspoon sage and sugar until light and fluffy. Beat in your eggs. In a separate bowl, mix together your flour, salt and baking powder. In alternating batches, add your flour mixture and buttermilk to the batter, finishing with the buttermilk. Fold in your poppy seeds, being careful not to over mix. Pour the batter into your prepared pan and bake for 40–50 minutes, or until golden and a skewer inserted into the deepest part of the cake comes out clean. Allow the cake to cool for 10 minutes in the pan, and then turn it out onto a wire rack to cool completely.

3 Remove the tough outer leaves from your cabbage and select ten of the biggest inner leaves. File down the ribs of the cabbage with a vegetable peeler so that each leaf is thin and flexible. Bring a large pan of salted water to a boil and blanch the leaves by submerging them in the boiling water for 8 minutes, then immediately plunge the leaves into ice water. The leaves should be very pliable but not mushy, and retain their shape. Keep the leaves submerged while you move on to the next steps.

4 Preheat your oven to 180°C/350°F/Gas 4. In a frying pan (skillet), melt your butter and sauté your shallot and garlic until soft and aromatic. Add your apples and cook for 2 minutes, then add your chestnuts to the pan. Turn the pan up to high heat until the pan is sizzling loudly. Stir together your wine and chicken stock and add to the pan. Simmer until the liquid is almost fully reduced and only a few tablespoons remain. Set aside to cool completely. Once cool, fold the chestnut mixture into your pork along with your thyme, and season with salt and pepper.

5 When the filling is evenly mixed, line an 18cm (7in) springform cake pan with your cabbage leaves. To do this, select the largest leaves for the top and bottom of the dish and set the largest leaf on the bottom, so that the edges of the leaf come 2.5cm (1in) or more up the sides of the dish. Line the sides of the dish with cabbage leaves, layering and overlapping them neatly, so that 7.5cm (3in) hangs over the sides of the pan. Fill the cabbage with your pork filling and fold the overhanging cabbage leaves over the top. Finally, with one last, large cabbage leaf, cover your pan and tuck the edges of the leaf into the sides of the pan with a knife. Press down on your cabbage to ensure no air bubbles are trapped inside and to compress the stuffed cabbage into shape. Bake for 30–40 minutes until the cabbage is browning and the filling is fully cooked.

6 Prepare your feast table. Burn herbs or incenses which facilitate communication with the dead – mullein, wormwood, tobacco, cypress, myrrh. Keep your feast room free of distraction and artificial light, using candles instead. The process of setting food on the table and beginning the feast should be performed in silence and the silence should be observed until the end of the meal.

7 Prepare the potion by measuring the ingredients into a cocktail shaker with ice. Shake until well chilled, then strain into a cocktail glass. Repeat for each guest. Since a silent supper is an austere occasion, leave the glasses ungarnished.

8 At serving time, remove your cabbage from the pan and slice wedges for each guest, setting aside one portion. This portion should be placed at a reserved setting, complete with flatware and napkins, in front of an empty chair. If dining alone, this seat should be directly across from you.

9 For dessert, prepare a quick frosting for the cake by mixing together your sour cream and icing sugar. Add your milk slowly, a little at a time, until the frosting is smooth but not runny. Pour over the cake and garnish with a dusting of sage powder and a sprinkle of poppy seeds.

Feast of the Stars

Cooking through the wheel of the zodiac

Feast of the Stars

Astrology is a fascinating art, which treads a narrow path between science and magic. For many, this study is an entry point to esoteric concepts, somewhat validated and removed from the rest of "woo woo" in the public consciousness, but offering many in-roads for those who wish to go deeper. In the era of pop astrology, these tools are useful in self-examination, calling us to think more deeply about who we are, what we're made of and what our connection to the macrocosm could be. As Instagram astrologers and zodiac memes conjure a renewed cultural interest in astrology, new frameworks and ideologies are continually emerging for experimenting with astrological concepts – and kitchen witchcraft is certainly among them.

As a gateway to magical thought, astrology is a brilliant example of the concept of *sympatheia*, one of the oldest magical concepts in the Western world, which formed the basis for much of how magic was practised in the ancient world. Within this worldview, the divine macrocosm of the heavens and the terrestrial microcosm of material reality are linked, echoed in the adage "as above; so below". Through *sympatheia*, chains of causality and correspondence are said to run between the heavens and earth, speaking to us in a cryptic, symbolic language of divine connectedness. Thus, both material reality and heavenly arrangements can be "read" as symbols emanating from one divine source, revealing information about the nature of reality and gesturing toward an interrelationship of the entire universe.

Though astrology is a strictly heavenly discipline, there is some precedence for correspondence between herbs, ingredients and the signs of the zodiac – particularly where early medicine is concerned. Medical astrology, or iatromathematics, was a school of cosmobiology which considered the ways in which physical and emotional ailments could be set in motion by heavenly transits. In this discipline, medicine and astrology were two sides of the same coin, and a detailed analysis of astrological movements was a key component in providing successful medical care. Even the famous herbalist and doctor Nicholas Culpeper practised his medicine in this way, once saying that astrologers "are the only men I know that are fit to study physic, physic without astrology being like a lamp without oil."[5] Many medical manuals of this

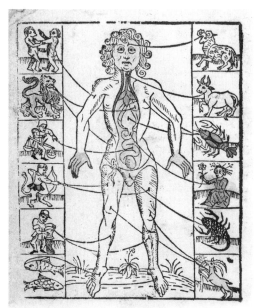

The Zodiac Man was a popular illustrative chart in early medical manuals, detailing how parts of the body were governed by the twelve astrological signs.

time even listed correspondences between human anatomy and the twelve signs of the zodiac, using these relationships to both diagnose and cure illnesses.

While an established framework for correspondence between food and the zodiac does exist within Vedic astrology and Ayurveda, a fully unified system is difficult to trace in the West. However, drawing from these connections within medical astrology, as well as elemental associations and planetary rulerships, we can begin to see the nature of astrological kitchen witchcraft take shape. As such, the charts and correspondences presented here draw their rulerships from various sources, considering the writings of medical astrologers and scholars such as Agrippa, William Lily and Nicholas Culpeper, as well as considerations about the ingredients themselves – their taste, texture, flavour, and even the bioregions where ingredients are found. What results is one perspective on the work of astrological cooking, which provides a useful new lens for our continued investigation into the tools of kitchen witchcraft.

Though the wheel of the zodiac has no true beginning or end, it is said to "start" on the vernal (spring) equinox, with the dawn of the sign of Aries. Aries is the cardinal fire sign, symbolized by the image of a ram. As such, Aries is associated with the virtues of confidence, motivation and intensity, propelled in forward momentum by the strength of its willpower. No surprise, then, that medical astrologers associated this sign with the head, face, brain and eyes – all parts of the body which we use to look ahead and plan our next adventure. Since it is ruled by the planet Mars, Aries is also associated with

the blood as a source of iron, and thus, with iron-rich foods like spinach, beetroot (beets), red meat and raisins. As plants go, we also find spiny and thorny plants under rulership of warlike Mars, such as artichokes, nettles, jackfruit, cactus pears and hearts of palm. Because of its fire sign designation, Aries is also frequently associated with spicy, warming ingredients, such as chillies and cinnamon, but this also gives Aries a rulership over sharp and bitter flavours as well, like we see with garlic, radishes, onions, horseradish and mustard. Finally, Aries is given rulership over open-fire cooking methods as well, such as broiling, barbecuing, or pit-roasting, which impart a deliciously smoky, charred flavour directly from the flames to the food.

Next in our progression is the sign of Taurus, the bull. Taurus is an earth sign, ruled by Venus, and as such is associated with tactile delight, harmony and domestic life. Here, there is an emphasis on that which is comfortable, familiar and pleasurable – things that ground us and promote a sense of peace. Among the foods of Taurus we find starchy vegetables like potatoes, yams and taro, as well as complex springtime flavours like mushrooms, wheatgrass and fresh herbs. Taurus is also associated with sweet and rich flavours, like dairy, honey, roasted garlic and chocolate. As a Venus-ruled sign, this comes as no surprise, and gives Taurus specific governance over luxurious cakes, pastries and desserts as well. In medical astrology, Taurus rules the thyroid, which promotes growth and balance within the body, as well as the throat, neck and vocal cords, which we use to advocate for ourselves and our boundaries. Taurus is certainly no stranger to speaking up, as this earth sign is famous for its stubborn wilfulness – but then again, knowing precisely what you want is a divine virtue.

Our third sign (in which I have a stellium!) is Gemini, the sign with two faces. Symbolized by an image of the famous twins, Castor and Pollux, Gemini is the sign of duality, polarity and curiosity. It is ruled by the planet Mercury and the element Air, and is known for being complex, intellectual and skilled with language and communication. It is a sign which is fully comfortable contemplating paradoxes and opposing ideas, as Geminis are known for their inquisitiveness above all else. The foods of Gemini share a similar flair for experimentation, favouring complex and inventive flavour pairings, like one might see in a salty/sour margarita. At a Gemini feast, one might find tropical fruits, wild meats and exotic specialities, all tantalizingly aromatic, served banquet-style on a long grazing table, so that guests can peruse and socialize as they explore. In medical astrology, Gemini governs the lungs, which generate our voice and communication, as well as our arms and hands, which we use to comprehend and interact with the world around us. No surprise, then, that Gemini also rules foods which support these pathways, especially the nervous system, such as broccoli, baked fish, nuts and seeds.

As spring wanes and summer fully arrives, we come to the sign of Cancer, symbolized by the image of the crab. This subaquatic mascot is apt, as Cancer is ruled by both the Moon and the element of water, which associates this sign with the emotional sphere, especially with love, intimacy and security. We see echoes of these virtues in the medical astrology of this sign, which corresponds Cancer with the stomach and diaphragm – which are activated in response to fear, anxiety and insecurity – as well as the chest and breast – which are the emotional centres associated with love and

tenderness. The ingredients of this sign typically have a very Lunar flavour profile, which is cooling, fresh and faintly sweet, as we see with cucumber, coconut, aloe, dairy or fennel. As a water sign, we also find many aquatic foods under Cancer's rulership, such as rice, lotus roots, sea vegetables, shellfish and crustaceans. As an archetype, Cancer is concerned with comfort and security, so we find favourite dishes of childhood nostalgia placed firmly under its rulership. These will vary from person to person, but the dishes which activate our emotional memories – chicken soup, ice cream cones, s'mores – will be the most Cancerian of all.

At the height of the summer season, we arrive at bright and shining Leo, the royalty of the zodiac. Leo is a fixed fire sign, ruled by the Sun itself and symbolized by the mighty and prideful image of the lion. In medical astrology, Leo governs the solar organ of the heart, as well as the spine and shoulders, which give us posture and carry us with grace though the world. This dignified sign governs expensive, luxury ingredients, like caviar and truffles, as well as grand, special-occasion dishes and fine Champagne. Here, we find traditional ingredients of the Sun, such as whole grains, pineapple, rosemary and sunflower seeds, as well as golden ingredients like dried apricots, peaches, honey and citrus fruits. As a fire sign, Leo is fond of a little spice, but prefers peppery greens like watercress, nasturtiums and rocket (arugula) to the heat of chillies. The ingredients of this sign are generally very vibrant and flavourful as Leo arrives during the climax of the agricultural year, especially ruling over summer nightshades like tomatoes and aubergine (eggplant), (bell) peppers, tomatillos, new potatoes and goji berries.

As summer begins her turn toward fall, we encounter the mutable earth sign Virgo, the virgin, symbolized by a young woman holding a stalk of wheat. This image comes from the Greek goddess Astraea, daughter of the Titanic dawn goddess Eos, who ruled over justice, precision and purity. Astraea shared the wheat symbol with Virgo, giving us the sign's first ingredients – whole grains, breads and wheat flour. In medical astrology, Virgo governs the abdomen, digestive system, intestines and spleen – the discerning, sorting aspects of the body, which extract nutrients from our food and discard the unnecessary. As such, we find that the ingredients of Virgo are simple, natural foods: raw fruits and vegetables, lean meats, and superfoods like quinoa, blueberries and açaí. However, we can be sure that Virgo's feast won't feature your average blasé "health food" menu – with Mercury as their ruler, this sign takes an experimental, exploratory approach to cooking, while its earth-sign designation hints toward a certain refinement and preference for traditional praxis. In the kitchen, you can expect Virgo to learn and experiment with every tool in the book, so that they can use them to break the rules and rewrite the entire game, as these unstoppable perfectionists are wont to do.

Beginning at the true start to fall, just around the autumn equinox, we arrive at Libra, symbolized by the scales of justice. Libra is a sign of balance and aesthetic, a cardinal Air sign governed by the planet Venus, making it one of the more artistically inclined signs of the zodiac. This means the dishes of Libra will be flashy and visually engaging, feeding both the eyes and the palate. Libra is also well known for its love of flirtation, hinted at in the sign's medical astrology rulerships – the skin, lower back and buttocks – which need no explanation as instruments of romance.

The foods of Libra also lean heavily toward this Venus designation, favouring caramelized flavours, fine cuts of meat, fresh fruit and edible flowers. As sugar is associated with both air and Venus as well, we find that Libra also rules cakes, pastries and desserts of all kinds, as well as special-occasion party dishes like cheese boards or baked brie en croûte. Libra's love of finery and substance also gestures toward an affinity for high-quality ingredients, like imported olive oil, French butter or artisanal finishing salt – a certain indicator that Libra feasts are meant to be classy affairs, with attention paid to every detail, as the master hosts that they are.

Just before Halloween, as the illuminated half of the year begins to wane, we arrive at Scorpio. Scorpio is a fixed water sign, symbolized by the scorpion and ruled by the planet Mars. As such, Scorpio can be quite reserved on the exterior, but privately, this sign can be quite deep, poetic and sensual within. A suggestion of these correspondences can be seen in the medical astrology of Scorpio, which corresponds this sign to the nose, blood and reproductive organs. These associations link Scorpio directly to ingredients which increase blood flow, like rosemary, chillies and cinnamon. It is also no surprise, then, to find aphrodisiac ingredients given squarely under Scorpio, such as oysters, asparagus, avocados, cardamom, black beans and wine. The flavour profile of Scorpio is bitter and aromatic, featuring ingredients like cumin seed, mustard, blood orange and coffee. A feast of Scorpio would be a sensual affair, incorporating a variety of textures – rich sauces, crisp greens, crusty bread and perhaps a perfectly silken panna cotta for dessert.

Next, we encounter Sagittarius, the sign of the hunter, symbolized by a bow-wielding centaur. This mutable fire sign is ruled by Jupiter, the great planet of expansion and progression. In medical astrology, Sagittarius rules the hips, thighs and legs, which give us mobility and carry us great distances as we explore the world around us. Known for its love of travel, Sagittarius rules complex, exotic dishes that represent a global palette. A Sagittarian chef might buy a cookbook of foreign cuisine and use it to immerse themselves in the culture, fragrance and flavours of a place they wish to someday visit. As a fire sign, Sagittarius rules spices with a numbing heat, like horseradish and Sichuan peppercorns. The flavours of Sagittarius tend to be pungent and complex, like blue cheese, truffles, curry or orange wines. As a testament to their self-sovereign nature, this sign is also associated with wild and foraged foods, particularly game meats and wild-caught fish.

In the deep of winter, we come to Capricorn, symbolized by the image of a mountain goat with a fish tail. This startling image reflects Capricorn's prowess at navigating both their practical reality (earth) as well as their emotional sphere (water). Capricorn is a fixed earth sign and a true sign of Saturn, occurring at the darkest and coldest part of the year in Northern hemispheres. In medical astrology, this sign corresponds to the Saturnian aspects of the body as well – bones, joints and teeth, gesturing toward Capricorn's love of simplicity and the basics. It is a sign which is refined but unpretentious, favouring simple, high quality ingredients prepared in familiar ways. The flavours of Capricorn would be time-honoured and comforting, built slowly in a pan over many hours without the use of exotic herbs or spices. This emphasis on old-fashioned sensibility hints at Capricorn's rulership of traditional fine dining fare, such as beef wellington, coq au vin or a top-quality sirloin at a steakhouse.

As the solar calendar transits from one year to the next, we arrive at Aquarius, the water bearer, symbolized by water flowing from one jug into another. Aquarius is the fixed air sign of the zodiac, traditionally ruled by Saturn but now governed by Uranus – an update which came after the discovery of the outer planets in the 17th century, changing the planetary designation for this sign as well as Pisces. This alignment with Uranus, the planet of surprise and innovation, makes Aquarius the mad scientist of the zodiac, known for shifting paradigms and changing the world with their big-picture ideas and perspectives. This means an Aquarius feast is likely to take a form you've never seen before – food as art, as storytelling, and yes, even as magic. Molecular gastronomy would certainly be the Aquarian approach to cooking and their flavours would be challenging and provocative, like savoury ice cream or candied bacon. Here, we also find plant-based proteins like tofu, seitan and tempeh, as well as versatile, flavourful ferments like miso, amazake or black garlic. In medical astrology, Aquarius rules our circulation, and so we see also stimulants and energizing ingredients clearly under its designation – coffee, tea, ginger, cayenne, ashwaganda or kola nuts.

Finally, the cycle of the zodiac comes to a close just before the spring equinox with the sign of Pisces, the fish. This last stop on the zodiac is a mutable water sign, and was traditionally ruled by Jupiter, though now it is designated under Neptune. As the most watery of all the signs, even more so than lunar-ruled Cancer, Pisces is associated with fish, shellfish, crustaceans and sea vegetables, as well as nutritious, hydrating foods like aloe vera, coconut, melons, cucumber and tomatoes. Pisces also rules water-based cooking methods like steaming and poaching, as well as soups, broths and sauces in general. The flavour palette of Pisces is delicate and salty, with creamy, starchy and fatty textures leading the way – as we might see in a salted caramel cheesecake, for example. However, because Pisces is aligned with the lymphatic system in medical astrology, there is a significant emphasis here on healthy foods which are easy to digest, even if Pisces is known for being easily swayed to indulgence. For this reason, Pisces has an association with dairy-free alternatives to milk and cheese, potatoes, pumpkin, taro and lotus roots, as well as all members of the brassica family – cauliflower, Brussels sprouts, broccoli, cabbage and kale.

As you explore the recipes in this chapter, the correspondences and charts presented here should provide a useful way of thinking about ingredients and dishes within an astrological framework. You may find some ingredients are given to multiple rulerships, and this is a feature, not a bug – the edges of correspondence designations are fuzzy and qualitative, and are the places where intellect ends and intuition begins in *sympatheia*. If you are unsure of an ingredient's designation, consider the qualities, cooking methods and flavours of each sign – cool, hot, starchy, saucy, spicy, etc – as a guide for making your considerations and follow your hands and heart from there.

Feast of Aries:
Chorizo meatballs with cheesy polenta; Cherry and Sichuan pepper truffles

When western astrologers consider the foods of the zodiac, it seems Aries always gets a predictable, limited menu – hot chillies, red meats, spicy mustard, cinnamon and all of the other sharp Mars-associated flavours that mark your designation as a cardinal fire sign. But there's more to you than fire, Aries! It's important to remember that in the Roman pantheon where he originates, Mars rules both war and agriculture, as both the iron of the sword and the iron of the plough. Under his rulership are the fruits of the field and pasture – grains, vegetables, meat and dairy – as well as his trademark heat-giving spices. While this feast is certainly spice-forward, these recipes focus on circulation-stimulating warmth instead of excessive heat, opting for sweet and smoked paprikas and tingly, mouth-numbing Sichuan peppercorns. Since Mars also

rules iron and bloodshed, you'll also find meat featured prominently in this feast, as well as foods which aid the absorption of iron into the blood – tomatoes, cherries, dark chocolate and parsley.

Since fire signs are known for their kinetic and fast-paced energy, you'll find this feast is surprisingly easy to prepare. Aside from the setting time of your truffles, the rest of this two-pot meal comes together in under an hour and requires no special skills or equipment. And while some of these flavours are flashy and bold, these dishes still feel traditional and comforting, with cheesy grains and rich chocolate providing a base for other flavours to unfold. Whipping up a creative feast in no time at all is so you, Aries, and will leave your guests in awe of your effortless mastery of flavour and spice.

Serves 4
Prep time for full feast: 4 hours
Cook time for full feast: 45 minutes

FOR THE MEATBALLS

* 450g (1lb) minced (ground) pork
* 225g (8oz) fresh chorizo, minced (ground)
* 1 medium yellow onion, finely chopped
* 4 cloves garlic, minced
* 60g (2oz/½ cup) breadcrumbs
* 1 large egg
* A handful of fresh parsley, chopped
* 3 sprigs of thyme, stems removed
* 3 tablespoons olive oil
* 400g (14oz) can chopped (crushed) tomatoes
* 1 teaspoon paprika
* ½ teaspoon smoked paprika
* 120ml (4fl oz/½ cup) chicken stock
* 120ml (4fl oz/½ cup) dry sherry
* Salt and pepper

FOR THE POLENTA

* 120ml (4fl oz/½ cup) chicken stock
* 85g (3oz/heaped ½ cup) stone-ground polenta
* 3 tablespoons olive oil
* 30g (1oz) manchego cheese, grated

FOR THE TRUFFLES

* 2 tablespoons Sichuan peppercorns
* 240ml (8fl oz/1 cup) double (heavy) cream
* 55g (2oz/¼ cup) granulated sugar
* 40g (1½oz) dark baking chocolate, chopped
* 20–25 brandied cherries, drained, rinsed and patted dry
* 5 tablespoons cocoa powder
* 2 tablespoons freeze-dried cherry powder (optional)
* ¼ teaspoon salt

1 Begin with your truffles. In a dry pan over medium heat, toast your peppercorns for about 3 minutes until aromatic and warm. Use a mortar and pestle or a coffee grinder to grind the peppercorns to a powder and set aside.

2 In a small saucepan, warm your cream and sugar over medium heat until the sugar dissolves, taking care not to boil or scald the cream. Remove from the heat and add your ground peppercorns, allowing to infuse for 10 minutes. Strain your cream and return to the stove once more until warm. Place your chocolate in a mixing bowl and pour the warm cream over the top to melt. Stir in your salt, and then continue stirring until smooth. Pour this ganache into a shallow storage container, cover the surface tightly with clingfilm (plastic wrap) and allow to chill in the refrigerator for 4 hours.

3 Once set, use a spoon or melon baller to portion 1-teaspoon balls of ganache. Make a depression into the balls and set a brandied cherry at the centre, then fold in the edges and roll the ganache into a sphere. Dust the finished truffles with cocoa powder, or freeze-dried cherry powder, and set in a cool, dry place until ready to serve.

4 Now start the meatballs. In a mixing bowl, knead together your pork and chorizo, onion, garlic, breadcrumbs, egg, parsley and thyme. Season with salt and pepper and roll into 2.5cm (1in) diameter meatballs.

5 In a skillet, heat your olive oil over high heat. When hot, add your meatballs and sear on all sides, evenly browning them. When browned, add your chopped tomatoes and paprikas, then stir in the stock and sherry. Simmer to reduce the sauce until thick. Set aside and keep warm.

6 To prepare the polenta, bring your chicken stock and 570ml (20fl oz/2½ cups) water to a boil in a saucepan. Lower the heat to a simmer and tip in your polenta, whisking continuously, and continue to stir as it begins to thicken. Stir in your olive oil and cheese, season with salt and pepper and mix until the polenta is smooth and creamy.

7 To serve, top your cheesy polenta with the meatballs and a generous helping of sauce. Reserve your truffles for dessert.

Feast of Taurus:
Spring onion gnudi with braised greens; Chamomile panna cotta with honeycomb candy

More than other Venus-ruled signs, Taurus is associated with sensuality and tactile pleasure. Taureans often gravitate toward experiences which arouse the senses, but are not unnecessarily complicated or fussy. Your approach to food is luxurious but deliberate, grounded in traditional and dependable approaches. Designed in this spirit, your feast features a minimalist flavour profile, which seeks to develop and explore the flavours of springtime – wild garlic, fresh cheese, chamomile and honey. You will find your senses and your love of process sated, as this feast challenges you to prepare from scratch what many prefer to buy ready-made. This is a small ask from you, Taurus, as you value the magic of homemade goods – especially when it comes to cooking.

While these recipes are straightforward, the dessert will take you out of your comfort zone (a high crime against Taureans!). If you've never made candy before, the honeycomb recipe is beginner-friendly – and one of my favourites. It has a dramatic wow-factor, but only takes 20 minutes and uses limited equipment. This recipe needs a sugar thermometer, to ensure your sugar sets firm and dry, instead of soft and sticky. Set up your workstation before you begin, read the recipe carefully, and always keep oven mitts or thick rubber gloves handy to protect your skin when working with hot sugar. While this may sound intimidating, trust me – this foray into the unknown will be worth it. Once you start making candy, you'll find it's addictive – especially for your Taurean sweet tooth!

TAURUS

♀ Venus ♈ Earth ▽

sweet flavours
tender, aromatic herbs
rich, creamy textures
starchy vegetables
nutrient-dense foods

honey
yogurt
cheese & butter
pasta & bread
wheatgrass
beans & lentils
lean meats
nuts & seeds
stone fruits
potatoes & yams

Serves 4
Prep time for full feast: 4 hours
Cook time for full feast: 45 minutes

FOR THE GNUDI
* 28g (1oz) spring onions (scallions) (chives may be used as an out-of-season substitute), finely chopped
* 225g (8oz/1 cup) full-fat ricotta cheese
* 30g (1oz/½ cup) grated Parmesan cheese
* 1 egg
* 130g (4½oz/1 cup) plain (all-purpose) flour, plus extra for flouring
* ¼ teaspoon dried cloves
* 4 tablespoons butter, chilled
* 115g (4oz) rapini (broccoli rabe), swiss chard or garlic scapes
* 60ml (2fl oz/¼ cup) dry white wine
* Chive flowers, to garnish (optional)
* Salt and pepper

FOR THE PANNA COTTA
* 240ml (8fl oz/1 cup) milk
* 480ml (16½fl oz/2 cups) double (heavy) cream
* 6 bags chamomile tea
* 1 tablespoon unflavoured gelatine
* 6 tablespoons honey
* Fresh chamomile flowers, to garnish (optional)

FOR THE HONEYCOMB

* 200g (7oz/1 cup) sugar
* 120ml (4fl oz/½ cup) honey
* 2 teaspoons bicarbonate of soda (baking soda)
* Cornflour (cornstarch), to store

1 Begin with the panna cotta, as this will take time to set. In a saucepan over medium heat, warm your milk and cream together, taking care not to boil or scald it. Remove from the heat and add your bags of chamomile tea, allowing to infuse for 15 minutes. Remove the tea bags, straining them by pressing them against the side of the pan, then discard. Remove 2 tablespoons of this mixture and transfer to a small bowl, then stir in your gelatine and leave for 5 minutes to bloom.

2 Stir the honey into the infused cream in the pan and turn the heat back on. Bring the mixture to 82°C (179°F), then remove from the heat. Stir in your gelatine mixture and whisk thoroughly to combine. Strain your panna cotta and pour into serving glasses until they are two-thirds full. Place the glasses on a tray in the refrigerator to chill and set, about 4 hours.

3 Next, prepare your honeycomb candy. Start by lining a deep 23 x 33cm (9 x 13in) casserole pan with baking parchment and liberally greasing the entire pan with vegetable oil or cooking spray. Keep this pan handy, as the next steps will move quickly.

4 In a medium saucepan, stir together your sugar, honey and 120ml (4fl oz/½ cup) water until evenly mixed. Place the pan over a medium heat and melt the sugar slowly, stirring only just until the sugar dissolves. It is important not to stir while melting your sugar, but to only swish the pan if necessary, as stirring could cause your sugar to crystallize. If you notice this happening around the edges of your pan, use a pastry brush or damp towel to wash down the walls of the pot with water and dissolve the crystals again. As the heat rises, your sugar will begin to darken and caramelize. A deep amber colour is ideal, and you may gently swirl the pot to distribute colour if one spot heats faster than the rest. Bring your sugar to 151°C/305°F (hard crack stage) and remove from the heat.

5 Working quickly, whisk your bicarbonate of soda into the sugar mixture. This will cause the sugar mixture to expand rapidly, so it is important to whisk and quickly transfer your candy to the prepared pan, using a rubber spatula to scrape down the walls of the pan. Set aside the tray of candy and allow it to cool at room temperature. (To clean your pan, fill with water and bring to a boil, which will dissolve any sugar left behind. Discard the water and clean as normal.)

6 To begin your gnudi, mix the spring onions with the ricotta, Parmesan, egg, three-quarters of your flour and the ground cloves in a large mixing bowl. Season with salt and pepper. Knead in enough of the remaining flour for the dough to form a smooth ball. Wrap in parchment or clingfilm (plastic wrap) and chill 30 minutes in the refrigerator.

7 To form your gnudi, you may choose to roll the dough into long, 1cm (½in) thick ropes, cutting your dumplings at 2.5cm (1in) intervals with a knife, or you may choose to roll them by hand. In either case, toss the dumplings with a little extra flour and lay in a single layer while preparing to cook them.

8 Bring a large saucepan of salted water to a boil. When it is at a rolling boil, drop your gnudi into the pot, a few at a time, and boil for 7 minutes or until the gnudi are fully cooked and floating. Adding too many to the pot will lower the temperature, so only cook 6–8 gnudi at a time depending upon the size of the dumplings and the pot. Strain, toss your gnudi in olive oil to keep them from sticking to one another, and set aside.

9 Finally, in a non-stick skillet over medium–high heat, brown 3 tablespoons of butter. Add the gnudi and gently sauté until just browning. Add your rapini, swiss chard or garlic scapes, and cook until the gnudi and greens are seared. Turn the heat to high, stir together your wine and an equal amount of water, then add this to the pan to deglaze. Reduce the sauce until thickened, 3–6 minutes, then remove from the heat and stir in the remaining tablespoon of butter, which will thicken the sauce and give it a velvety finish. Serve immediately, garnished with chive flowers.

10 At dessert, remove your panna cotta from the refrigerator. Crumble about a generous handful of your honeycomb candy and sprinkle liberally on top of your panna cotta. Garnish with chamomile flowers and serve immediately. To store your leftover honeycomb, gently dust with cornflour and store in a cool, dry place for up to 2 weeks.

Feast of Gemini:
Herbed fondue;
Lemongrass pavlova with summer berries

How do you turn a meal into an experiment, or even a game? This is the question I've tried to answer with our feast of Gemini. I myself have three Gemini placements in my chart (sun, rising, Venus) so I understand how our mercurial spirits crave stimulation, excitement and variety. This feast was created in this spirit and leaves things a bit open ended, so you can choose your own adventure. Classic fondue is an unexpected centrepiece these days, and centres the meal around sharing, experimentation and social interaction. For dessert, a bright, herbaceous pavlova cake provides a buffet of textures and flavours – crunchy meringue, luscious summer fruits, tart lemon curd and soft, unsweetened

cream – and will feed all of your guests without being overly saccharine or rich.

To delight your love of trivia, Gemini, here's a fun fact: pavlovas, which are pillowy meringue cakes from New Zealand, were mythically created almost a century ago in honour of the Russian ballerina, Anna Pavlova. I love this symbol of whirling, kinetic ballerinas as inspiration for our Gemini feast, and it doesn't hurt that these cakes are essentially made of eggs and air – Gemini's ruling element. After a rich, first course of cheese fondue and crudités, this cake is a light, refreshing end to the meal, finishing the feast with a dish that is definitely not an afterthought.

GEMINI

☿ Mercury ♈ Air △

inventive flavour pairings
foods for brain & nerve heath
grazing tables
omnivorous diets
aromatic herbs & flowers

---

cured meats
nuts & seeds
mint, lavender & hyssop
broccoli
baked fish
dark chocolate
berries
wine & grapes
oats & whole grains
nightshades

Serves 4
Prep time for full feast: 1 hour
Cook time for full feast: 3 hours

FOR THE FONDUE

* 1 tablespoon olive oil
* 1 clove garlic, minced
* 2 tablespoons finely chopped chives
* 2 tablespoons finely chopped parsley
* 2 tablespoons dried marjoram
* 1 tablespoon dried lavender flowers, crushed
* 290ml (10fl oz/1¼ cups) dry white wine
* 450g (1lb) Gruyère cheese, grated
* 1 tablespoon plain (all-purpose) flour
* Juice of ½ lemon
* Salt and pepper

FOR DIPPING

* Crudités, cherry tomatoes, crusty bread, roasted new potatoes, broccoli, chicory (endive), etc

FOR THE LEMON CURD

* 4 large egg yolks
* 130g (4½oz/⅔ cup) sugar
* 1 tablespoon lemon zest
* 80ml (2½fl oz/⅓ cup) freshly squeezed lemon juice, strained
* 90g (3¼oz/6 tablespoons) butter, softened

FOR THE PAVLOVA

* 4 large egg whites
* 1 stalk lemongrass, outer leaves removed, beaten with the side of your knife and thinly sliced
* 270g (13½oz/1⅓ cups) granulated sugar
* 2 teaspoons cornflour (cornstarch)
* 120ml (4fl oz/½ cup) double (heavy) cream
* A handful each of your favourite summer berries (raspberries, blackberries, currants, gooseberries, blueberries, etc)

1 Begin by preparing the lemon curd. In a double boiler (or heatproof bowl set over a pan of simmering water) over medium heat, whisk together your 4 egg yolks, sugar, lemon zest and lemon juice. Whisk for 10–12 minutes as the mixture heats and thickens, keeping an eye on the texture of your sauce. When it resembles the consistency of hollandaise or béchamel, remove the bowl from the heat.

2 Immediately stir your butter into the curd, whisking until fully melted and incorporated. Pour your curd into a bowl or storage box and place in the refrigerator to set, covering the top with clingfilm (plastic wrap) so that it touches the surface of the curd, which prevents a skin from forming. Refrigerate for at least 1 hour, or until set.

3 Next, start your pavlova by infusing your egg whites with lemongrass. In a blender, add your lemongrass and 4 egg whites and pulse for 2 minutes. The eggs should be frothy, but not whipping into foam. Allow the mixture to sit for 5 minutes, then strain through a fine mesh sieve, squeezing as much of the egg white from the lemongrass as possible.

4 Preheat your oven to 180°C/350°F/Gas 4. Place your infused egg whites in the bowl of a stand mixer and whip until soft peaks form. Slowly add in your sugar, a little at a time, while the mixer runs, whipping until very stiff peaks form and the bowl can be upturned without meringue spilling out. Add your cornflour, beating just a minute more until combined.

5 Trace a 23cm (9in) circle on a piece of baking parchment and

set it on a baking sheet. Spoon your meringue into the circle and use a pastry knife or spatula to spread it into an even circle, leaving a slight depression in the middle. Place the pavlova in the oven and immediately turn the heat down to 100°C/200°F/Gas ½. Bake for 90 minutes, then turn the oven off, leaving the pavlova in the oven as it cools for 2 hours. This pavlova can be made up to 24 hours in advance and stored wrapped in plastic wrap until ready to serve.

6 Closer to serving time, begin your fondue. In a saucepan over a medium heat, warm your olive oil and sauté your garlic until soft and fragrant. Add your herbs, sautéing for 30 seconds more, then stir in your wine. Bring the pot to a simmer.

7 In a small bowl, toss your grated cheese with your flour, then begin slowly adding the cheese to your pot, whisking continuously. When all of your cheese is added, whisk for 2 minutes more to ensure the cheese is emulsified. Stir in your lemon juice, season with salt and pepper, and keep warm until ready to serve, stirring occasionally.

8 At serving time, set your fondue to warm in a fondue pot or crock pot, or elevated over a small sterno or burner. Surround the fondue with your selected crudités and dipping snacks and provide your guests with fondue forks or skewers.

9 At dessert, whip up your cream to stiff peaks (no sugar needed, the cake is sweet enough). Spread this on top of your pavlova, followed by your lemon curd and a generous helping of summer fruit. Serve immediately.

Feast of Cancer:
Poppyseed chicken bake;
Coconut and lotus seed crispy bars

For the feast of Cancer, it's natural we should be working with ingredients of the moon. Since the moon rules water, you'll find aquatic plants featured prominently in these dishes – rice and lotus seeds. This feast also calls for a generous helping of poppy seeds, which are regarded as a plant of the moon because of their great capacity to bring sleep, sedation and dreams. With your lunar allies in abundance, Cancer, this feast is sure to bring the same warmth and comfort that is so characteristic of your sign.

Cancerians have a reputation for their love of generosity and caregiving, and it's likely that this also makes you an incredible host. I'm sure no one at your dinner table goes hungry, and this feast was created in that same spirit, with a focus on comfort food and family-style sharing. These recipes are humble, but traditional favourites always please a crowd and these dishes have enough personality to set them apart from the status quo. You may have had chicken casserole and crispy treats before, but this feast puts a few twists on the classics. This poppyseed-laden chicken bake is scented with fresh herbs and enriched with wild rice, while the bars are packed with crunchy puffed lotus seeds and warmed with a dash of cardamom. While they still feel traditional, these recipes will intrigue your guests, and definitely leave them full and satisfied.

CANCER

☽ The Moon ♈ Water ▽

aquatic plants
cooling fruits & vegetables
sweet, fresh flavours
steamed dishes
comfort foods

---

rice & beans
sea vegetables
cucumbers
water spinach & watercress
natural sugars
melons
brassicas
lotus seeds & roots
aloe & agave
coconut

Serves 4
Prep time for full feast: 30 minutes
Cook time for full feast: 1 hour

FOR THE CHICKEN BAKE

* 100g (3½oz/7 tablespoons) butter
* 3 chicken breasts
* 3 cloves garlic, sliced
* 1 shallot, diced
* 1 leek, sliced
* 4 tablespoons plain (all-purpose) flour
* 480ml (16½fl oz/2 cups) chicken stock
* 120ml (4fl oz/½ cup) dry white wine
* 200g (7oz/1 cup) dried wild rice
* 5 tablespoons poppy seeds, plus more for topping
* Juice of 1 lemon
* 4 tablespoons finely chopped fresh dill
* 90g (3¼oz/2 cups) panko breadcrumbs
* 35g (1¼ oz/½ cup) grated Parmesan cheese
* 1 small bunch parsley, chopped
* Salt and pepper

FOR THE BARS

* Non-stick cooking spray, for greasing
* 4 tablespoons butter
* 280g (10oz) marshmallows
* 85g (3oz/5 cups) puffed rice
* 40g (1½oz/1½ cups) puffed lotus seeds, toasted
* Seeds from 1 vanilla pod (bean)
* ½ teaspoon ground cardamom
* ¼ teaspoon salt

1 Begin with your poppyseed chicken bake. Preheat your oven to 180°C/350°F/Gas 4. In a large frying pan (skillet), melt 1 tablespoon of your butter over high heat. Season your chicken breasts with salt and add them to the pan, searing them for 6–8 minutes on each side until golden brown. Turn the heat down to medium and continue cooking for an additional 6–8 minutes per side until fully cooked. Once done, transfer your chicken to a chopping (cutting) board and use two forks to pull the breasts into shreds. Set the chicken aside.

2 Return the same skillet to a medium–high heat and sauté your garlic, shallot and leek until tender and aromatic – about 5 minutes. Add 2 more tablespoons of your butter and melt them in the pan. Whisk in your flour, then slowly add your chicken stock and wine to the pan, whisking evenly so no lumps of flour remain. Stir in your wild rice and chicken, followed by the poppy seeds, lemon juice and dill. Season with salt and pepper, then transfer the chicken mixture to a 28 x 18cm (11 x 7in) baking dish.

3 To make the casserole topping, mix together your breadcrumbs, Parmesan and parsley, and season with salt and pepper. Melt your remaining butter and stir into the breadcrumb mixture. Top your casserole with the breadcrumbs and bake for 30–40 minutes, or until the filling is bubbly and the topping is golden.

4 Next, begin the crispy bars by preparing a 23 x 33cm (9 x 13in) brownie pan, liberally greasing the bottom and sides with non-stick cooking spray. In a saucepan over medium heat, melt your butter. Stir in the marshmallows and cook until fully melted, stirring continuously. Remove the pan from the heat and stir in your puffed rice, lotus seeds, vanilla seeds, cardamom and salt.

5 Tip your rice mixture into the prepared pan and use a spatula to press it into an even layer. Allow to cool completely, then cut into bars.

6 At serving time, both of these dishes are best served family-style, with the crispy bars reserved for dessert.

Feast of Leo:
Heirloom tomato salad with nasturtium vinaigrette; Cantaloupe and Champagne popsicles

For the royalty of the zodiac, it felt only right to prepare a dish that looks and feels like a plate of shining jewels. In your feast, Leo, you'll be dining on flowers, Champagne-spiked ice pops and the ripest fruits of your season. This salad is one I eat all summer long, especially when corn and tomatoes are in season and at their most flavourful and nutritious. The melon pops are also a summer go-to, since they're effortless to prepare but still feel luxurious on a hot day. Summer produce is such a rare, annual treat that it feels right to serve this feast almost completely raw, allowing each ingredient space to shine. Only the best for you, Leo.

But while this feast is a perfect snapshot of Leo season in-action, it may be hard to source a few of these ingredients once summer fades. For those holding their feasts out of season, substitute nasturtiums with other peppery, tender greens, such as watercress or rocket (arugula). Otherwise, the recipes for both salad and popsicles can be adapted to suit your favourite fruits and vegetables – just keep your quantities consistent and adjust your flavours as needed.

♌

LEO

☉ The Sun ♈ Fire △

colourful fruits & vegetables
fruit sugar & natural sweeteners
ripe, in-season foods
spicy, peppery flavours
open-fire cooking methods

citrus
stone fruits
sunflower seeds
bitter greens
legumes & tofu
shellfish & caviar
olives
beetroots (beets) & radishes
pineapple
quinoa & super grains

Serves 4

Prep time for full feast:
4 hours 15 minutes

Assembly time for full feast:
20 minutes

FOR THE SALAD

* 60ml (2fl oz/¼ cup) olive oil
* A handful of fresh nasturtium leaves and flowers (about 15g/½oz), plus extra flowers for garnish
* 30ml (1fl oz/2 tablespoons) Champagne vinegar or white wine vinegar
* 2 teaspoons Dijon mustard
* 1 ear of corn
* 1 small shallot, sliced
* 2 cloves garlic, finely minced
* 30g (1oz) feta cheese, crumbled
* 680g (24oz) heirloom tomatoes, cubed or cut into wedges
* 50g (6 tablespoons) sunflower seeds
* Salt and pepper

FOR THE POPSICLES

* 175g (6oz/heaped ¾ cup) granulated sugar
* 1 tablespoon chopped fresh mint leaves
* 1 tablespoon chopped fresh basil leaves
* 2 tablespoons honey
* 240g (8½oz/1½ cups) diced cantaloupe melon
* 250ml (9fl oz/1 cup) Champagne

I Begin with the popsicles, as these will take time to freeze. In a small saucepan, bring 250ml (9fl oz/1 cup) water to the boil with the sugar and fresh herbs. Stir to dissolve the sugar, then remove from the heat. Stir in the honey, strain and let cool to room temperature.

2 In a blender, purée your cantaloupe until smooth. Stir this into your cooled sugar mixture, followed by your Champagne. Fill 8–10 lolly (popsicle) moulds with your Champagne mixture and insert a lolly (popsicle) stick into each one. Freeze for 4 hours, or until ready to serve.

3 Begin the salad by preparing your vinaigrette. In a blender, combine your olive oil, nasturtium leaves and flowers, vinegar and mustard. Blend until evenly incorporated, then season with salt and pepper. Set your vinaigrette aside.

4 At serving time, wash and dry your vegetables. If you have a barbecue, grill your ears of corn until blackening; otherwise boil them in a large pot of salted water for 3 minutes. Once cooked, cut the kernels away from the cob. Place these in a large serving bowl, along with your shallot, garlic, feta, tomatoes and sunflower seeds. Toss to combine, then dress with your nasturtium vinaigrette and serve, garnished with extra flowers. Serve the popsicles for dessert.

Feast of Virgo:
Lemon lavender roast chicken;
Russian honey cake

The feast of Virgo features some of the most eye-catching recipes in this book. Both centrepieces in their own right, these dishes are show-stoppers – tried-and-true favourites which, if executed to perfection, will be the rock stars of any feast table. That's very much your nature, Virgo – to make all others look like they didn't even try. But while this feast is certainly impressive, it is also (almost) effortless, and will be one you can whip up quickly between your many other projects. And while you may be surprised not to see Virgo's trademark ingredient – wheat – featured prominently in this feast, it takes a back seat to feature flavours of your ruling planet, Mercury – lavender and strong, spicy honey.

A quick note about dessert: if you're used to baking your cakes in pans, this honey cake will likely feel a bit unfamiliar at first. Each layer of this eight-layer cake is baked individually, by spreading the batter on sheets of parchment instead of baking in a cake pan. Once baked, these thin layers are easy to assemble and the cake can be frosted as normal. There are a few extra steps, Virgo, but I know you don't mind – you know the value of complex dishes executed to perfection, and this feast is sure to present an exciting challenge and a delicious reward.

VIRGO

☿ Mercury ♀ Earth ▽

simple, whole foods
fatty, nutritious nuts & seeds
red meats
salads & raw dishes
vitamin-rich ingredients

---

wheat & whole grains
lamb, beef & veal
fruit juices
apples
turmeric
hazelnuts & pistachios
pomegranate
beans & legumes
sprouts & sprouted grains
corn

Serves 4
Prep time for full feast: 45 minutes
Cook time for full feast: 90 minutes

FOR THE CHICKEN

* 1 whole chicken
* 4 tablespoons fresh or dried lavender buds
* Leaves from 2 sprigs of thyme
* 90g (3¼oz/6 tablespoons) butter, softened
* 1 lemon
* Salt and pepper

FOR THE CAKE

* 6 tablespoons honey
* 1 teaspoon bicarbonate of soda (baking soda)
* 100g (3½oz/7 tablespoons) butter
* 3 eggs
* 175g (6oz/heaped ¾ cup) granulated sugar
* 260g (9oz/2 cups) plain (all-purpose) flour
* ½ teaspoon salt
* 300ml (10fl oz/1¼ cups) double (heavy) cream, cold
* 180ml (6fl oz/¾ cup) sweetened condensed milk

1 Begin with your honey cake. Preheat your oven to 180°C/350°F/Gas 4 and place a small saucepan over medium-low heat. Add your honey, bring it to a simmer, then stir in your bicarbonate of soda. Cook for 4–5 minutes or until the honey darkens and has a deep caramel aroma. Stir in your butter until completely melted, then remove from the heat and allow to cool.

2 In the bowl of a stand mixer, beat your eggs until foamy. Slowly add your sugar and beat on medium-high speed until the mixture is light and aerated – about 6 minutes. Stream the honey mixture into the bowl and beat just until fully combined. Fold in your flour and salt in 3–4 additions, working slowly to keep as much air in the eggs as possible.

3 When ready to bake the layers, use a 23cm (9in) cake pan or a compass to trace 23cm (9in) circles on 9 sheets of parchment paper. Using 4–5 tablespoons of batter, spread a ½cm (¼in) thick circle of batter onto one of the sheets of parchment paper. Bake until firm, about 6–10 minutes, then repeat for the rest of the parchment and batter until you have 9 layers in total.

4 Make your frosting by whipping the cream in the bowl of a stand mixer until stiff peaks form. Fold in your sweetened condensed milk, then season with salt.

5 To assemble the cake, select your least perfect cake layer and crush it into crumbs using a ziplock bag and a rolling pin. Spoon a dab of frosting onto your serving plate, and then place your first cake layer. Spread a thin layer of frosting on top, then add another layer of cake. Continue until all the layers are used, then cover the top and exterior of the cake with your frosting. Dust the cake with your crumbs and chill in the refrigerator until ready to serve.

6 Next, prepare your chicken. Preheat the oven to 180°C/350°F/Gas 4 (or just keep it on if proceeding after the cake is finished). Wash your bird and, working from the cavity toward the neck, use your fingers to gently loosen the skin away from the flesh. Stir your lavender and thyme into the softened butter and use it to liberally coat the chicken, both under and over the skin, as well as within the cavity.

7 Slice your lemon in half crosswise and, working from the centre, slice 6–8 thin slices of lemon from the widest part. Slip these slices under the chicken skin, so that they show through elegantly. Quarter the lemon ends which remain, and place these inside the cavity of the chicken. Season with salt and pepper, then roast for 45–60 minutes, or until golden and cooked through.

8 At serving time, remove the lemons from within the cavity of your chicken. Carve the chicken and serve alongside salad or side dishes, reserving your cake as a sweet reward afterward.

Feast of Libra:
Floral papardelle with pistachio sauce; Roasted pineapple with basil mousse

Ruled by the laughter-loving planet Venus, the feast of Libra is a joy to behold. These dishes are herbaceous, surprising, and rely upon naturally bold and botanical flavours to deliver Libra's classic people-pleasing charm in spades. It doesn't get much simpler than pasta and roasted fruit, but this feast channels Libra's flair for theatre and love of aesthetic, turning something humble into something dramatic. For a polished look, take care to reserve a few extra flower petals from your pasta to garnish the finished plate. For dessert, use two warm spoons to form a smooth, even scoop or "quenelle" from your mousse. These little finishing touches will impress your guests, which comes as no surprise, since you're already known for being a fabulous host.

But it's not all about looks, Libra. As a sign of Venus, sensory indulgence is the name of the game, so your feast will naturally be a pleasure to the eyes, the nose and, of course, the palate. The deeply Venusian flavours of pistachio, caramelized pineapples, flower petals and cream are incredibly rich, making these dishes feel almost like comfort food – if they weren't so obviously fancy. But these dishes are not needlessly frilly, nor fancy for its own sake. Instead, the beauty of these recipes is how they highlight the natural, exquisite shapes and textures of their ingredients. That's one of your best qualities, Libra – your ability to focus on the beauty of ordinary things. It's why everyone can't get enough of you – and why you won't be able to get enough of this feast.

LIBRA

♀ Venus ♈ Air △

edible flowers
fancy, special-occasion treats
caramelized fruits & vegetables
beautifully presented meals
sweet, tart & zesty flavours

berries & forest fruits
(bell) peppers
apples, pears & quinces
cured meats
cakes & desserts
olive oil
squash & sweet potatoes
vanilla
bananas & mangoes
peas

Serves 4
Prep time for full feast: 4 hours
Cook time for full feast: 30 minutes

FOR THE PASTA
* 225g (8oz/1¾ cups) 00 flour
* 85g (3oz/½ cup) semolina flour, plus extra for dusting
* 3 eggs
* 85g (3oz) mixed fresh edible flowers and herbs (rose, borage, calendula, tiger lily, sage leaves, nasturtium, dill, parsley, cornflower, poppy petals, etc), plus extra to serve

FOR THE SAUCE
* 200g (7oz/2 cups) shelled pistachios, chopped, plus 3 tablespoons to serve
* 1 handful fresh parsley, washed and stems removed (about ½ cup)
* 2 tablespoons olive oil
* 120ml (4fl oz/½ cup) double (heavy) cream
* 225g (8oz/1 cup) ricotta cheese
* ½ teaspoon crushed chilli (red pepper) flakes
* ½ teaspoon salt
* ½ teaspoon black pepper

FOR THE MOUSSE AND PINEAPPLE

* A bunch of basil (about 60g/2oz)
* 290ml (1¼ cups/10fl oz) milk, plus 2 tablespoons
* 2¼ teaspoons powdered gelatine
* 115g (4oz) white chocolate, chopped
* 240ml (8fl oz/1 cup) double (heavy) cream
* 85g (3oz/scant ½ cup) sugar
* 1 pineapple
* 3 tablespoons honey

1 Begin with your mousse, as this will take some time to set. Bring a small pan of water to a boil and blanch your basil leaves for 5 seconds, then submerge in ice water. Strain and wring the leaves as dry as possible. In a blender, purée the basil leaves with your milk until the milk takes on a delightful green colour, then strain to remove the basil. Add your gelatine to the basil milk and leave to bloom for 5 minutes.

2 In a bain marie, melt your white chocolate. Whisk in your basil milk until evenly combined and all gelatine is dissolved. Remove from the heat and cool to room temperature.

3 In the bowl of a stand mixer, whip your cream and sugar together until stiff peaks form. Gently fold the whipped cream into your chocolate mixture, then transfer the mousse to a large storage container. Chill in the refrigerator until fully set, at least 3 hours.

4 In a food processor, combine your 00 and semolina flours, then add your eggs. Blend until the dough is crumbly and sandy. Turn the dough out onto a work surface and knead until it comes together into a soft, smooth ball. Divide the dough into 4 pieces and cover lightly with a damp towel so they do not dry too quickly.

5 Using a pasta machine, roll one portion of the dough to a 3mm (⅛in) thickness, keeping the other portions of dough covered while you do. Decorate your sheet of dough with a single layer of flower petals and fresh herbs, but do not press them into the dough. Roll out one more portion of dough to 3mm (⅛in) thickness, then lay this second layer on top of the first and press them together gently so that they adhere. Pay special attention to the edges of your dough, making sure both sheets are fully adhered before proceeding. Divide this herbed pasta dough in half, then run each half through the pasta machine until they are 3mm (⅛in) thickness once more. Repeat this process with the other two portions of dough, then use a pizza cutter to slice the dough into 5mm (¼in) thick strips of fettuccine. Toss the pasta with semolina flour and set aside.

6 Preheat your oven to 200°C/400°F/Gas 6 and line a baking sheet with baking parchment. Remove the crown and base from your pineapple, then trim down the sides to remove all the skin and spines. Slice your pineapple from top to bottom into 2.5cm (1in) wedges, separating the flesh from the core. Place your pineapple wedges on the prepared baking sheet. Mix your honey with 3 tablespoons water and brush the pineapple pieces with half of the honey mixture. Roast for 15 minutes, then flip your slices, brush with remaining honey mixture, and roast for another 15 minutes until golden and caramelized. Remove from the oven and set aside.

7 To make the pistachio sauce, use a food processor to pulse your pistachios and parsley together. Heat your olive oil in a skillet over medium heat and when it is hot, add your nut mixture to the pan. As the mixture warms, stir in your cream, ricotta and seasonings, simmering until the sauce is thickened. Take care not to overheat your sauce, as this can cause your cream to split.

8 Bring a large stock pot of salted water to a boil and add your pasta. Cook for 3–4 minutes, stirring occasionally, until tender. Strain your pasta, then transfer it to the skillet, tossing in the pistachio sauce to coat.

9 Serve your pasta immediately, topped with chopped pistachios, flower petals and sprigs of herbs. For dessert, plate your slices of caramelized pineapple and top with a scoop of chilled basil mousse.

Feast of Scorpio:
Pork loin with pickled mustard seeds;
Blood orange sorbet with Fernet-Branca

The feast of Scorpio is serious and refined – not overly rich, but deeply infused with bitter-leaning flavours that tread the line between savoury and sweet. Scorpio has a reputation for being reserved on the outside but privately passionate, and these dishes are also much more complex than they appear at first glance. Roasted pork loin is infused with herbs and spices, sweetened with a touch of honey, and accompanied by pickled mustard seeds, which pop and explode in the mouth like caviar to lend a tangy, sweet acidity to the dish. If you've never pickled mustard seeds before, they're about to become your new favourite condiment and are perfect for roast meats, sandwiches, salads and alongside charcuterie. For dessert, bitter winter citrus meets complex, syrupy Fernet – a fruit-forward

departure from traditional desserts, which falls somewhere between a cocktail and a palate cleanser. You will need an ice cream machine for this recipe.

Taking inspiration from the foods of Scorpio season, this feast explores the darker side of the palate, working with flavours that can sometimes be challenging to control – bitter blood orange, botanical amaro and spicy whole mustard seeds. But just as Scorpio teaches us how to temper what is revealed or concealed, these dark and potent flavours are balanced with tart vinegar and sweet honey so that they can challenge the palate – not dominate it. Even in their bitterness, these dishes highlight Scorpio's early-winter flavours and remain faithful to the Scorpio's love of simplicity and sensuality.

♏
SCORPIO

♇ Pluto ♈ Water ▽

pungent, aromatic dishes
braising & poaching
rich sauces
red meats & shellfish
bitter & complex flavours

---

asparagus
black beans
dark leafy greens
squid, oysters & lobster
smoked meats
grapefruit
beer & hops
blackberries
beef & pork
horseradish

Serves 4
Prep time for full feast: 1 hour
Cook time for full feast: 1 hour

FOR THE PORK LOIN

* A 1.4kg (3lb) pork loin
* 3 tablespoons olive oil
* 1 sprig fresh rosemary, finely chopped
* 1 teaspoon sweet paprika
* 4 cloves garlic, minced
* 3 tablespoons honey
* 4 tablespoons soy sauce
* 1 tablespoon Dijon mustard
* Salt and pepper

FOR THE MUSTARD SEEDS

* 120ml (4fl oz/½ cup) apple cider vinegar
* 3 tablespoons sugar
* 1 teaspoon salt
* 30g (1oz/¼ cup) mustard seeds, white and black

FOR THE SORBET

* 700ml (24fl oz/3 cups) freshly squeezed blood orange juice
* 150g (5½oz/⅔ cup) honey, agave syrup or light corn syrup
* 25ml (1fl oz) vodka
* Fernet-Branca (or another amaro), for topping

1 Ahead of making the sorbet, freeze or otherwise prepare your ice cream machine as per the manufacturer's instructions. In a small saucepan over medium heat, warm your blood orange juice to a simmer. Stir in your honey or syrup and whisk until dissolved. Remove from the heat and stir in your vodka. Place the syrup into your ice cream machine and run until the sorbet is prepared, about 1–2 hours depending on your ice cream maker. When ready, store in the freezer until serving time.

2 Next, wash and pat dry your pork loin and place it in a roasting pan. Preheat your oven to 190°C/375°F/Gas 5. In a small saucepan, heat your olive oil over medium–high heat. When warm, add your rosemary, paprika and garlic, and cook until the garlic is soft and fragrant. Stir in your honey, soy sauce and Dijon and remove from the heat once fully combined. Season with salt and pepper.

3 Brush the pork loin liberally with the sauce and place in the oven. Roast for 60 minutes or until the loin is cooked through, pausing every 20 minutes during cooking to brush the loin with the remaining sauce. If using a larger or smaller pork loin, the general rule for cook times is 20 minutes per pound, plus an additional 20 minutes. Please keep this in mind.

4 While the loin roasts, prepare the mustard seeds. In a medium saucepan over high heat, combine your vinegar, sugar and salt with 120ml (4fl oz/½ cup) water. Bring to a boil, then stir in your mustard seeds. Turn the heat down to low and simmer for 30 minutes, or until the seeds are plump and tender. Remove from the heat and store in an airtight jar for up to 1 month in the refrigerator.

5 At serving time, carve your loin and serve with the pickled mustard seeds, alongside salad or side dishes. For dessert, place a scoop of your sorbet in each glass, top each with 2 tablespoons of Fernet and serve immediately.

Feast of Sagittarius:
Fig, prosciutto and blue cheese flatbreads; Hibiscus brownies

As a Gemini, there are so many qualities of Sagittarians that I deeply relate to – their love of culture and travel, their quest for new ideas, and their yearning to experience the entire world in meaningful, action-oriented ways. Ruled by Jupiter, Sagittarius loves expanding their worldview and experimenting with new perspectives, and prefers tactile engagement with their environment to theoretical consideration. You don't just want to think about the world, Sagittarius – you want to see it for yourself! But as their quest for stimulation and experience tends to keep them in motion, Sagittarians are also known for their laid back and unfussy nature – going with the flow and taking each new experience as it comes.

In keeping with these themes, your feast features big, Jupiter flavours – figs, prosciutto, olive oil – as well as the exotic addition of Jupiter-ruled hibiscus, which adds a botanical tartness to otherwise classic brownies. These recipes are unpretentious and fun, and appeal to your inquisitive inner child's sense of play. If preparing this feast for a group, allow each guest to prepare their own flatbread, letting them have their own adventure in choosing flavours, textures and ingredients. This feast also comes together quickly, feeding a crowd in under two hours of work, giving you time to get back to your busy schedule of travel, experience and exploration. It is my hope that this feast is an extension of your infectious *joie-de-vivre*, and brings a bit of that classic Sagittarian charm and playfulness to your table.

Serves 4
Prep time for full feast: 30 minutes
Cook time for full feast: 1 hour

FOR THE FLATBREADS

* 4 flatbreads
* 1 tablespoon olive oil
* 450g (1lb) fresh figs, washed and quartered
* 1 small red onion, sliced
* 115g (4oz) blue cheese, chilled
* Needles from 2 sprigs rosemary
* 225g (8oz) thinly sliced prosciutto di Parma
* A bunch of fresh rocket (arugula)
* 2 tablespoons balsamic reduction (optional)

FOR THE BROWNIES

* 30g (1oz/½ cup) dried hibiscus flowers
* 225g (8oz/1 cup) butter, melted, plus extra for greasing
* 280g (10oz/scant 1½ cups) sugar
* 170g (6oz/¾ cup plus 2 tablespoons) brown sugar
* 4 eggs
* 85g (3oz/scant 1 cup) unsweetened cocoa powder
* 130g (4½oz/1 cup) plain (all-purpose) flour
* ½ teaspoon baking powder
* 1 teaspoon salt
* 120g (4oz/1 cup) fresh raspberries, sliced in half
* 230g (8oz) dark chocolate chips
* 240ml (8oz/1cup) double (heavy) cream

1 Begin by preparing the brownies. Preheat your oven to 180°C/350°F/Gas 4 and grease a 23 x 33cm (9 x 13in) brownie pan. In a mortar and pestle or spice grinder, grind your hibiscus flowers to a powder and set aside, reserving 1 tablespoon in a separate dish.

2 In a large bowl, whisk together your melted butter and sugars to combine. Beat in your eggs, then the cocoa powder. In a separate bowl, mix together the flour, baking powder, hibiscus powder and salt, then fold this into the egg mixture.

3 Transfer the brownie batter to the prepared pan. Top the batter with your raspberries and bake for 35–45 minutes, or until a toothpick inserted into the centre of the brownies comes out clean. Remove from the oven and allow to cool in the pan.

4 While the brownies bake, lay your flatbreads on a baking parchment-lined baking sheet and brush with your olive oil. Toast these in the oven alongside your brownies for 8–10 minutes, or until crisping at the edges. Remove from the oven and set aside.

5 Place your dark chocolate chips in a large bowl, and set your cream in a small saucepan over medium high heat. Heat your cream until it just begins to bubble, then pour over your chocolate and allow to sit for 10 minutes. Stir together until combined, then pour the ganache over the top of your cooled brownie pan. Garnish with a dusting of your reserved hibiscus powder, then set the pan in the refrigerator for at least 20 minutes, or until the ganache is set.

6 Decorate your flatbreads with the figs, red onion, cheese, rosemary, prosciutto and rocket. Return to the oven for an additional 10 minutes, or until the cheese is softened and melting. Remove from the oven, drizzle with your balsamic reduction, if using, and serve immediately. Cut your brownies and set them out for dessert.

Feast of Capricorn:
Sausage and plum hunter's stew; Blackberry meringues

The feast of Capricorn is a simple, rich meditation on the sign of the goat, with qualities befitting a beast of the deep earth and mountain heights such as yourself. Your planetary ruler, Saturn, suggests you have very fine taste but prefer simple ingredients and preparations. Your unmatched ambition and attention to detail call for refinement in cooking, but your earth aspect demands luscious flavours and textures as well. Flashy dishes will fail to impress you if they lack substance and your discerning eye will be sure to know the difference.

This feast features Saturn's classic ingredients – mushrooms, meats, blackberries and ferments –

but gives them nowhere to hide. There is an art to withholding, even with flavour, and Saturn teaches this well. In this spirit, the stew of meats and wine cuts its richness with creamy white beans, and the meringues set tangy, warm blackberries against a pillow of unsweetened cream. The quality of your ingredients will deliver in the final result, so treat yourself to high-quality produce and meats for this feast. Both main and dessert also feature slow cooking methods, so Saturn's requisite patience is an essential ingredient as well. This feast is unpretentious at first glance, but if anyone can take the fruits of the earth and elevate them to great heights, it's you, Capricorn.

♑

CAPRICORN

♄ Saturn ♈ Earth ▽

deep, luxurious flavours
dark-coloured foods
high-protein dishes
slow cooking methods
natural ferments

---

mushrooms
cured meats
beer & wine
forest fruits
allium vegetables
vinegar
whole grains
pickles & kraut
unsweetened cream
root vegetables

Serves 4

Prep time for full feast: 30–40 minutes

Cook time for full feast: 90 minutes

FOR THE STEW

* 2 tablespoons olive oil
* 1 large shallot, sliced
* 225g (8oz) sliced oyster or maitake mushrooms
* 2 slices thick-cut smoked bacon, chopped into 1cm (½in) strips
* 450g (1lb) smoked kielbasa (or similar coarse, smoked sausage), thickly sliced
* 2 black plums, cut into wedges
* 2 cloves garlic, sliced
* 350g (12oz) jar of red cabbage, drained
* 2 pinches ground cloves
* ½ teaspoon Dutch process cocoa powder (unsweetened)
* 3 tablespoons chopped fresh dill
* 350ml (12fl oz/1½ cups) dry red wine
* 1 x 400g (14oz) can giant white beans or butter beans, drained and rinsed
* 1 teaspoon salt
* Black pepper
* Crusty bread, to serve

FOR THE MERINGUES

* 225g (8oz/generous 1 cup) granulated white sugar
* 1 tablespoon cornflour (cornstarch)
* 4 egg whites, at room temperature
* 1 teaspoon lemon zest, grated
* 60g (2oz/3½ tablespoons) blackberry preserve

FOR THE MERINGUE TOPPING

* 225g (8oz/1¾ cups) fresh blackberries
* 3 tablespoons honey
* 3 tablespoons balsamic vinegar
* 240ml (8fl oz/1 cup) double (heavy) cream, chilled

I For the meringues, preheat your oven to 120°C/250°F/Gas ½. Line two baking sheets with baking parchment and trace two 10cm/4in diameter circles on each. Flip the parchment over so that your pen marks are on the back of the paper, face-down. In a small bowl, mix together the sugar and cornflour. Add the egg whites to the bowl of a stand mixer and whisk until frothy. With the mixer running, gradually add the sugar and cornflour mixture and whisk until stiff peaks form. Fold in your lemon zest and blackberry preserve, leaving streaks of purple through the meringue. These streaks will remain visible inside the cooked meringues.

2 Using a piping bag or two spoons, pile the meringue onto your prepared parchment paper, making a 5cm (2in) tall mound of meringue in the circles you drew, then use a spoon to make a depression in the centre of each mound. Bake the meringues for 60–75 minutes, rotating the pan halfway through the cooking time, until they are slightly golden and firm to the touch. Turn off your oven and allow the meringues to cool inside the oven for 2 hours.

3 Next, make the meringue topping. In a small saucepan, combine the blackberries, honey, balsamic vinegar and 2 tablespoons water. Bring to a boil, then reduce the heat and simmer over medium–low heat. When the sauce is thick and bubbly and coats the back of your mixing spoon, remove the berries from the heat and set aside.

4 Begin the stew by heating your olive oil in a large sauté pan over high heat. Add the shallot and mushrooms and turn the heat down to medium–high, cooking until the mushrooms lose water and begin to brown. Add the bacon and cook until browning, then add the sausage, plums and garlic. Sauté until the garlic is soft, then add the red cabbage to the pan. Cook for 2 minutes, then add the cloves, cocoa and dill, followed by the wine. Simmer on medium-low until the stew is reduced by half, about 20 minutes. Stir in the beans and allow to simmer until the stew has thickened, about 10–15 minutes more. Season with the salt and black pepper and serve with crusty bread.

5 When you are ready to serve dessert, whip the cream in the bowl of a stand mixer until stiff peaks form. Remove the meringues from the oven and set them on serving plates. Spoon the cream over the meringues and make a well in the top with the back of your spoon. Spoon the berries over the top, and drizzle with any remaining sauce. Serve immediately.

Feast of Aquarius:
Duck breast with blueberry balsamic sauce; Honey, walnut and goat's cheese tart

One of the key archetypes for Aquarius is the mad scientist – the one who creates for the sake of creativity, the innovator and maverick, and the revolutionary. To give your inventive side a culinary challenge (I know you love a challenge!), this feast swaps dinner and dessert, delivering a sweet, fruit-forward entrée and an almost-savoury final course. Both feature the favoured ingredients of your traditional planetary ruler, Saturn, who loves natural ferments like cheeses, soy sauce, vinegars and wines. The flavours of each dish are complex. Each of the five tastes are represented, seeking to challenge the palate with new experiences – the salty caramelization of crispy duck skin, the bitterness of toasted walnuts, the sweetness of blueberries and honey, the tartness of vinegar, and the savouriness of fatty meat and cheese.

This feast will call on some specialized techniques as well, appealing to the Aquarian love of gadgetry and learning new skills. First, you will be called upon to score your duck breast in a classic cross-hatch pattern. You may find this easier to do with a very sharp knife, and also if your duck has been chilled or briefly frozen first so that the fat stiffens and the skin is easier to slice. Additionally, this recipe calls for the use of pastry weights, to blind bake your tart shell. If you have no weights, use dry beans or rice to weigh down your tart shell; they will help the dough keep its shape while it bakes. Of course, if you have your own invention or contraption you'd like to use instead, be my guest, Aquarius. With these recipes as a starting point, your creative vision and sense of radical play will transform this feast into something really out of this world.

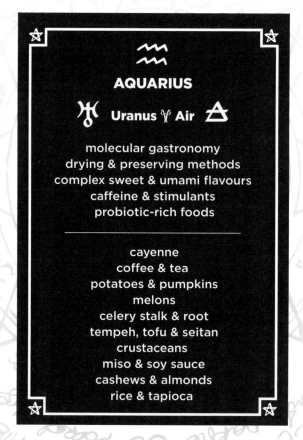

AQUARIUS

♅ Uranus ♀ Air △

molecular gastronomy
drying & preserving methods
complex sweet & umami flavours
caffeine & stimulants
probiotic-rich foods

cayenne
coffee & tea
potatoes & pumpkins
melons
celery stalk & root
tempeh, tofu & seitan
crustaceans
miso & soy sauce
cashews & almonds
rice & tapioca

Serves 4

Prep time for full feast: 1 hour
Cook time for full feast: 1 hour

FOR THE DUCK AND SAUCE

* 1 tablespoon olive oil
* 450g (1lb) fresh blueberries
* 90ml (3fl oz/6 tablespoons) balsamic vinegar
* 60ml (2fl oz/4 tablespoons) red wine
* 2 tablespoons honey
* 2 tablespoons soy sauce
* 4 duck breasts, skin on
* Salt and pepper

FOR THE TART

* 200g (7oz/1¾ cup) whole walnuts, toasted
* (4½oz/1 cup) plain (all-purpose) flour, plus extra for dusting
* 1 tablespoon granulated sugar
* 4 tablespoons butter, chilled and cut into 5mm (¼in) cubes
* 90–120ml (3–4fl oz/6–8 tablespoons) ice-cold water
* 115g (4oz/½ cup) cream cheese, softened
* 175g (6oz) goat's cheese, softened
* 115g (4oz/½ cup) sour cream
* 4 tablespoons honey, plus extra to drizzle
* 1 large egg
* 70g (2½oz/½ cup) walnut halves
* Salt

I Preheat your oven to 180°C/350°F/Gas 4. Begin by preparing your tart shell. Use a food processor or mortar and pestle to chop your toasted walnuts as finely as possible. In a large bowl, mix together the walnuts, flour and sugar. Using your hands or a pastry cutter, cut your butter into your flour mixture until no large clumps of butter remain. Slowly add your cold water, 1 tablespoon at a time, mixing just until the dough comes together in a smooth ball. Wrap in baking parchment or clingfilm (plastic wrap) and chill in the refrigerator for 20 minutes.

2 When the dough has chilled, remove it from the refrigerator and place it between two sheets of floured baking parchment. Roll the dough into a 5mm (¼in) thick circle with a 30cm (12in) diameter. Carefully transfer the dough to a 25cm (10in) tart dish with a loose base and press the dough into place, then trim away the excess dough. Set a layer of baking parchment over your dough and fill the tart case with pie weights or dried beans. Bake for 8 minutes, then remove from the oven and allow to cool. Remove the parchment and weights/beans when cool.

3 In the bowl of a stand mixer fitted with a paddle attachment, or using a spatula, beat together your cheeses and sour cream. Add your honey and season with salt, then beat in your egg. Transfer the batter to your tart shell, and level off the surface with a palette knife. Carefully set your walnut halves around the rim of the tart. Bake for 25–30 minutes, or until just set in the centre. Remove the tart from the oven and allow to cool in the dish.

4 Next, prepare your blueberry sauce. Heat your olive oil in a saucepan over medium heat and add your blueberries. Stir until the berries are darkened and swelling, then add your vinegar, red wine, honey, soy sauce and 6 tablespoons of water. Bring the sauce to a simmer, then turn the heat to low. Cook to reduce the sauce until it is thick and syrupy and coats the back of your mixing spoon. Season with salt and pepper, and set aside.

5 Finally, prepare your duck breasts. Directly after removing them from the refrigerator, score the skin in parallel lines across the breast, then turn the breasts 90 degrees and score in parallel lines again, creating a crosshatch pattern of cuts. Keep your cuts shallow, about 5mm (¼in) deep. Season the breasts with salt and set aside.

6 Place your duck breasts, skin-side-down, into two cold frying pans, with two breasts per pan. You may choose to use one pan, but this method will save you time and ensure that the food is ready at the same time. Turn the heat to medium–low, and allow the breasts to gently sizzle. Keep the heat balanced so the fat doesn't spit. Cook for 15 minutes, or until the skin is crispy and golden brown, pouring off any rendered fat as required. Bring the heat up to medium and flip the breasts, cooking for another 3–5 minutes, or until an instant-read thermometer shows an internal temperature of 60°C/140°F (for medium doneness). Remove the breasts from the pan and set aside to rest.

7 At serving time, slice your duck breasts and serve with the blueberry sauce over the top. Drizzle the tart with honey before serving. You may reserve your tart for dessert, but this almost-savoury pastry would make a fine accompaniment to the duck as well. Make your own rules, Aquarius!

Feast of Pisces:
Roasted cauliflower with miso and yogurt; Elderflower pâte de fruit

Associated with Neptune, the heady sphere of spirituality and visions, Pisces is known for an imaginative approach to life and I wanted this feast to feel just as dreamy. These dishes appear as if from another world, in colours and textures that feel exotic and alien. Thick-sliced cauliflower steaks, slathered in miso and honey, are drizzled with herb-infused yogurt, producing a dish that bursts with flavour and texture. For dessert there are perfect squares of translucent pâte de fruit, which look like cut gems but melt on the tongue, delighting with the strange sweetness of elderflower liqueur. Your guests will be transported by this feast to someplace far from home – someplace deep within the visionary realm of your own creation.

However, building dreamworlds on earth is no easy task, as any Pisces can attest, and this feast features one of the more process-based recipes in my personal grimoire. Pâte de fruit, sometimes called "dry jam", is a French confection made using sugar, apple pectin and citric acid to create sweet and bouncy fruit jellies, like an elevated cousin to gummy sweets. This recipe summons Pisces' love of liquor and spirits, and uses pears simmered in elderflower liqueur as a botanical base. If you've not worked with apple pectin or citric acid before, they can both typically be found in the baking aisle of your supermarket, and most health food stores will carry them. This recipe also requires some special equipment – a cooking thermometer and silicone baking mat, which can both be found at baking supply shops. While it may sound complex, the pâte de fruit comes together quickly in just a few short steps, allowing you to create something truly otherworldly.

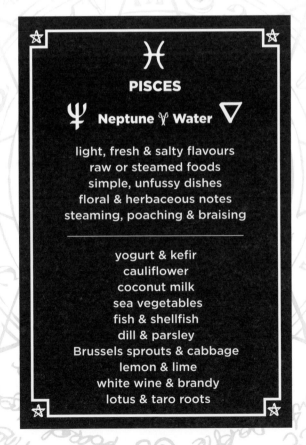

PISCES

♆ Neptune ♓ Water ▽

light, fresh & salty flavours
raw or steamed foods
simple, unfussy dishes
floral & herbaceous notes
steaming, poaching & braising

---

yogurt & kefir
cauliflower
coconut milk
sea vegetables
fish & shellfish
dill & parsley
Brussels sprouts & cabbage
lemon & lime
white wine & brandy
lotus & taro roots

Serves 4
Prep time for full feast: 3 hours
Cook time for full feast: 40 minutes

FOR THE CAULIFLOWER

* 4 tablespoons olive oil
* 2 tablespoons white miso
* 2 tablespoons tahini
* 1 tablespoon red wine vinegar
* 2 teaspoons honey
* A head of cauliflower, cut into 2.5cm (1in) thick "steaks"
* 175g (6oz/¾ cup) plain Greek yogurt
* 4 tablespoons chopped fresh mint
* 4 tablespoons chopped fresh dill
* 1 clove garlic, chopped
* Juice of 1 lemon
* 1 tablespoon sesame seeds
* Salt and pepper

FOR THE PÂTE DE FRUIT

* 750ml (26fl oz/3¼ cups) elderflower liqueur
* 2 Williams (Bartlett) pears, peeled, cored and cut into rough chunks
* Non-stick cooking spray, for greasing
* 500g (1lb 5oz/3 cups) granulated sugar, plus extra for coating
* 23g (about 2 tablespoons) apple pectin powder
* 90g (3¼oz/6 tablespoons) light corn syrup or liquid glucose
* 1 rounded teaspoon (about 7g/¼oz) citric acid

1 Begin with your pâte de fruit. In a medium saucepan, combine your elderflower liqueur and pears. Bring the liquid to a boil, then reduce the heat so it is simmering. Reduce the liquid by half, cooking slowly to ensure as much alcohol is cooked off from the liqueur as possible. When finished, transfer the mixture to a blender and purée your pears and syrup together. Strain the purée and return to the saucepan once more. You should have 450ml (16fl oz/2 cups) of finished purée – if there is slightly less, you may add a small quantity of water to compensate.

2 Line a 46 x 33cm (18 x 13in) sheet tray with a silicone baking mat and grease thoroughly with non-stick cooking spray. (Ordinarily, wiping down the surface of your tray with vegetable oil would suffice, but here an even, thorough coating of fat is essential and so cooking spray is preferable.)

3 Bring the purée to a simmer over medium heat. In a separate small bowl, stir together 50g (1¾oz/¼ cup) of your sugar and the apple pectin, then slowly add the sugar mixture into your bubbling purée, whisking continuously to ensure there are no lumps. Whisk in your remaining sugar, the corn syrup and citric acid, and bring the mixture to 107°C/225°F. Continue to hold the mixture at this temperature for 2 minutes, carefully monitoring your heat, then pour the mixture onto your prepared sheet tray to firm up at room temperature. When the pâte has cooled, slice neatly into cubes and toss with sugar to coat. Lay the sweets (candies) in a single layer on baking parchment and store in a cool, dry place at room temperature for up to 3 days.

4 To prepare your cauliflower steaks, preheat your oven to 180°C/350°F/Gas 4 and line a baking sheet with baking parchment. In a small bowl, whisk together 2 tablespoons of your olive oil with the miso, tahini, vinegar, honey and 1 tablespoon water. Lay your cauliflower steaks down on the prepared baking sheet and use a brush to liberally coat both sides of the steaks with the miso sauce, and season with salt and pepper. Bake for 30 minutes, or until the cauliflower is tender when pierced through the stem with a fork. I recommend flipping the steaks halfway through baking to ensure they are crispy and toasted all over.

5 While the cauliflower bakes, prepare the yogurt sauce. In a blender, combine your remaining olive oil with your yogurt, mint, dill and chopped garlic. Blend on high until combined, then stream in your lemon juice. Season with salt and pepper and set aside.

6 When your cauliflower steaks are done, serve immediately with a drizzling of your mint yogurt sauce and a garnish of sesame seeds. After dinner, offer your guests the pâte de fruit as a palette cleanser. These candies keep for up to 3 days, especially when stored in a cool dry place and tossed with granulated sugar. These also make a great take-home party favour for guests!

Feast of the Heavens

Planetary magic in the kitchen

Feast of the Heavens

T here exists an engine in the heavens; an ever-churning wellspring of power that has swirled above our heads in perfect synchronicity since before life came to earth – older than man, older than magic. This mechanism is comprised of our closest planetary spheres – Mercury, Venus, Mars, Jupiter and Saturn, along with the luminous Moon, and the Sun around which they all revolve. A working knowledge of these spheres and their properties forms the basis for planetary magic, which draws its power and inspiration from the fabric of the cosmos itself. This branch of magic originates deep within ancient history, and walks a line between astrology and practical magic in its inquiry of how the planets can be used for our work as witches. However, when we think about the role of these planets in the ancient world, it's important to remember the way the cosmology of ancient magicians differs from the one we have today.

In their foreword for the *Picatrix*, an 11th-century book of astrological magic dealing with these very spheres, John Michael Greer and Christopher Warnock describe this older perspective, stating that "the sources of magical power [were] in the macrocosm rather than the microcosm; power is native to the universe, not to the mage."[6] Here, the art of magic is to study and interpret these currents of creative power descending from above, and through proper timing and the use of sympathetic materia, capture these forces for their own ends.

While this is not a complete expression of how magic worked throughout the entire ancient world, it certainly describes the way the world worked for ancient planetary magicians, especially those who practised during classical antiquity, where this practice became solidified in the western system of magic. In this view of magic, the magician or witch is not the engine of the working, but rather a hunter or huntress using their knowledge of astrology and correspondences to capture heavenly energies, as filtered through the seven spheres.

When we talk about planetary magic today, we're talking about a specific paradigm through which we can make our magic manifest in the world. Every aspect of magic and the human experience can find a correspondence among the heavenly spheres, and we can use these planets as archetypal focal points for harnessing their specific influence in our work. We can call their influence into our work through rites of veneration and invocation, where the planet is exalted with petitions and offerings in the hope of receiving its more benevolent virtues. For example, many witches seek to calm the unpredictable and troublesome energy of Mercury in retrograde by performing acts of veneration to the planet itself, in the hope of channelling its more agreeable aspects. A witch might burn a Mercury incense during this time, read a charm requesting Mercury's benefits, or even create a talisman which captures Mercury's more positive qualities, in the hope of staving off the planet's challenging retrograde effects.

For our purposes in kitchen witchcraft, planetary magic could mean the careful selection of ingredients associated with these spheres, prepared at auspicious times and in conjunction with appropriate symbols, to produce a meal worthy of celestial honour. Through this work of preparing, cooking and consuming dishes as an act of invocation or veneration, we literally take these planetary virtues into ourselves, and are transformed as they fuse into the fabric of our bodies. Through this simple practice, we can use their influence via sympathetic magic to alter our current reality, plan the timing of spellwork with precision, help us embody certain aspects of their rulership or to navigate the effects of astrological weather.

Through most of human history, people have only been aware of the "classical planets" – Mercury, Venus, Mars, Jupiter and Saturn, along with the Sun and the Moon. The outer planets were not discovered until the late 18th century and onward. For this reason, much of our classical writing on the associations and correspondences of the planets in magic is limited to the seven planetary spheres. From these original seven spheres, each was designated rulership over one day of the week, and the etymology of our names for the days of the week reflects this – Saturn rules Saturday, the Sun rules Sunday, the Moon rules Monday, and so on.

These are the days when the effect of this planet is said to be the strongest, and magical work done on the day of a planet's greatest influence will bear the strongest imprint of its energy.

Additionally, each planet is assigned rulership to particular hours of the day, and calculating these planetary hours can be incredibly useful in finding precise times for spellwork under ideal astrological conditions. For example, it would be best to work our love spells under the influence of Venus, perhaps on Venus' day of rulership (Friday) and at the hour of Venus as well. You can find a complete chart of planetary correspondences within this chapter. To use this chart to calculate planetary hours yourself, you'll need to find the precise times for sunrise and sunset for the day you wish to calculate. From there, divide the time between sunrise and sunset into twelve segments, or "planetary hours", and then use the chart to determine the rulership of the hour in question. Using these correspondences, along with moon phases and other astrological weather, can help us choose precise timing for our magical work that is the most aligned with our desires – and can, hopefully, provide the energetic boost we need to secure results.

In examining these heavenly spheres, we can begin closest to the sun with the planet Mercury.

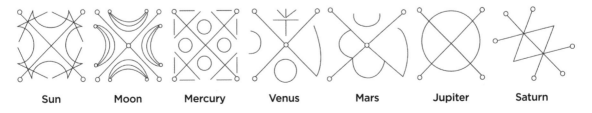

| Sun | Moon | Mercury | Venus | Mars | Jupiter | Saturn |

Planetary seals given by Heinrich Cornelius Agrippa in the 16th century, from Three Books of Occult Philosophy

☿ Mercury is the "first in line" from the centre, with the shortest orbit and quickest rotation through the solar system. Mercury rules communication, travel, information, language, decision making and our intellectual selves. It is associated with the element of air, the sword suit in the tarot, and rules over the zodiac signs Gemini and Virgo. Mercury embodies the archetypes of the messenger and the magician, and thus governs the actualization of ideas and the use of magic itself. Because of its association with opposites and dichotomies, Mercury is also viewed as being archetypally dual-gendered, logical rather than emotional, and amoral in its embodiment of the trickster archetype. In classical mythology, Mercury is equated to the psychopomp Hermes, who traverses the spheres of the heavens and the underworld with ease. Hermes governs roads, medicine, mathematics, the alphabet, and other intellectual pursuits, while also embodying the trickster aspect with cunning pranks on his half-brother, the sun god Apollo. This close relationship between Hermes and Apollo mirrors the proximity of Mercury and the Sun, which are really never too far apart.

♀ Second from the Sun is Venus, the famed planet of love, poetry and tactile pleasures. Venusian energy is romantic, domestic, beautiful, harmonious, resilient, lavishly comfortable and pleasing to the senses. If Mercury rules the powers that bring people together in communication, it is Venus that binds them together in community and love. Venus is archetypally feminine and associated with the element of earth and the zodiac signs of Taurus and Libra. She is mirrored in the Empress card of the tarot, which bears her symbol prominently, and reflected in the classical goddess Aphrodite, who bestows great powers of love, beauty and ecstatic joy to her devotees. Generally speaking, when Venus appears in relationships, she brings peace and tranquillity, encouraging comfort, safety and egalitarian resolutions to conflict. However, because of the extremely charming and seductive nature of Venus, her archetype is sometimes given an amoral connotation, in that her powers can be used to both give pleasure to lovers and secure emotional domination over men and gods alike. We can see a hint of this correspondence in one suspected root of her name – *venes* in Latin, which means "poison"; a compound which can be medicinally valuable in some doses, and lethal in others.

♂ Our third sphere from the Sun (excluding Earth, of course) is that of Mars, the potent, warlike, archetypally masculine planet. Mars governs boundaries, injury, self-assertion, aggression, sexuality, adventure, impulsiveness, physical strength and competition. Where Venus signifies love and connection, Mars is passion, conflict and action. Mars is associated with the element of fire and the zodiac signs of Aries and Scorpio, as well as the Emperor card of the tarot. In classical mythology, Mars is the god of war and bloodshed, and shares its correspondence to iron weapons and red, iron-rich blood with the iron-filled soils of Mars itself – the "red planet". Mars is considered to be the lesser of the malefic planets, meaning Mars bears challenging, restrictive and negatively-aspected energy wherever he goes. However, Mars also grants blessings of protection, safe boundaries, confidence and security, so there are certainly benevolent virtues to be accessed through this sphere as well.

♃ Our fourth planet is the great ruler Jupiter. Jupiter is the good king, the just judge, great protector and guardian. Jupiter's energy is megalithic, as mirrored in Jupiter's outstanding size among the planets, and rules growth, expansion, opportunity, success, miracles, prosperity, luck, justice and good fortune. Jupiter is associated with the elements of both air and fire, as well as the Wheel of Fortune in the tarot and, to a lesser extent, the Hierophant as well. Where Mars is a malefic planet, full of restriction and challenges, Jupiter is the greater benefic planet, more potent in this regard than the minor benefic, Venus. This means its energy is generally helpful, fortuitous and magnanimous, leading toward the greater good at all times. Because Jupiter moves through such a royal archetype as well, it also rules ascendance through higher education, spiritual progress and career success. While our earlier planets have been slightly amoral in their correspondences, Jupiter is a planet very concerned with what is good, right and just, and as such is also very concerned with the law, both legal and moral.

♄ Finally, we come to the outermost of the classical planets, ringed Saturn. In classical mythology, Saturn is the proto-Olympian god Kronos, a leader among the Titanic deities, who rules the cyclical sowing and reaping of crops, social order, precision and conformity. This planet rules Capricorn and, to a lesser extent, Aquarius, and is the great planet of limits, focus, tradition, reckoning, responsibility, endurance, the value of hard lessons, and collection on what is owed. Saturn is associated with the element of earth, but less like the green fecundity of Venus' realm, and more like the everlasting minerality of mountains and caves. Because of these virtues, Saturn is deeply associated with death as a function of cosmic justice; when depicted as the god Kronos, his trademark symbol is the scythe. If Mars rules the act of dying and bloodshed, then Saturn is the inevitable rot that follows, where the components of life are recycled for future use and the borrowed elements of our bodies are returned to the planet once more. This greater malefic planet can certainly be difficult and challenging to navigate, as many of his aspects are brutally harsh, but the return on Saturn's slow and often painful lessons are gifts that stand the test of time. On the other hand, when he is well-aspected, Saturn can be immeasurably creative, dedicated beyond compare and able to survive anything.

☉ Returning to the centre of the solar system, we encounter the powerful presence of the Sun, our home star. This luminary body is regarded as the "king of the cosmos", being both the grand, unknowably powerful engine of our solar system, and also the sphere which most directly impacts our daily lives. We feel the wax and wane of the sun's influence in the cycles of day and night, the course of the seasons and the currents of the winds and the oceans – all of which make the impact of the Sun's energy more tangible than that of the other planets. This sphere is regarded as archetypally masculine, and corresponds with purification, passion, exorcism, enlightenment, the delivery of prophecy and the pure creative principle. In the tarot, the Sun card clearly represents this sphere, and he also rules both the physical organ of the heart and the zodiac sign of Leo.

☽ If the Sun represents our external selves and our ego, then the moon is our internal selves and our intuitive aspects. The moon is Earth's satellite, another heavenly luminary, formed from Earth's own flesh when Theia, a Mars-sized asteroid, struck our planet and sent a significant portion of its vaporized mass flying into space.

Planetary hours table

	MONDAY	TUESDAY	WEDNESDAY	THURSDAY	FRIDAY	SATURDAY	SUNDAY
RULING PLANET	Moon	Mars	Mercury	Jupiter	Venus	Saturn	Sun
Day Hours 1	☽	♂	☿	♃	♀	♄	☉
2	♄	☉	☽	♂	☿	♃	♀
3	♃	♀	♄	☉	☽	♂	☿
4	♂	☿	♃	♀	♄	☉	☽
5	☉	☽	♂	☿	♃	♀	♄
6	♀	♄	☉	☽	♂	☿	♃
7	☿	♃	♀	♄	☉	☽	♂
8	☽	♂	☿	♃	♀	♄	☉
9	♄	☉	☽	♂	☿	♃	♀
10	♃	♀	♄	☉	☽	♂	☿
11	♂	☿	♃	♀	♄	☉	☽
12	☉	☽	♂	☿	♃	♀	♄
Night Hours 1	♀	♄	☉	☽	♂	☿	♃
2	☿	♃	♀	♄	☉	☽	♂
3	☽	♂	☿	♃	♀	♄	☉
4	♄	☉	☽	♂	☿	♃	♀
5	♃	♀	♄	☉	☽	♂	☿
6	♂	☿	♃	♀	♄	☉	☽
7	☉	☽	♂	☿	♃	♀	♄
8	♀	♄	☉	☽	♂	☿	♃
9	☿	♃	♀	♄	☉	☽	♂
10	☽	♂	☿	♃	♀	♄	☉
11	♄	☉	☽	♂	☿	♃	♀
12	♃	♀	♄	☉	☽	♂	☿

This cloud of earth-dust coalesced through gravity to form the moon we know today, one of the largest moons in our solar system. This violent origin hints at some of the moon's archetypal characteristics, which can often be amoral and two-handed. For example, while the moon is relied upon as a symbol of constancy and light in the darkness, it is also deeply embedded within the trickster archetype, which it shares with Mercury. The tarot also speaks to this dichotomy, wherein the moon corresponds to both the High Priestess and the Moon cards. The former represents our psychic self and all the deeply hidden knowledge it can reveal, while the latter speaks to a fear of the unknown and unfamiliar. The moon is also archetypally feminine and associated with the element of water and the zodiac sign of Cancer. It is said to rule over all dreams and divinations, and well as our deeply-hidden emotional and intuitive selves. For these reasons, and for its proximity to Earth, the moon has been relied upon as a particularly powerful ally in spellwork and witchcraft.

As the moon revolves around the Earth, its shifting position gives us the moon's trademark phases. These phases mark the life and death, or wax and wane, of the lunar cycle, and represent the heightening and diminishing of her influence over the world. While the phases are cyclical, the new moon is generally regarded as the start of the cycle, with the moon appearing to be "born" from darkness as she waxes into view. As the moon illuminates and gathers power, she soon arrives at the half moon, a time when the moon is equal parts dark and light. This phase straddles a liminal place, making available to us a doorway to the psychic and intuitive self, strengthening the communication between this part of ourselves and the external world. Finally, before the moon makes her slow descent into darkness once more, she culminates in her fullest expression on the full moon, the height of the lunar cycle. The full moon, whose energy is typically coloured by her position within the wheel of the zodiac, is a time of heightened illumination, culmination, expression and release. If we focus intentions and plant the seeds of future magic on the new moon, the full moon is the reap tide, when we come to collect on what we have nurtured to fruition.

While these are very general examples of how the lunar phases and planets can be worked into magic, your own experience and experiments with these virtues will yield more complex correlations that will be more meaningful to your work. If this technology still seems too theoretical, the tables on the following page should be playgrounds for your imagination, where you can look at how these planetary correspondences and qualities line up with ingredients and recipes within the chapter. As is always the case, your beliefs and practice will colour the specifics of your rituals, but this outline should prove useful in forming an understanding of how planetary magic works. You can read them as examples of how this technology can be put into practice – a jumping-off point for you to fully explore planetary magic within the kitchen. Prepare dishes in veneration of the planets to gain their favour, consecrate your cookware with seals and symbols of the planets, and use their motions to be deliberate and precise in your work.

SUN

THEMES: Success, exorcism, fame, joy, prophecy, physical healing, identity

---

FLAVOURS: Bright, sweet, aromatic

HERBS: Angelica, bay, chamomile, cloves, marigold, rosemary, saffron, sunflower

---

FOODS: Almond, butter, cereal grains, corn syrup, dates, frangipane, gooseberry, hearts of palm, lime, jams, mulberry, pasta, peanut butter, oranges, quinoa, rose hips, sugarcane, turmeric, wheat, whiskey

MOON

THEMES: Cleansing, second sight, conquering fear, divination, healing from trauma

---

FLAVOURS: Mild, crisp, fresh

HERBS: Anise, dittany, hops, jasmine, mugwort, oat straw, poppy, sage, yarrow

---

FOODS: Agave, aloe, bamboo, banana, cabbage, cheese, coconut, cucumber, duck, eggs, leafy greens, lotus seeds, marshmallow, melons, milk, potato, pumpkin, rice, salt, seaweeds, shellfish, yam, yogurt

MERCURY

THEMES: Progress, inspiration, communication, clarity, persuasion, transformation

---

FLAVOURS: Floral, herbaceous, complex

HERBS: Caraway, carrot seed, dill, ginkgo, lavender, parsley, sassafras, tarragon

---

FOODS: Beans, bean shoots, carrot, cashew, cauliflower, celery, coffee, confectionery (candy), courgette (zucchini), fennel, honey, game meats, lemon, lemongrass, millet, peas, rabbit, spinach, tamarind, tea leaves, tofu, wheatgrass

VENUS

THEMES: Romance, pleasure, love, home, blessing, artistic expression, beauty, glamour

---

FLAVOURS: Indulgent, sweet, caramelized

HERBS: Bergamot, cardamom, clover, hibiscus, lemon balm, mint, orchid, rose

---

FOODS: Apples, avocado, barley, berries, bread, burdock, cacao, cherry, chocolate, dumplings, desserts, edible flowers, fenugreek, fish, grapes, legumes, oysters, peaches, pistachio, pomegranate, sorrel, wine, violet

♂
MARS

THEMES: Boundaries, protection, curses, courage, sexuality, domination, victory

---

FLAVOURS: Savoury, spicy, warm

HERBS: Basil, black pepper, borage, cinnamon, nasturtium, pine, thistle, wormwood

---

FOODS: Alcohol, artichokes, asparagus, red meat, beer, cactus pear, cranberry, curry, dandelion greens, fried foods, ginger, horseradish, leeks, mustard, nettle, okra, (bell) peppers, radicchio, radishes, raspberry, red lentils, watercress

♃
JUPITER

THEMES: Appeals to authority, abundance, justice, good fortune, expansion, wisdom

---

FLAVOURS: Nutty, rich, deep

HERBS: Grape leaf, holy basil, hyssop, liquorice, linden, nutmeg, sumac

---

FOODS: Aubergine (eggplant), broccoli, Brussels sprouts, butternut squash, chicken, chickpea, figs, flax, ginger, grapefruit, lamb, molasses, maple syrup, olive oil, pears, red and white plums, pineapple, rhubarb, rye, turmeric

♄
SATURN

THEMES: Survival, resilience, rebirth, return, discipline, limits, breaking addictions

---

FLAVOURS: Bitter, salty, sour

HERBS: Coriander (cilantro), blackberry leaf, elder, hemp, mullein, thyme, valerian, willow

---

FOODS: Amaranth, beetroot (beets), blackberry, black plums, black rice, blue corn, capers, corn, eel, fermented foods, fiddleheads, garlic, gin, hempseed, hickory, mushrooms, onions, pickles, quail, sesame, vinegar

NEW MOON

Darkness ⚥ Rebirth

MAGIC: Bless new projects, protection magic, refresh altars, set intentions, shadow work

FOODS: Eat dark foods and those which come from underground: figs, beetroot (beets), mushrooms, garlic, kale, black beans, squid ink, seaweeds, pumpernickel bread

FULL MOON

Light ⚥ Fulfilment

MAGIC: Cast spells, cleansing, consecration, dreamwork, love magic, strength

FOODS: Eat pale, white or silver foods: honeydew, cabbage, fennel, fish, white beans, lotus root, yogurt, eggs, sage, pine nuts, coconut, banana, tofu

HALF MOON

Liminality ⚥ Balance

MAGIC: Communication with spirits, divination, glamour magic, prophecy, sorcery

FOODS: Eat herbs and foods which relax the body and promote the intuitive senses: mugwort, dittany, yarrow, chicken, duck, elderberry, lemongrass, anise, almond

WAXING MOON

Increase ⚥ Gain

MAGIC: Attraction, financial magic, luck magic, manifestation, opening roads

FOODS: Eat sweet, light, nutritious foods: dried fruits and nuts, berries, whole grains, sugar, honey, cured meats, chillies, tempeh, whipped cream

WANING MOON

Diminishing ⚥ Loss

MAGIC: Banishing, binding, curses, exoticism, grounding, invisibility, purification

FOODS: Eat bitter, rich, fermented foods: pickles, sauerkraut, dark leafy greens, black tea, cheeses, beer, onions, grapefruit, roast meats, dark bread

Full Moon Feast:
Mushroom and parsnip soup;
Gnocchi with sage blossom pesto;
Black sesame cake

The evening of the full moon is significant for European witchcraft traditions and for religions the world over. On this night, the illuminated face of the moon is *nyktophaneia*, "night-shining", and pulls upon the Earth to swell the tides to their fullest. She gives a rare light to the nighttime and inspires the hearts of poets, artists and witches as she casts her strange glow down to Earth. Since the moon observes a predictable orbit and resides so close to Earth, her influence is more palpable than that of other planets, and in the pinnacle of her cycle, the moon is said to give her gifts in excess – dreams, visions, and the possibility to slip from linear reality.

In the ancient world, any obscuration of the moon was viewed as an ill-omen, with eclipses and new moons being especially dangerous. On the other hand, the full moon was said to embody the moon's more luminary aspects, but it was still not without its dangers. In ancient Greece, it was believed that

people could exhibit madness or lunacy as a direct consequence of the full moon. In the middle ages, it was believed that European witches would transgress their physical bodies during the full moon to meet their devil-lover in the wilderness. In 16th-century France, a full moon that fell on a Friday had the power to turn humans into werewolves simply with its shining rays.

Feared and revered, the full moon continues to inspire us, and offers modern witches a powerful time to conduct their rituals beneath her otherworldly light. The following feast was designed to be served in ceremony on the full moon, and to be a meditation on herbs and ingredients that share the moon's more luminary virtues. While this feast serves only two, you may multiply the ingredient quantities for the soup and gnocchi recipes as many times as needed to feed the whole coven. The black sesame cake, on the other hand, will serve up to 10 guests, so keep this in mind as you plan the guest list for your next full moon feast.

Serves 2

Prep time for full feast: 1 hour
Cook time for full feast: 2 hours

FOR THE SOUP
* 2 tablespoons olive oil
* 225g (8oz) mixed mushrooms – chestnut (cremini), oyster, shiitake, maitake, portabello, or any mix you like!
* 1 leek, split, washed, and sliced into 5mm (¼in) slices
* 2 cloves garlic, sliced
* 1 celery stalk, diced
* 2 parsnips, peeled and cut into 1cm (½in) cubes
* 1 pinch ground cloves
* 1 teaspoon salt
* ½ teaspoon ground white pepper
* 700ml (24fl oz/3 cups) chicken stock (broth)

FOR THE GNOCCHI
* 350g (12oz) potato gnocchi
* 85g (3oz) fresh sage blossoms or leaves, plus extra blossoms to serve
* 60g (2oz) fresh parsley
* 1 large clove of garlic, minced
* 40g (1½oz/¾ cup) grated Parmesan cheese
* 60g (2oz/½ cup) pine nuts, toasted
* 90ml (3fl oz/6 tablespoons) olive oil
* Salt and pepper

FOR THE CAKE
* Butter, for greasing
* 90ml (3fl oz/6 tablespoons) extra virgin olive oil
* 200g (7oz/1 cup) granulated sugar
* 3 large eggs

* 1 teaspoon vanilla extract
* 210g (7½oz/1½ cups) plain (all-purpose) flour
* 1½ teaspoons baking powder
* ¼ teaspoon salt
* 2 tablespoons black sesame seeds
* 120ml (4fl oz/½ cup) buttermilk

FOR THE FROSTING
* 115g (4oz/½ cup) butter, softened
* 225–280g (8–10oz/1⅔–2 cups) icing (confectioner's) sugar
* 3 tablespoons milk
* 6–8 tablespoons black sesame seeds, ground fine in a coffee grinder or mortar and pestle
* Salt

Full Moon Feast

I On the eve of the full moon, begin by starting your cake and frosting. Preheat your oven to 175°C/350°F/Gas 4 and prepare two 15cm (6in) cake pans by lining them with baking parchment. For each pan, cut out a circle of parchment to fit the base, and inscribe upon the parchment Agrippa's seal of the moon (see right). Set this parchment in the base of each pan and grease both pans thoroughly.

2 In the bowl of a stand mixer, beat the olive oil and sugar until light and fluffy. Beat in the eggs and vanilla. In a separate bowl, combine the flour, baking powder, salt and sesame seeds. In alternating batches, add your flour mixture and the buttermilk to the oil and egg mixture, ending with the buttermilk. Divide the batter evenly between the prepared cake pans and, using a knife or skewer, trace the lunar sigil again into the surface of both cakes. Bake for 25–30 minutes or until a toothpick inserted into the centre of the cake comes out clean.

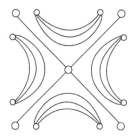

3 In the bowl of a stand mixer, make the frosting by whipping the soft butter until light and fluffy. Add the icing sugar in small batches, making sure it is fully incorporated before adding more. Stir in the milk and sesame powder, and season with salt to taste. Allow your cakes to cool fully before frosting. To frost your cake, place one round onto your serving plate, and cover evenly with a quarter of your frosting. Place your second round on top of the first, and frost the top and sides of the cake with the remainder of your frosting.

4 Begin the soup by heating the olive oil in a medium saucepan. Add the mushrooms and sauté until browning. Add the leek, garlic and celery and sauté until soft. Finally, add the parsnips, cloves and seasonings, sautéing for 2 minutes before covering with the stock. Bring the pot to a boil, then turn the heat down to medium-low and allow to simmer for 20 minutes or until the parsnips are tender. Remove the pot from the heat and carefully ladle your soup into a blender, or use an immersion blender to process until smooth.

5 Lastly, make the gnocchi. Bring a large pot of salted water to a boil and add the gnocchi, cooking until tender; about 4 minutes, or until the gnocchi float to the top of the pot. Wash the sage blossoms and parsley and trim away the stems. Add these to a food processor with the garlic, Parmesan and pine nuts. Blend until finely chopped, then stream in the olive oil, blending until the pesto is smooth. Season with salt and pepper. Toss the gnocchi in your pesto, garnishing with extra sage blossoms, and serve.

6 Before eating, set aside a small, sacrificial portion of the meal and place it upon your working altar, the altars of lunar deities, or upon a moonlight-soaked windowsill. Burn frankincense and dedicate your meal in honour of the moon by reading aloud one of her many invocations, charms or hymns. Consider the "Homeric Hymn to Selene", the goddess who personified the moon in classical antiquity. Use this hymn as both an invocation and a powerful meditation on the qualities of the moon as she shows her face in fullness.

And next, sweet voiced Muses... tell of the long-winged Moon. From her immortal head a radiance is shown from heaven and embraces earth; and great is the beauty that ariseth from her shining light. The air, unlit before, glows with the light of her golden crown, and her rays beam clear, whensoever bright Selene having bathed her lovely body in the waters of Ocean, and donned her far-gleaming, shining team, drives on her long-maned horses at full speed, at eventime in the mid-month: then her great orbit is full and then her beams shine brightest as she increases. So she is a sure token and a sign to mortal men...
THE HOMERIC HYMN TO SELENE [7]

Sun:
Dandelion and orange fritule

Since the sun rules our personalities and identities, I've decided to pull a special recipe from my ancestral cookbook for this feast. *Fritule* are ricotta doughnuts, similar to Italian *zeppoles*, though smaller and chewier, and are beloved on the Dalmatian coast of Croatia where my family is from. The basics of this recipe were given to me by my grandmother, who has been making *fritule* since she was 10 years old. This recipe has been a treasured part of family holidays for my entire life, and I'm excited to present it now as homage to my Croatian identity, and to the long line of ancestors behind me who have carried this recipe through history, to deliver the version you see on this page.

While traditional *fritule* are flavoured with lemon zest, raisins and whiskey (all ingredients of the Sun in their own right) this version receives a modern, solary update. Fresh ginger and candied orange peel bring a brightness to the recipe, while the dough itself is packed with nutty sunflower butter and golden dandelion petals. These little heliotrope flowers have a gentle flavour of their own, and the petals run ribbons of colour through the dough that look like little shards of light. Dandelions can be gathered fresh from spring through autumn, or substituted for other edible, solar flowers – calendula, sunflower, acacia, etc.

Consider serving this dish on a Sunday, during the hour of the sun, accompanied by solar incenses of frankincense, labdanum, angelica, saffron or rosemary.

Makes about 50 *fritule*
Prep time: 30 minutes
Cook time: 30 minutes

* 700ml (24fl oz/3 cups) vegetable oil
* 450g (1lb/2 cups) ricotta cheese
* 3 tablespoons sunflower butter
* 1 egg, plus 1 egg yolk
* Zest of 2 lemons
* 3 tablespoons whiskey
* 260g (9oz/2 cups) flour
* ½ teaspoon salt
* 120ml (4fl oz/½ cup) milk
* 4 tablespoons sugar
* 1 teaspoon baking powder
* 15g (½ cup) fresh dandelion petals
* 115g (4oz/½ cup) candied orange peel, finely minced
* 1 tablespoon finely grated fresh ginger
* Icing (confectioner's) sugar, for dusting

1 In a medium saucepan, set your vegetable oil over medium heat to warm up.

2 In a large bowl, combine your ricotta, sunflower butter, whole egg, egg yolk, lemon zest and whiskey. Use a wooden spoon or spatula to stir until combined. Sift your flour and salt over the ricotta mixture and set aside.

3 In a cup, use a fork to whisk together your milk, sugar and baking powder until frothy and bubbly. Pour the milk mixture into the large bowl and use a wooden spoon to stir together until combined. Stir in your petals, orange peel and ginger, then continue to stir by hand until some gluten has developed and the dough begins to become smooth and tacky, about 10 minutes.

4 Drop a small amount of the dough into your oil to check the temperature. The dough should sizzle upon contact, but the bubbles should be small and fizzy, not rolling and spitting. If your heat is too high, the doughnuts will cook unevenly, so adjust your heat accordingly to stay at a steady medium flame.

5 Using a spoon and your fingertips, form small, 3cm (1in) balls of dough and drop them into the oil in small batches so as not to crowd the pan, frying for 5–8 minutes, or until the outside of each *fritule* is golden and the inside is cooked through. Toss in icing sugar and serve immediately.

Moon:
Creamy mugwort soup

This dish is best served in the evening, within a few hours of going to bed. Mugwort is a herb which can bring vivid dreams and visions, especially during the new and full moons, and so this feast can be an assistive prelude to an evening of dream divination. While mugwort itself can be quite bitter, the astringent flavours are softened a bit by the comforting richness of potato, mushrooms and cream. It is certainly an exotic treat, although wild foods like mugwort can often be a challenge to the palate; but this soup still feels hearty and familiar when all is finished – and the added boost of mugwort's dream-enhancing power is the perfect side effect for a lunar feast.

To maximize the lunar quality of this meal, prepare this recipe in the evening on a Monday, with an incense of lunar fragrances – poppyseed, storax, seaweed, black frankincense – accompanied by libations made from the plants of the moon, such as rice wine or mugwort beer.

Serves 4
Prep time: 15 minutes
Cook time: 30 minutes

* 180g (6oz/6 cups) fresh, wild mugwort
* 60g (2oz/2 cups) fresh spinach
* 1 tablespoon butter
* 2 cloves garlic, minced
* 200g (7oz/2 cups) white mushrooms, sliced (about 12–15 mushrooms)
* 1 large, starchy potato, peeled and diced
* ¼ teaspoon grated nutmeg
* 1.4 litres (48fl oz/6 cups) vegetable stock (broth)
* 240ml (8fl oz/1 cup) double (heavy) cream
* Salt and pepper

I Wash your mugwort thoroughly and separate the leaves from the stem. Chop the mugwort and spinach leaves and set aside.

2 In a saucepan, melt your butter over a medium heat and add the garlic, stirring just until fragrant. Add your sliced mushrooms and cook until they have released their water and are beginning to brown – about 8 minutes.

3 Add your mugwort and spinach to the pot, followed by your potato and nutmeg. Cook for 1 minute, then add your stock. Bring the pot to a boil, then turn the heat to low and simmer uncovered for 20 minutes.

4 Add your cream slowly, stirring clockwise as you do, and season with salt and pepper to taste. Simmer gently for 3 more minutes, stirring occasionally. Remove from the heat and carefully blend your soup, either in a standing blender or with an immersion blender. Ladle into bowls and serve immediately.

Mercury:
Lavender butter with herbed seed crackers

The archetype of Mercury is known for its fast-paced energy, so it felt right to serve a dish in Mercurial honour that felt a bit more light and informal. This dish is one you can set out at the start of a party, but it is also a perfect afternoon snack that provides energy and stimulation during the day. The seed crackers are richly aromatic and give a crunchy, textural contrast to soft, herb-infused butter. I recommend serving this dish alongside freshly sliced vegetables of Mercury – radishes especially – or as an accompaniment to charcuterie, encouraging a Mercurial experimentation with a variety of flavour combinations.

To maximize the Mercurial virtue of this meal, serve this dish on a Wednesday, alongside Mercurial incense of benzoin, lemongrass, anise seed or lavender. You may choose to begin this meal with a small Mercurial ritual, like reading, journalling or reciting charms, since Mercury rules the spoken word. Consider reading aloud some useful Greek epithets of Hermes (the god linked with Mercury in the Greek pantheon):

AGORAIOS – "Of the Marketplace"
for money magic
DIAKTOROS – "Messenger, Guide"
for clarity and communication
FORTUNUS – "Of Fortune"
for good luck
INTERPRES – "The Mediator"
for reconciliation and negotiation

Serves 6–8
Prep time: 30 minutes, plus chilling and resting the dough
Cook time: 10 minutes

FOR THE BUTTER

* 115g (4oz/½ cup) salted butter, softened
* 2 tablespoons each of chopped fresh dill, and sage
* 1 tablespoon cracked black pepper
* 5 tablespoons dried lavender

FOR THE CRACKERS

* 210g (7½oz/1½ cups) plain (all-purpose) flour, plus extra for dusting
* 2 tablespoons black sesame seeds
* 2 tablespoons white sesame seeds
* 2 tablespoons caraway seeds
* 1 tablespoon anise seeds
* 1 tablespoon poppy seeds
* 1 tablespoon salt
* 1 teaspoon sugar
* 1 teaspoon black pepper
* 2 tablespoons olive oil

1 In a large bowl, whip your soft butter with the fresh herbs, pepper and 1 tablespoon of the dried lavender. Spoon your butter onto a sheet of clingfilm (plastic wrap) and roll gently into a log, making sure the butter is rolled tightly. Once shaped, set the butter in the refrigerator to firm up.

2 For the crackers, preheat your oven to 200°C/400°F/Gas 6.

3 Combine your flour, seeds, salt, sugar and pepper in a large mixing bowl. Add your olive oil and 120ml (4fl oz/½ cup) cold water slowly, mixing just until the dough comes together. Press the dough into a smooth ball and allow to rest, uncovered, for 15 minutes.

4 On a floured piece of baking parchment, roll out the dough as thin as possible – at least 3mm (⅛in) thick. Transfer the parchment to a baking sheet and bake the crackers for 8–10 minutes, turning the sheet halfway through cooking. When the cracker is golden brown, remove it from the oven and allow to cool. Once cool, use your hands to break the large cracker into smaller rough pieces.

5 At serving time, remove the butter from the refrigerator. Sprinkle the remaining 4 tablespoons of lavender onto a plate and carefully roll the butter into the flowers, so that they coat the outside completely. Serve your butter with the crackers.

Venus:
Edible flower dumplings

♀ When constructing the recipe of Venus, the question I asked myself was not if we should serve a feast of flowers, but *how* we should serve a feast of flowers. Flowers, whose charismatic chemical signals entice the bees to dance, are the reproductive aspect of plants, making them more closely aligned with Venus than other plant materia. However, Venus is more than just her flirtatious blush, but also rules all tactile pleasure and the sensuality of existence. Perhaps it's the American in me, but when I think about the sensuality of existence, I think about fried food. And if fried food is an expression of Venusian sensuality, then fried cheese dumplings are the pinnacle of luxury and decadence.

On the other hand, Venus also rules comfort and peace, so I knew that our Venusian recipe should fall somewhere between comfort food and fine cuisine. This recipe accomplishes just that, yielding neat, dainty, crispy pastries, which conceal a gooey parcel of cream cheese and flower petals. This recipe has been a favourite of mine since I was 16 as it walks a delicate line between being a curio and a crowd pleaser. These dumplings are unpretentious, but still feel exciting and exotic. Most of all, they are beautiful, and as an offering for the queen of aesthetic, Venus is sure to be pleased.

This dish is best prepared on a Friday, at the hour of Venus, accompanied by a fumigation of Venusian scents: amber, benzoin, violet, jasmine or rose.

Serves 4
Prep time: 20 minutes, plus 20 minutes chilling
Cook time: 10 minutes

FOR THE DUMPLINGS
* 225g (8oz/1 cup) cream cheese, softened
* 3 tablespoons honey
* ½ teaspoon rosewater
* 1 tablespoon grated lemon zest
* 60g (2oz/1 cup) chopped fresh flower petals (for example, roses, lavender, cherry blossom, honeysuckle, elderflower, etc)
* 3 tablespoons strawberry jam
* 1 x 450g (16oz) package frozen wonton wrappers, thawed
* 2 tablespoons vegetable oil

FOR THE SAUCE
* 6 tablespoons soy sauce
* 4 tablespoons rice vinegar
* 2 tablespoons honey

I In a large bowl, mix together your cream cheese, honey, rosewater and lemon zest. Fold in the chopped flower petals. Swirl in your jam, leaving ribbons in the mixture. Set in the refrigerator to chill for 20 minutes.

2 When the filling has chilled, remove it from the refrigerator. Fill each dumpling wrapper with 1–2 teaspoons of filling, making sure to wet the edges of the wrapper before closing and pressing tightly to seal. Lay the dumplings on a baking parchment-lined baking sheet in a single layer. (You may freeze your dumplings like this and store for up to 1 month, or proceed to the following steps if serving immediately.)

3 Heat your oil in a frying pan and arrange your dumplings in the pan. Turn the flame to high and when the dumplings begin to sizzle, add 120ml (4fl oz/½ cup) of water. Cover and steam for 3 minutes (4 minutes if frozen), then remove the lid and fry until the bottom is crispy and golden.

4 In a small bowl, mix the sauce ingredients together. Serve the cooked dumplings immediately with the sauce.

Mars:
Roasted artichokes
with feta and harissa spread

Mars, the warrior planet, is associated with blood in the human body. This Martial feast focuses on herbs and plants which support the blood – iron-rich red (bell) peppers and artichokes, as well as circulation-stimulating chillies and citrus. Artichokes are especially Martial as they are the flower of a spiny, thistle-like plant, grown in a circle of thorns.

While this recipe comes together fairly quickly, it does call for two uncommon ingredients worth mentioning before we begin. Harissa is a North African spice blend, made of hot chillies, smoked paprika and cumin seeds. It is one of my favourite flavours, but those who are sensitive to spice should adjust their seasonings as needed, because harissa is known to be fiery. Another North African staple features here and it's an ingredient I always keep in the pantry – preserved lemons. Preserved lemons are salty-sweet, fermented with bay and sea salt until the rinds are tender and edible. If you don't have preserved lemons at home for this recipe, you can approximate the flavours by mixing 2 tablespoons lemon pulp, 1 tablespoon salt and 1 teaspoon lemon zest and allowing the mixture to sit for 15 minutes.

Serve this meal on a Tuesday at a Martial hour, accompanied by the incenses of Mars – dragon's blood, cinnamon, cardamom, safflower or wormwood.

Serves 4
Prep time: 20 minutes, plus marinating
Cook time: 30 minutes

FOR THE ARTICHOKES
* 400g (14oz) can or jar of artichoke hearts, drained and dried
* 2 tablespoons olive oil
* 1 teaspoon ground black pepper
* 3 tablespoons chopped preserved lemon

FOR THE DIP
* 1 red (bell) pepper, deseeded
* 175g (6oz) feta cheese
* 3 tablespoons olive oil
* 2 teaspoons harissa powder or 1½ tablespoons harissa paste
* 1 clove garlic, chopped
* Juice of 1 lemon
* Salt and pepper

1 Preheat your oven to 200°C/ 400°F/Gas 6 and line a baking sheet with baking parchment.

2 In a large bowl, toss the artichokes with the olive oil, pepper and preserved lemon. Allow to marinate for 20 minutes, then transfer the artichokes to the prepared baking sheet. Drizzle with any extra marinade and bake the artichokes for 15 minutes. Remove the baking sheet from the oven and flip each artichoke, then bake for an additional 10–15 minutes or until the artichokes are crispy and browning.

3 Begin your feta dip by charring your pepper. (If you do not have a gas stovetop or a grill/broiler, you can purchase roasted red peppers in advance.) Begin by blackening your pepper over a medium flame, turning with tongs to ensure it is completely charred. If you are using a grill/ broiler, set at the highest heat and grill/broil for 15 minutes, turning once. Place your pepper in a bowl and cover tightly with a lid. Allow to steam for 15 minutes, then remove the lid and wipe away any charred skin from the pepper with a paper towel.

4 Slice your pepper and add it to the bowl of a food processor with the feta cheese, olive oil, harissa, garlic and lemon juice. Season with salt and pepper, and blend until smooth.

5 Serve the roasted artichokes with the dip.

Jupiter:
Braised lamb shanks with juniper and red wine

4 Jupiter is often described as the just king and benevolent ruler, so this feast is one of luxury. Braised lamb shanks feel like a regal addition to the feast table and are accompanied here by a number of Jovian allies – chief among them, juniper berries. These tiny, aromatic fruits possess Jupiter's ruling metal, tin, and are used to give a sanctifying, purifying fragrance that is so typical of Jupiter herbs. However, Jupiter also loves tradition, as evidenced by his association with the tarot's Hierophant card, and so this recipe is also unwaveringly committed to classic, timeless flavours – lamb, rosemary, red wine – which have been staples of European gourmet food since the Renaissance.

Serve this meal on Thursday at a Jovian hour, particularly at celebrations of advancement – graduations, award ceremonies, birthdays, promotions, etc. Use a yellow tablecloth and burn an incense of storax, bayberry bark, oak leaves or juniper.

Serves 4

Prep time: 15 minutes

Cook time: 3 hours 30 minutes

* 4 x 450g (1lb) lamb shanks
* 2 tablespoons olive oil
* 1 shallot, finely diced
* 4 cloves garlic, sliced
* 1 carrot, peeled and chopped
* 1 stalk celery, finely chopped
* 3 bay leaves
* 2 tablespoons juniper berries
* 2 sprigs rosemary, beaten
* 1 tablespoon whole black peppercorns
* A 75cl bottle of red wine
* 120ml (4fl oz/½ cup) ruby port
* Salt and pepper

1 Preheat your oven to 170°C/325°F/Gas 3 and season your shanks with salt and pepper. In a large frying pan, heat the olive oil over a high heat. Sear the shanks on all sides until evenly browned, then transfer to a plate and set aside.

2 Add the shallot and garlic to the pan and sauté until fragrant and soft. Add the carrot and celery and cook until softened as well. Stir in the bay leaves, juniper, rosemary and peppercorns, followed by the wine. Place the shanks into a casserole dish and pour the braising liquid over the top. Cover with the lid and cook in the oven for 3 hours, or until meat is tender and cooked through.

3 When the lamb is cooked, remove the shanks from the casserole dish and set on a serving tray. Strain the braising liquid into a saucepan and stir in the port. Bring the saucepan to a simmer and reduce the liquid until about 250ml (9fl oz/1 cup) remains. Season to taste, spoon the sauce over the shanks and serve immediately.

Saturn:
Blackberry pulled pork sandwiches

As the greater malefic of the heavenly bodies, Saturn rules all that is forbidden and taboo, and so it is only right that our feast for Saturn should feature one of the most ill-omened foods – blackberries. These berries are maligned in folklore, believing to bring bad fortune and ill health to those who partake of them. In Europe, blackberries were believed to be fruits of the Fae, and the Devil was reputed to lurk among the brambles. In Biblical lore, it was the blackberry that cushioned Lucifer after his fall from heaven and he is said to reclaim them every year on Michaelmas, after which eating blackberries was said to cause bad luck, demonic harassment and even instant death. Blackberry canes were also used as apotropaic charms, placed on windowsills to force invading demons to stop and count each thorn, distracting them from their destruction.

In addition to featuring the ingredients of Saturnian magic and lore, this feast also calls for another classic Saturnine addition – time. Keep in mind that this recipe calls for a slow cooker to gently roast the pork for 8 hours until it is tender and entirely infused with flavour. As Saturn always suggests, it will be worth the wait.

Serves 6–8
Prep time: 20 minutes
Cook time: 9 hours

FOR THE PORK
* 2 tablespoons olive oil
* 1 tablespoon ground cumin
* 1 tablespoon ground cinnamon
* 1 x 1.8kg (4lb) bone-in pork shoulder
* 260g (9¼oz/2 cups) blackberries
* 3 tablespoons tomato purée (tomato paste)
* 60ml (2fl oz/¼ cup) balsamic vinegar
* 50g (1¾oz/¼ cup) brown sugar
* 120ml (4fl oz/½ cup) peaty Scotch whisky (Laphroaig or similar)
* 6 cloves garlic, minced
* Bread buns, to serve

FOR THE CABBAGE SLAW
* 2 tablespoons mayonnaise
* 2 tablespoons apple cider vinegar
* 1 tablespoon honey
* 1 tablespoon Dijon mustard
* 1 teaspoon finely chopped fresh dill

* A pinch of ground cloves
* 140g (5oz/2 cups) red cabbage, thinly sliced
* Salt and pepper

1 In a large frying pan over medium-high heat, heat the olive oil. Mix the cumin and cinnamon together and rub them into the pork. When the oil is hot, use tongs to sear the pork on the top, bottom and all sides, searing and browning it as completely as you can. Remove from the heat and set aside.

2 In a small saucepan, heat 120ml (4fl oz/½ cup) water and add the blackberries. Cook them down while stirring occasionally until they have collapsed and the liquid has thickened – about 15 minutes. Strain the berries through a fine mesh sieve into a bowl, discarding the seeds, then whisk in your tomato purée, vinegar, sugar, Scotch and garlic.

3 Place the pork into your slow cooker and pour the blackberry mixture over the top. Cook for 8 hours at a medium heat, until cooked through and falling apart.

4 Closer to serving time, whisk together the mayonnaise, vinegar, honey, mustard, dill and cloves for the slaw in a large bowl. Toss in your cabbage and season with salt and pepper.

5 Remove your pork from the slow cooker and use two forks to shred the meat completely, discarding any bones or gristle. Transfer the cooking liquid to a small saucepan and reduce until the sauce is thick and bubbly. Season with salt and pepper, then stir the sauce into the shredded pork.

6 Serve the pork on buns topped with the red cabbage slaw.

Saturn:
Blackberry pulled pork sandwiches

New Moon
Feast

New Moon Feast:
Kale salad with hazelnuts and black garlic;
Five-spice fried mushrooms;
Chocolate poppyseed cake

The new moon is a point on the lunar cycle that represents the moon's more chthonic, obscured aspects. It is sometimes called "the dark moon", and is the time when the moon "disappears", as she is fully without her usual luminary graces. It is also a time sacred to fearsome, chthonic lunar deities, like Hekate of the Ancient Greeks or Khonsu of the Ancient Egyptians – both depicted in bestial and cannibalistic forms. As this phase of the moon is traditionally accompanied by a kind of primeval terror, it is often celebrated in introspective ways. While the full moon is a period of heightened senses and external activity, the new moon instead turns inward and focuses on meditation, divination and devotional work.

This feast features foods that represent this darker, more earth-bound aspect of the lunar cycle. Black garlic, vinegars, dark leafy greens, wild mushrooms and narcotic poppy seeds are all sacred to the moon and correspond to chthonic themes of rot and rebirth. Serve this meal with your coven on the eve of the new moon, as a prelude to rites of divination or as you strategize for the upcoming lunar cycle.

Serves 4
Prep time for full feast: 1 hour
Cook time for full feast: 90 minutes

FOR THE SALAD

* 6 cloves black garlic
* 120ml (4fl oz/½ cup) olive oil
* 60ml (2fl oz/¼ cup) red wine vinegar
* ½ teaspoon Dijon mustard
* ½ shallot, finely chopped
* A bunch of kale (or cavolo nero), washed and stems removed
* 3 sprigs thyme, stems removed
* 30g (1oz/¼ cup) toasted hazelnuts, chopped
* A handful of shaved Parmesan cheese
* Salt and pepper

FOR THE MUSHROOMS

* 450g (1lb) mushrooms – shimeji (beech), maitake, oyster, enoki or hen of the woods
* 2 tablespoons soy sauce
* 2 tablespoons balsamic vinegar
* 700ml (24fl oz/3 cups) vegetable oil

* 50g (1¾oz/½ cup) cornflour (cornstarch)
* 3 tablespoons Chinese five spice
* 2 cloves garlic, quartered
* 8–10 fresh sage leaves
* Juice of ½ lemon
* 225g (8oz/1 cup) mayonnaise
* Salt and pepper

FOR THE CAKE

* 300g (10½oz/2½ cups) poppy seeds
* 180ml (6fl oz/¾ cup) sweetened condensed milk
* 170g (6oz/¾ cup) butter, cold
* 40g (1½oz/¼ cup) semolina flour
* Zest of 1 lemon
* 6 tablespoons granulated sugar
* 1 egg
* 200g (7oz/1½ cups) plain (all-purpose) flour
* 25g (1oz/¼ cup Dutch process cocoa powder
* ½ teaspoon salt
* Icing (confectioner's) sugar, for dusting

I Begin with your cake. Preheat the oven to 180°C/350°F/Gas 4. Grease and flour a 25cm (10in) springform pan or a 23 x 33cm (9 x 13in) baking dish.

2 In a medium saucepan, combine your poppy seeds and 700ml (24fl oz/3 cups) water and bring to a boil. Boil for 5 minutes, then strain the poppy seeds with a fine mesh sieve. Place the poppy seeds in a blender, add the condensed milk and 45g (1½oz/3 tablespoons) of your butter, and blend until the seeds are partially ground. Transfer the seed mixture to a medium bowl and stir in your semolina flour and lemon zest. Set aside.

3 In another bowl, cream together your sugar and the remaining butter. Beat in the egg. In a separate bowl, mix together your flour, cocoa powder and salt. Stir this into the butter mixture and combine into a smooth ball.

4 Spread your chocolate mixture into the bottom of the pan and spoon the poppy seeds over the top, flattening with the back of a spoon. Bake for 25–35 minutes, or until the top is dry and set. Allow to cool fully in the pan before removing and dusting with icing sugar.

5 Next, begin your mushrooms. Trim away any dense pieces of mushroom stem, then rinse your mushrooms and dry them on paper towels. Place the mushrooms into a large bowl, then pour the soy sauce and balsamic vinegar over the top. Toss the mushrooms in the sauces and marinate for 5 minutes.

6 In a deep frying pan, heat your oil over medium-high heat. On a plate, stir together your cornflour and five spice powder. Shake any excess marinade from the mushrooms, then toss in the cornflour mixture thoroughly to coat. Immediately drop the coated mushrooms into the hot oil and fry until golden and crispy.

7 When the mushrooms are done cooking, add the garlic and sage to the oil and fry for an additional 3 minutes. Fish out the garlic and sage and leave to cool, then add to a blender with the lemon juice and mayonnaise. Blend together until evenly combined, then season with salt and pepper and set aside.

8 Finally, begin your salad. Combine your black garlic, olive oil, vinegar, mustard and shallot in a blender and blend until smooth and emulsified. Season with salt and pepper and set aside.

9 Tear your kale or cavolo nero leaves from the thick stalks and put them in a large mixing bowl, then massage with your hands until they tenderize. Toss the kale/cavolo nero with your thyme, hazelnuts, Parmesan and black garlic dressing. Serve the fried mushrooms alongside the kale/cavolo nero, with the sage aioli on the side. Reserve the poppyseed cake for dessert.

Feast of the Earth

Seasonal meals for the solstices and equinoxes

Feast of the Earth

in examining the religions of the ancient world, we often find the rhythms of nature personified, even deified, to reveal various aspects of spiritual mystery. In Greece, Persephone rises from the underworld, breaking spring upon the Earth with her return. In Egypt, Osiris dies and is reborn as the Nile waters spill over the riverbanks and begin the fertile growing season. But behind these various dramas and cultural expressions, we can sense a single rhythm, rocking the Earth gently between extremes as it pulls us through our annual cycle of seasons. This is the rhythm of the Sun, king of the cosmos and the central star in our galactic neighbourhood. Holding the Earth in a gravitational embrace, the Sun sends gifts of light and warmth to our planet through its own self-immolation in nuclear fusion. The fantastic clockwork of these solar motions did more than mystify ancient peoples; it held a firm grip on their daily lives. As the motions of the Sun brought freezing winters, scorching summers, fierce winds, storms and lightning, humans have always lived and died by its cycles.

For this reason, the Sun often held a central position in the cosmologies of ancient religions. While grand solar cults like those of ancient Egypt and Aztec Mexico are rare, motifs of solar worship can be found in practically every culture, particularly in landscapes dominated by farming and agriculture. In these, the Sun is regarded as the bestower of life to the Earth, the ruler of the heavens, and the arbiter of cosmic justice. It personified the vitality of life, symbolized the quest for wisdom and illumination, and was regarded as a constant companion to the living creatures of the Earth. Many of these ancient cults mapped the motions of the solar cycle and venerated the Sun at its most extreme points – the solstices and the equinoxes. These events marked peak points on the Sun's cycle of wax and wane. At the solstices, the effects of the Sun are polarized, giving us both the longest and shortest days of the year. On the equinoxes, night and day are of equal length and the Sun holds the Earth in a perfect balance of light and dark. These dates are regarded as liminal times, when the ordinary laws of reality are suspended, softening the boundary between the material and subtle spheres and allowing greater powers of divination, spirit communication and spellcraft. In European traditions, the solstices and equinoxes were often of extreme religious import, and many cults throughout history are believed to have organized their ritual calendars around these dates, using their passage to track the seasonal cycle and tap into the liminality and magic of these rare moments. Across the globe, some ancient societies even erected massive temples and stone structures to capture and focus the holy beams of light from these precious days, as seen at Stonehenge, Machu Picchu, the Great Pyramids and many other solar-oriented megaliths that still stand today.

While complex astrological calculations posed challenges in the ancient world, the motions of the stars were used to calculate precise dates for these celestial events. In the tropical zodiac, which is ruled by the motion of the Sun, the vernal equinox traditionally begins in spring when the Sun enters the first degree of Aries. Here, the constellation of

Orion the Hunter slips below the horizon into the southern hemisphere, making way for his replacement, Boötes the Herdsman. In June, the Sun enters the first degree of Cancer, bringing with it the summer solstice and the longest day of the year. In September, Orion begins his return to the night sky, and as the Sun enters the first degree of Libra, day and night stand as equals on the autumn equinox. Finally, in the deep winter, the Sun enters the first degree of Capricorn, delivering the winter solstice and the longest night of the year. In the pagan traditions of Northern Europe, many traditions also mark midpoints between these events, called the cross-quarter days, with feasts and religious celebrations meant to honour and track the Sun's annual course. While they don't signify grand celestial events, these cross-quarter days also hold significant religious import for many traditions, with the festivals in spring and fall being the "hinge" dates around which the rest of the year turns. However, it is worthwhile to note that the tropical system of astrology is based on the positions of the constellations in the ancient world, which have shifted significantly in the thousands of years since. As a result of the Earth's wobbling rotational axis, the astrological signs of these events have shifted from their traditional designation – the vernal equinox now rises in Aquarius, the summer solstice in Gemini, the autumn equinox in Virgo, and the winter solstice in Sagittarius.

While this book is written from my perspective in the Northern hemisphere, it's worth noting that not all regions will experience these solar events in the same way. Many of these traditional feasts are based around the seasonal cycle of Europe, while people in the Southern hemisphere will experience these holidays in opposite. For example, as the summer solstice swells the Northern hemispheres with blooming verdancy, the Southern hemispheres are plunged into the darkness of the winter solstice. For readers living in other parts of the world, please keep these complex rhythms in mind as you plan your solstice and equinox feasts.

Spring Equinox

The spring or vernal equinox is also called Ostara, mythically derived from the Germanic goddess of spring, Eostre. While Eostre's cults in Europe only date back to the 2nd century CE, her name is also believed to form the root of another traditional spring ceremony, Easter. In the Northern hemispheres, the spring equinox occurs as the land experiences the first days of warmth after winter. Across the land, the earth cracks open as shoots and blossoms erupt from their chthonic slumber. Snakes uncoil in their subterranean nests, rabbits kick their feet against the earth, and the landscape reawakens for a kinetic, vibrant new season. It is a time when fresh vegetables and tender greens are finally available once more and edible flowers bloom in psychedelic sprays against the grey-green of early spring. With returning colour come vitamins, nutrients and medicinal herbs, which have been missing from the landscape since last fall. The once-quiet planet riots with life, and all of Earth's living beings – humans, animals and especially plants – are revitalized by the first blush of the Sun's life-giving warmth upon the ground.

In many folk traditions, this time of rebirth comes with an emphasis on cleansing and purgative rituals. We can think of this now as "spring cleaning", but in many traditions this cleansing had a holistic approach. Windows were opened, homes swept, and even the body itself was cleansed, usually by ingesting purgative herbs in an effort to "cleanse the blood" of winter's fat, salt and stagnancy. This detoxification was necessary to begin the new year fresh, as the spring equinox was in many places regarded as the true start of the annual calendar. In fact, the earliest recorded "new year" celebration, from the Babylonian calendar in 2000 BCE, places the start of the year on the vernal equinox. This rebirth and renewal is described beautifully in one of the equinox's most powerful European symbols, the egg, in which the hard earth of winter (the shell)

SPRING EQUINOX

March ♈ Aries

THEMES: Cleansing, purging, blessing, quickening, preparation, growth, awakening the land

raw foods, edible flowers, tender greens, fresh herbs, salads

---

HERBS: dill, mint, hyssop, juniper, clover, dandelion, plantain, cattail, nettle, willow, yarrow, lavender, lilac, elfwort, chives

---

FOOD: cherry blossoms, lettuce, rocket (arugula), eggs, lamb, bamboo shoots, asparagus, spring onions (scallions), ramps, wild mushrooms, cabbage, artichokes, cherries, carrots, peas, fiddleheads, new potatoes, radishes, rhubarb, fennel, plums, apricots, broad (fava) beans, watercress

cracks and gives way to the new life of spring (the nutritious egg within). In Slavic countries, the equinox is celebrated with a number of egg-breaking games, in which children sing songs in praise of Lazarus, the resurrected saint, and tap eggs against one another to see which breaks first. These egg charms are seen throughout Europe and usually come with the recitation of prayers and blessings to open the land and grant a fertile harvest to those who

| March 20–22 SPRING EQUINOX | Late March HOLI the colourful Hindu "festival of love" | Early April ADONIA the ancient Greek festival honouring Adonis, Aphrodite, and Persephone | April 30th HEXENNACHT "night of the witches" or the feast of St Walpurga | May 1st BELTANE | June 7th VESTALIA the Roman festival of Vesta, goddess of the hearth |

depend on it for survival. For this reason, eggs are a traditional part of spring equinox rituals the world over and feature prominently in feasts for this holiday.

Summer Solstice

The summer solstice is also called midsummer or Litha, and it was one of the significant fire festivals among the ancient peoples of Northern Europe. The word "solstice" derives from the Latin *sol* (sun) and *sistere* (to stand still). While the vernal equinox was regarded as the start of the new year in most places, the summer solstice was the first day of the calendar in much of ancient Greece. In Athens, the solstice was celebrated with Kronia, the festival of Kronos (Saturn), honoured there in his agricultural aspect as a harvest god, complete with his trademark scythe. Later, in the Roman era, the summer solstice was opened with Vestalia, the festival of the hearth goddess Vesta, attended by her bread-baking virgin priestesses. In ancient Egypt, the summer solstice heralded the flooding of the Nile river and was celebrated with the new year's festival of Wepet Renpet, a large feast where singing, dancing and revelry continued for several days.

This day is the climax of the solar calendar, marking the longest day and shortest night of the year. On the summer solstice, the earth is in full bloom, generating fruits, flowers, vegetables and plant medicine

SUMMER SOLSTICE

June ♈ Cancer

THEMES: creativity, tactile pleasures, movement, action, divination, enchantments, love magic

open-fire cooking methods, berries, nightshades, grains, sweet vegetables

---

HERBS: rose, calendula, basil, bay, poppy sunflower, lemon balm, St John's wort, wild carrot, borage, oregano, dittany,

---

FOOD: summer squashes, corn, raspberry, tomatoes, (bell) peppers, strawberry, aubergine (eggplant), squash blossoms, melon, peaches, cucumber, garlic, blueberry, okra, celery, beetroot (beets), avocado, seafood, kiwi, mango, chicken, kale, collards, chard, hearts of palm, chillies, limes

in excess. In the liturgical year, midsummer is syncretized with the feast of Saint John the Baptist on 24 June. While this is certainly a Christian feast, the lore of this night's mystical importance is preserved within the traditions of Saint John's Day, which include protection rituals, divination rites, and the creation of magical charms from hypericum and the ox-eye daisy, both sacred to Saint John the Baptist. This solstice epitomizes the

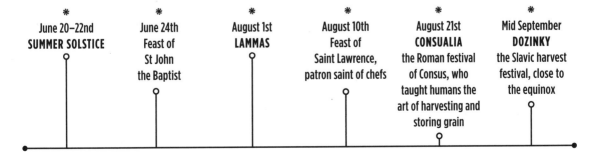

| June 20–22nd **SUMMER SOLSTICE** | June 24th Feast of St John the Baptist | August 1st **LAMMAS** | August 10th Feast of Saint Lawrence, patron saint of chefs | August 21st **CONSUALIA** the Roman festival of Consus, who taught humans the art of harvesting and storing grain | Mid September **DOZINKY** the Slavic harvest festival, close to the equinox |

notion that these sacred days carry magical potency, with midsummer being the day with the greatest volume of folklore, attesting to its liminal nature. On this night, witches and spirits transcend worlds, maidens are visited by visions of future lovers, and even the morning dew of the summer solstice is said to possess miraculous healing powers. It is a day when mortal humans could cast off the limitations of material reality, receive prophecy, treasure, and make pacts and allegiances with spirits. In Europe, this festival is still celebrated today with towering bonfires, colourful theatrical displays and rites of protection, divination and astral travel.

Autumn Equinox

In the fall, summer's heat wanes and the autumn equinox splits the day equally between light and darkness once more. The word "equinox" derives its root from the Latin terms *aequus* (equal) and *nox* (night), describing the balance of night and day that the equinox brings. This holiday also takes the name Mabon and heralds the wane toward winter and the coming death of the earth. Many ancient religions celebrated death and rebirth mysteries at this time of the year, with the focus on autumn's descent into darkness. In Sumerian legend, the earth goddess Inanna undergoes an autumn death at the hands of her jealous sister and goes to the underworld to await her spring rebirth. In ancient Greece,

AUTUMN EQUINOX

September ♍ Libra

THEMES: spirit communication, gathering, ancestral magic, reaping, sacrifice, setting wards, giving thanks

roasted foods, baked goods, tree fruits, starchy vegetables, brassicas

---

HERBS: elderberry, rose hip, wild grape, hawthorn, sumac, mullein, mugwort, sassafras, goldenrod, mallow, ginger, black walnut

---

FOOD: apples, squashes, nuts, grapes, blackberry, pumpkin, pears, pomegranates, figs, honey, Brussels sprouts, fennel, sunchokes, broccoli, soybeans, horseradish, persimmon, radicchio, quince, swede (rutabaga), yams, shallots, lychee, mulberries, spinach, kohlrabi

Persephone is dragged to Hades while harvesting flowers. She is permitted to return on the vernal equinox but must descend to Hades and rule as Queen of the Dead when the autumn equinox returns again. In cultures across the globe, this day is a time to hold space for death mysteries, and to celebrate loss and endings as a natural, necessary aspect of the human experience.

September 20–22
AUTUMN EQUINOX

September 29th
MICHAELMAS
or the Feast of
St Michael
the Archangel

October 31st
SAMHAIN

November 17th
Feast of
Saint Elizabeth
of Hungary, patron
saint of bakers

December 17th
SATURNALIA
the Roman feast
of decadence and
opposites

December 19th
OPALIA
the Roman festival
which concluded the
agricultural year

In the folk customs of the autumn equinox, this night is celebrated in Europe with feasting, dancing, music and accounting. Grand balls and festivals were held to share the summer's harvest and to gather one last time before the winter chill sets in. Michaelmas, the Catholic feast of St Michael the Archangel, was sometimes celebrated alongside the equinox. As one of the significant end-of-quarter days for the financial and judicial year, Michaelmas was a time of settling debts, paying farmhands and securing work for the long winter ahead. It was also a time to celebrate the fermentation of spirits, as the equinox heralded the end of the grape and hop harvests, when wine and beer were traditionally brewed. While autumn festivals were known for being rowdy and jolly as a result, the death current running through this season is inescapable. As such, the autumn equinox is primarily regarded as a holiday of ancestral veneration and feeding one's beloved dead, with many harvest feasts including the practice of leaving table settings and chairs empty to seat the spirits of the dearly departed.

Winter Solstice

As summer's warmth fades into memory and the earth is gripped in snow and ice, the winter solstice offers the promise of light within the darkness. After the equinox's balancing act between day and night, darkness overtakes the solar cycle and delivers shorter days and longer nights.

> ## WINTER SOLSTICE
>
> ### December ♑ Capricorn
>
> **THEMES:** introspection, calling forth light into darkness, storytelling, protection magic, survival, resilience, prophecy
>
> ferments, slow cooking methods, meat, dairy, dried beans and grains
>
> ---
>
> **HERBS:** pine, rosemary, thyme, sage, dock, burdock, sea vegetables, chicory, lichen, wintergreen, sorrel, caraway, birch, chicory
>
> ---
>
> **FOOD:** mushrooms, root vegetables, onions, pork, cranberries, lemons, oranges, grapefruit, turnips, leeks, parsnips, potatoes, beef, pickles, sauerkraut, whole grains, dried beans, cheese, cured meats, papaya, passion fruit, currants, dates, winter squashes

On the longest of these cold, dark nights, the winter solstice occurs – the climax of the Sun's wane and the deepest point in the underworld of the year. Here, the Sun turns on its heels and the days begin to lengthen once more as the Earth ascends into spring. Called Yule or Jul among pagans, the winter solstice is a time characterized by troublesome spirits, the delivery of prophecy and an inversion of

| December 20–22 WINTER SOLSTICE | December 23rd LARENTALIA the Roman feast of the Lares, the hearth-dwelling ancestral spirits of the home | January 22nd Feast of St Vincent of Saragossa, patron saint of vintners and vinegar-makers | February 2nd IMBOLC | February 17th FORNACALIA the Roman feast of bread | Mid February MARDI GRAS or Fat Tuesday, the carnival feast before Lent | Early March MASLENITSA the Russian Butter Festival |

social norms. In ancient Greece, two festivals celebrated the solstice in December – the smaller feast of Haloea, dedicated to the lascivious god Poseidon, and the week-long romp of Saturnalia, the topsy-turvy feast of Saturn. During Haloea, women were separated from men and encouraged to hedonism – drinking wine and eating genital-shaped cakes, while priestesses whispered Sapphic suggestions in their ears. Participants would remain segregated by gender for one night, before the women would rejoin the men, who had been building towering, celebratory bonfires. During Saturnalia, small gifts were exchanged between friends and family, taboo behaviours such as gambling and public drunkenness were permitted, and power structures were inverted. Servants could command their masters, enslaved people walked free, and one among them was elected the "King of Saturnalia", who would preside over the day giving orders to encourage continued debauchery. While this may seem an odd festival for the god Saturn, who usually rules limitations and responsibility, this holiday was viewed by some in the Roman Empire as alluding to the golden age of Saturn's rule as king of the gods, when there is said to have been order and peace on Earth.

After the Christianization of Europe, many of these traditions continued to live on and were absorbed into Christian festivals. The Saturnalian traditions of ritual feasting, drunkenness, the giving of gifts, and the celebration of a trickster-king or "Lord of Misrule" became established folk traditions of Christmas and the Epiphany, both occurring around the winter solstice. In addition, special logs of birch or oak were cut as Yule logs, to be burned within the home, and the shadows read to portend omens of the coming year. It was also understood that humans were

especially vulnerable to troublesome spirits during this liminal time, and great care was taken to protect the home and its inhabitants from their influence. Caraway seeds were strewn upon doorways, set under cradles and sprinkled around butter churns to prevent witches from stealing food and children. A large bread or bannock was often baked – round and plaited, in the appearance of a wreath – as a sacrificial offering to spirits of the land. Chief among these traditions, however, was gathering close with loved ones to share in ceremony a feast, good drink and fantastic stories, to entertain and inspire as the world waited in silence for the Sun's spring return.

There is great beauty and magical potency to be found in following these crucial cycles, but there is also deep wisdom. The living earth is an intelligent being and it provides what is necessary when we need it most. In spring, the return of fresh produce and herbs supplies much-needed vitamins, enzymes and fibre after a season of salt, fat and starch. In summer, fresh fruits and vegetables are cooling and hydrating to the body, helping us to withstand the scorching heat and providing energy for summer's kinetic pace. At the return of fall, richer foods appear – fatty nuts, starchy vegetables, meats and cheeses, all of which prepare the body for the slow pace and frigid temperatures of the coming season. Here, we also see living ferments return to our diets – pickles, kraut, vinegars and wines, which provide crucial enzymes and probiotics during a season with little fresh food available. Even in deep winter, the earth continues to provide, giving us nutrient-dense vegetables and foods that store easily at low temperatures, like beetroots, pumpkins and carrots, ensuring that fall's harvest will sustain us all winter long. Consuming these foods when they are in season will not only ensure that they are at their most delicious and nutrient-rich, but is also proven to strengthen the immune system and help our bodies navigate the flux of seasons. While seasonal eating has become a trend in recent years, this wisdom is ancient, deriving from our ancestors' deep interrelationship with the land that gave them life.

As you examine these traditions and correspondences, consider the role of the solstices and equinoxes in your own practice. In the following pages, you will find a unique table of correspondences and associations, as well as a complete feast for each of these high points in the solar cycle. These dishes will celebrate seasonal foods, herbs and cooking

methods, and they share some of the grandest recipes from my personal grimoire. Use these dishes and the chart provided as a template, inspiring yourself creatively as you plan your own solstice and equinox gatherings, continuing the ancient tradition of honouring the Sun in feast and ceremony at these powerful, liminal times.

Feast of
the Spring Equinox

Feast of The Spring Equinox:
Ricotta and spring pea spread;
Herb and allium quiche in a potato crust;
Shaved radish salad
with a cherry blossom vinaigrette;
Jasmine tea shortbread

One of my favourite vernal equinox rituals is the creation of egg talismans, traditional to Eastern Europe and my ancestral Croatia. These are traditionally prepared for both the vernal equinox and Easter, especially across Europe, and act as a symbol of renewal in the still-greening landscape of early springtime. In my practice, these eggs are a sacrificial offering given in exchange for the springtime promise of rebirth. I mark the eggs in wax, drawing symbols and sigils relating to desires I have for the coming year, and also to those things which I wish to discard. The eggs that represent desires are dyed blood-red in a dye of black tea, alkanet root and vinegar, and the eggs that represent discarded things are dyed black with black walnuts, myrrh, and vinegar as well. I prepare these talismans the day before the equinox and rise early the next day to continue the work.

When I rise, I dress in clean, light-coloured clothes and pin flowers in my hair. I pack the eggs in a backpack, along with fresh bread, candles and something good to drink, and hurry away to the woods. When I arrive, I search out a place where wild flowers are beginning to grow – dandelions, crocuses, and violets this time of year. The suitable place will be quiet and hidden, and will usually reveal itself after some wandering. When I arrive, I set the eggs in a small circle around the wild flowers and begin gathering buds, mushrooms, and aromatic leaves from the area around me. I circle the eggs in these gathered offerings, light candles and tear the bread in two, setting each half on either side of the eggs – one half for what came before, and one half for what is to come. I speak openly and honestly with the spirits of this place, detailing both my desires and my regrets, asking plainly for support in the year ahead. I inscribe the loaves with sigils marking their purpose and, with a copper spoon, I dig two holes in the earth and bury the loaves where they sit. I share the drink with the plants, with the forest, with the entire strangeness of existence, and pour more than half into the open holes with the bread. When all is said and sung, I close the holes, snuff the candles and leave the eggs to encircle the flowers in secret, returning home in silence as day creeps over the land.

This feast was created as a meditation on the flavours and fruits of the spring equinox season, and highlights ingredients sacred to spring festivals – eggs, dairy and fresh herbs. Our feast calls for a special preparation of plums – the umeboshi, a variety of salt-pickled plum from Japan. We will use both the vinegar of the umeboshi and the fruits themselves, along with Japanese salt-cured cherry blossoms. These ingredients can be found at most Asian speciality markets, ordered online or made at home the old fashioned way, if you happen to have the plums and blossoms on hand.

Serves 4
Prep time for full feast: 2 hours
Cook time for full feast: 2 hours

FOR THE PEA SPREAD
* 1 baguette
* 4 tablespoons olive oil, plus extra to serve
* 125g (4½oz/1 cup) fresh or frozen peas
* A handful of fresh mint leaves, plus extra to serve
* 115g (4oz/½ cup) ricotta cheese
* Zest and juice of 1 lemon
* 1 teaspoon roughly ground pink peppercorns (optional)
* Salt

FOR THE QUICHE
* 1 large shallot, sliced crosswise into 6mm (¼in) thick rings
* 85g (3oz/¾ cup) peeled white baby (pearl) onions
* 60ml (2fl oz/¼ cup) umeboshi vinegar
* 1 head of garlic
* 1 tablespoon olive oil
* 3 large, starchy potatoes of similar size
* 6 eggs
* 700ml (24fl oz/3 cups) goat's milk or whole cow's milk
* 240ml (8fl oz/1 cup) double (heavy) cream
* 3 tablespoons chopped fresh chives
* 3 tablespoons chopped fresh oregano
* 2 tablespoons chopped fresh dill
* 1 pinch ground cloves
* 225g (8oz) Gruyère cheese, grated
* Salt and pepper

FOR THE SALAD
* 60ml (2fl oz/¼ cup) olive oil
* 60ml (2fl oz/¼ cup) umeboshi vinegar
* 2 umeboshi plums, pitted and minced or ground to a paste
* ¼ shallot, minced
* 2 small watermelon radishes
* 1 grapefruit or 2 oranges
* 1 large bunch (about 225g/8oz) rocket (arugula)
* 37g (¼ cup) crumbled goat's cheese
* 33g (¼ cup) toasted pine nuts
* 10g (¼ cup) salt-cured cherry blossoms
* Fresh cherry blossom petals, to garnish (optional)
* Salt and pepper

FOR THE SHORTBREAD
* 3 tablespoons jasmine tea leaves
* 225g (8oz/1 cup) butter, softened
* 100g (3½oz/¾ cup) icing (confectioner's) sugar
* 1 teaspoon vanilla extract
* 240g (8½oz/1¾ cups) plain (all-purpose) flour
* ½ teaspoon salt
* 3 tablespoons large-crystal sugar

1 Begin with the shortbread. Preheat the oven to 150°F/ 300°F/Gas 2 and grease a 23cm (9in) cake pan or tart dish with a removable base. Using a spice grinder or mortar and pestle, process your tea leaves into a powder. In a large mixing bowl, combine the tea leaves with your softened butter and icing sugar. Beat the butter mixture until light and fluffy, then fold in the vanilla, flour and salt until the dough just comes together.

2 Press the dough into the prepared pan. Sprinkle the dough with the crystal sugar, and lightly press the crystals into place. Score the dough into 12 long, slender wedges, and bake for 10 minutes or until beginning to brown. Remove from the oven and transfer the shortbread, in its pan, to a cooling rack. Use a butter knife to cut along the score marks while the shortbread is warm and allow to cool to room temperature.

3 Next, begin the quiche. In a medium bowl, toss together your shallot, onions and umeboshi vinegar and allow to stand for 10 minutes. Meanwhile, raise the heat in your oven to 200°C/400°F/Gas 6 and lightly grease a 23cm (9in) springform pan. When the onions are ready, drain the vinegar and transfer them to a foil-lined baking sheet. Set aside.

4 Slice the head of garlic crosswise and place it on a sheet of kitchen foil. Drizzle the garlic with 1 tablespoon of oil, wrap it securely in the foil and transfer it to the baking sheet with the onions. Bake the onions and garlic for 20 minutes, or until the garlic is soft and the onions are beginning to brown. Remove the garlic paper and discard, reserving the cloves.

5 Next, use a mandoline or sharp knife to cut the potatoes lengthwise into even slices, as thin as possible. The potatoes should be flexible and translucent, but not shredding. Line the prepared springform pan with the potatoes to create a pie crust. Start by fanning a single layer across the base and then layering them up the sides of the pan, covering the pan completely, with each slice overlapping the last by at least 1cm (½in). Continue layering until all the slices are used. Set aside.

6 In a medium mixing bowl, beat your eggs and milk together until homogenous. Stir in your cream, fresh herbs, ground cloves and roasted onions and garlic. Season with salt and pepper.

7 In your potato-lined pan, sprinkle a layer of your grated cheese over the base of the crust. Bake the crust for 15 minutes, and then allow to cool to almost room temperature. Turn your heat down to 180°C/350°F/Gas 4.

8 Stir the rest of your cheese into your custard, then fill the crust as high as you can. If the potato crust tries to float with the custard, hold it down with the back of a spoon. Bake the quiche for 30 minutes, or until the eggs are set and the potato crust has browned. Set aside to cool.

9 Next, begin the spread. Use a sharp serrated knife to slice your baguette into 1.5cm (½in) slices and lay the slices in a single layer on a baking sheet. Brush the bread with 2 tablespoons of your olive oil, season with salt and pepper, and toast in the oven for 8–10 minutes.

10 Meanwhile, combine the peas, mint, ricotta, lemon zest and juice and the remaining olive oil in the bowl of a food processor. Blend until smooth, then season with salt and a little pink pepper, if using. When the seasoning is perfect, transfer the spread to a shallow serving dish, and garnish with torn mint leaves, cracked pink pepper and a drizzle of olive oil.

11 Finally, prepare the salad. In a blender or using a mixing bowl and whisk, combine your olive oil, umeboshi vinegar, pulverized plums and minced shallot. Season with salt and pepper and set aside.

12 Using a mandoline or very sharp knife, slice your radishes thinly. Set these in a bowl of water while you prepare the rest of your ingredients. Next, supreme your grapefruit or oranges by slicing off the top and bottom of the fruit, then using a sharp knife to carve away the peel and pith from the sides. Cut out each slice of the fruit, leaving the membrane behind. Combine your radishes and citrus segments in a large serving bowl with your rocket, goat's cheese, pine nuts and cherry blossoms. Drizzle with the dressing and toss to combine, garnishing with fresh cherry blossoms if using.

13 At serving time, set a small, shallow dish of wine upon your table, in which you have floated violets or other early-blooming flowers, and around this place a ring of pussywillow branches. Set a line of candles dividing the table lengthwise, as a symbol of the sun's light straddling the dark and light halves of the solar year. Burn an incense of cinquefoil, cedar, dandelion, frankincense, wild strawberry leaves and dried honeysuckle. Serve the salad, pea spread and quiche together, reserving the shortbread for dessert.

Feast of
the Summer Solstice

Feast of the Summer Solstice:
Burrata panzanella with lemon balm vinaigrette;
Summer corn risotto with basil and olives;
Roasted beetroot with labneh, sumac and crispy shallots;
Baked peaches with buttermilk gelato

The summer solstice is undoubtedly the climax of the solar year, both astronomically and magically. Days are long, food is abundant and humans are energized in a way that only the warm, gentleness of summer could permit. Each year on the solstice, I perform one small ritual of divination, as it is believed that prophecy is readily revealed on this day more than any other. I spend the day before the solstice meditating on the questions I have, selecting them keenly and honing their words so that I waste no time during my rituals.

When I am ready to begin, I dress in white and gold and head to the woods to pick flowers. I gather a generous amount, leaving offerings as I do, and arrange for myself a colourful bouquet of blossoms when all is said and done. I bring these to the appointed place, where I have set a sturdy cauldron or fire pit filled with birch bark and dried hazel leaves. I light the fire, and when it has finally caught, I transfer my fresh-picked blossoms to the cauldron and they roll up in flames immediately. Sipping a tea of vision-giving herbs – damiana, calendula and bay – I watch the burning flowers keenly, scrying upon the coals and clouds of smoke as I read aloud the questions I have prepared. When I have received my answers, I burn the fire down completely and ferry the charcoal home with me, to be used in incense and crafting for divinatory rites throughout the coming year.

While this feast in particular may appear to be quite demanding on paper, I assure you it cooks up quickly, and the ripe fruits and vegetables of summer make it hard to go wrong with flavours. However, this recipe does call for the creation of smoked buttermilk, and the smoking process may be unfamiliar to some. Follow the instructions carefully, and once you get the hang of this simple process, I promise you will fall in love with it! Truly, there is no flavour more quintessentially summertime than the rich smokiness of foods prepared over an open fire, grilled to perfection, and this feast does its best to capture those powerful flavours in an at-home setting.

Serves 4
Prep time for full feast: 2 hours
Cook time for full feast: 2 hours

FOR THE PANZANELLA

* 6 tablespoons olive oil
* 60ml (2fl oz/¼ cup) Champagne vinegar or white wine vinegar
* A bunch (about 30g/1oz) of fresh lemon balm, stems removed
* Juice of 1 lemon
* 1 teaspoon lemon zest
* 85g (3oz/2 cups) croutons
* A bunch (about 225g/8oz) of watercress, washed
* 2 large heirloom tomatoes, cut into wedges
* 1 handful fresh rose petals
* 2 large balls of burrata cheese
* Salt and pepper

FOR THE RISOTTO

* 3 ears fresh corn
* 120ml (4fl oz/½ cup) single cream (half and half)
* 280g (10oz/1 pint) cherry tomatoes
* 2 tablespoons olive oil
* 950ml (32fl oz/4 cups) chicken stock
* 3 tablespoons butter
* 280g (10oz/1½ cups) arborio rice
* 2 cloves garlic, sliced
* 1 bay leaf
* 23g (¼ cup) grated Parmesan cheese
* A handful of fresh basil leaves, chopped
* 85g (3oz/½ cup) pitted green olives, Castelvatrano or similar
* 1 tablespoon preserved lemon, minced

FOR THE BEETROOT

* 2 large red beetroot (beets), peeled and cubed
* 2 large golden beetroot (beets), peeled and cubed
* 2 tablespoons olive oil
* 1 small shallot, sliced thinly crosswise
* 2 tablespoons cornflour (cornstarch)
* vegetable oil, for frying
* 225g (8oz/1 cup) labneh
* 2 tablespoons torn fresh mint
* 2 tablespoons finely minced chives
* 1 teaspoon ground sumac
* Juice of 1 lime

FOR THE PEACHES AND GELATO

* 52g (½ cup) smoking chips, applewood or similar, soaked overnight
* 300ml (10½fl oz/1¼ cups) buttermilk
* 8fl oz (240ml/1 cup) double (heavy) cream
* 200g (7oz/1 cup) granulated sugar
* 3 tablespoons cornflour (cornstarch)
* 1 tablespoon whiskey
* 4 peaches, pitted and halved
* 4 tablespoons butter, cut into 8 pieces
* 8 teaspoons brown sugar
* Salt to taste

1 Begin with the gelato, as this will take the longest to set properly. Freeze or otherwise prepare your ice cream maker as per the manufacturer's directions.

2 Set a large stock pot with a lid on the stove, and line the bottom of the pot with kitchen foil. In the pot, place two small bowls – one upside down on the bottom, and one right side up on the top, stacked in an hourglass shape. Place your soaked applewood chips on the bottom of the pot and fill the raised bowl with your buttermilk. Cover the pot and set over a medium heat until the chips begin to release their fragrant smoke. Smoke the buttermilk for 10 minutes, then taste-test for desired smokiness. You may choose to continue smoking for an additional 5–7 minutes for a bolder flavour. When the buttermilk has reached the desired flavour, remove from the pot and discard the wood chips.

3 In a medium saucepan, stir together the smoked buttermilk, cream and all but 3 tablespoons of your granulated sugar. Simmer over a low heat, stirring constantly, until the sugar is dissolved, then remove the pot from the heat. Toss together your remaining sugar and the cornflour in a small bowl, then add the sugar mixture to the pan, stirring constantly so no lumps form. Finally, stir in your whiskey, then pour the mixture into your ice cream maker. Run the machine for 1 hour, or until the gelato is set, then transfer the ice cream to a lidded storage container and freeze until serving time.

4 Next, begin the risotto. Preheat your oven to 180°C/350°F/ Gas 4. In a broiler or over a stove burner, grill your corn until blackening. Slice the kernels from the cobs and set aside. In a blender, purée your grilled corn and cream. Strain, and set aside. Set your cherry tomatoes on a baking sheet, drizzle with your olive oil and season with salt and pepper. Roast the tomatoes for 30 minutes, then set aside.

5 Pour your chicken stock into a medium saucepan and set over a low flame to keep the stock warm but not simmering. On another burner, set a deep skillet or sauté pan over medium heat. Melt your butter and add your dry rice and garlic. Sauté for 2 minutes, or until the rice releases a nutty fragrance, then add 120ml (4fl oz/½ cup) of your warm stock and your bay leaf. Cook until the liquid is mostly absorbed, then add another ½ cup of stock. Continue in this fashion until all of the stock has been used, about 40 minutes, then stir in your Parmesan cheese and corn-infused cream. Simmer until the liquid is mostly absorbed, season with salt and pepper, then remove from the heat. Keep warm until serving time.

6 Next, begin your beetroot. Set the cubed beets on a sheet of kitchen foil and drizzle with your olive oil, then wrap tightly. Prick the foil with a fork to create steam holes and roast the beets for 30–45 minutes, or until tender. If preparing this entire feast at once, you may wish to roast these beets alongside your tomatoes to maximize efficiency. Once done, set aside to cool.

7 In the meantime, toss your shallot slices with the cornflour. In an air fryer, deep fryer or a pan filled 1cm (½in) deep with vegetable oil, fry the shallots until crispy. Set aside on a plate lined with paper towel to drain and cool.

8 Before your guests arrive, prepare the feast table properly; sprinkle crushed roses or bay leaves in a spiral across your table and fill the house with as many candles as you can manage. Burn an incense of St John's wort, sunflower petals, copal, roses and verbena, and open all windows as the smoke permeates the home and your guests begin to filter in.

9 Finally, prepare the panzanella at serving time. In a blender, make your vinaigrette by blending the olive oil, Champagne vinegar, lemon balm, lemon juice, and lemon zest together. Season with salt and pepper and set aside.

10 In a serving bowl, toss together your croutons, watercress, heirloom tomatoes and rose petals. Drizzle with the dressing and toss together. Tear the two burrata cheeses into rough wedges, set these atop the salad and serve immediately.

II To serve the beets, spread a thick layer of labneh on a serving platter. In a medium bowl, toss together your roasted beets, fresh mint and chives, sumac and lime juice. Heap the beets in the centre of the platter, atop the labneh, and garnish generously with your crispy fried shallots.

I2 To serve the risotto, toss together in a medium bowl your warm, roasted tomatoes, fresh basil leaves, chopped olives and the preserved lemon. Transfer the risotto to a serving bowl, top with the vegetables and serve.

I3 At dessert, lay out your peaches in a single layer on a baking sheet, cut side up. Place a cube of butter in the centre of each peach half and sprinkle each one with 1 teaspoon of brown sugar. Roast for 15–20 minutes at 190°C/375°F/Gas 5, or until the peaches are soft and browning. Serve immediately with a scoop of your smoked buttermilk gelato.

Feast of
the Autumn Equinox

Feast of the Autumn Equinox:
Crostini with roasted grapes;
Roast pumpkin stuffed with sausage, fennel and wild rice;
Curried apple soup;
Pear and red wine tarte tatin

The autumn equinox is a symbol for many things – death, responsibility, endings – and in my practice, it also signifies invisibility. For most of the year, my botanical and spirit allies are readily accessible in the wild world, with their leaves, branches and flowers extending into reality as tangible manifestations of themselves. When the autumn equinox comes, it is a final chance for me to touch and experience these tangible manifestations of nature, and to reacquaint myself with their immaterial intelligence through a ritual of nightwalking.

This ritual was inspired by my friend and mentor, Damon Stang, who wrote on this practice in *Venefica Magazine*'s autumn equinox issue (Vol 2). In his writing, Damon recommends preparing the body on the eve of the equinox by taking a candlelit bath in an infusion of birch bark. He then suggests meditating "in as much darkness as can be gathered", preparing to stretch and extend the psychic senses into the gloomy night. When the proper moment arrives, one must rise and gather suitable offerings – fruits, fresh bread and good drink – and ferry these to a place of power that one knows well. During the walk, the purpose is to see without eyes and speak without tongues; to gain knowledge and communion with the subtle and numinous spirits that reside in one's own backyard – some of which are known, and some of which are not yet known. In my personal practice, this ritual presents an exciting opportunity to begin the immaterial relationship with my allies, particularly the plants, as they return to the subterranean underworld for the duration of the winter months.

This feast of the autumn equinox is a sumptuous display of autumn's most decadent flavours, nurtured through roasting and baking to caramelized perfection. While the procedure is pretty straightforward, for readers who have never encountered a tarte tatin before, this step may be less than intuitive. Tarte tatins are marvellous pies which are baked upside down, so that the fruit within can sear and caramelize on the bottom of the pan while it bakes. The appearance is certainly rustic, but the flavours are unlike any other pastry. Besides this uncommon addition, this feast cooks up the fastest of all, and can make even novice chefs look like professionals when they bring these treats to their equinox feast tables.

Serves 4 guests
Prep time for full feast: 2 hours
Cook time for full feast: 1 hour

FOR THE CROSTINI

* 2 bunches (about 900g/2lb) seedless red grapes
* 4 tablespoons olive oil
* 3 cloves garlic, sliced
* 2 sprigs rosemary, stems removed
* 1 baguette
* A 225g (8oz) wedge of brie cheese
* Honey, for drizzling

FOR THE PUMPKIN

* 2 tablespoons butter
* 2 celery stalks, sliced
* ½ yellow onion, sliced
* 1 fennel bulb, cored and diced
* 450g (1lb) smoked sausage, sliced into 5mm (¼in) rounds
* 195g (7oz/1 cup) wild rice
* 450ml (16fl oz/2 cups) chicken stock
* 85g (3oz/½ cup) dried cherries
* 1 medium pumpkin, top cut off, seeds and pulp removed
* Salt and pepper

FOR THE SOUP

* 1 tablespoon olive oil
* ½ yellow onion, sliced
* 2 celery stalks, sliced
* A 2.5cm (1in) piece of ginger, peeled and minced
* 2 cloves garlic, peeled and minced
* 1½ tablespoons curry powder
* 2 teaspoons chilli paste, Sriracha or similar
* 2 large apples, peeled, cored and cubed
* 1 medium starchy potato, peeled and cubed
* 700ml (24fl oz/3 cups) chicken stock (broth)
* 120ml (4fl oz/½ cup) double (heavy) cream
* 1 handful coriander (cilantro), chopped
* 120ml (4fl oz/½ cup) sour cream

FOR THE TARTE TATIN

* 60g (2oz/4 tablespoons) butter
* 4 tablespoons sugar
* 2 tablespoons red wine
* 1 x 450g (16oz) sheet ready-rolled puff pastry, thawed if frozen
* 7 pears of similar size, peeled, halved, and cored
* ½ teaspoon ground cinnamon
* ½ teaspoon grated nutmeg

1 Begin with your pumpkin, as this will take the longest to cook. Preheat your oven to 180°C/350°F/Gas 4. In a frying pan (skillet) over a medium–high flame, melt your butter and add your celery and onion to the pan. Sauté until the vegetables are translucent and soft, then add your fennel and cook for an additional 2 minutes. Add your sausage to the pan and cook until browning – about 5–8 minutes.

2 Next, add your wild rice to the pan and cook for 1 minute. Stir in your stock and dried cherries and cook for an additional 2 minutes, stirring as you do. Season with salt and pepper. Transfer the mixture to the pumpkin and set the pumpkin in a casserole or pie dish. Bake the pumpkin for 50–60 minutes, or until the rice has fully cooked and the pumpkin itself is tender when pricked with a fork. Keep warm until serving time.

3 Now begin the tarte tatin. In a 23cm (9in) oven-safe frying pan (skillet), stir together your butter, sugar and red wine and set them over a medium heat until the sugar is dissolved and the mixture begins to caramelize. Meanwhile, lay out your puff pastry and trace a 28cm (11in) circle in the dough. Cut this circle of pastry out and keep cool in the refrigerator until ready to use.

4 In a mixing bowl, toss your pears with the cinnamon and nutmeg, then place them cut side down into the pan with the red wine caramel. Simmer until the caramel is bubbly and deepening in colour, about 5 minutes. Cover the pears with the puff pastry, rolling and tucking in the edges to form a crust. Place the skillet in the oven and bake for 30–40 minutes, or until the pastry is golden.

5 Next, begin your soup. In a 4-litre (4-quart) saucepan, heat your olive oil over a medium–high heat. Add your sliced onion and celery to the pan and sauté until translucent, then add your ginger, garlic, curry powder and chilli paste. Sauté for 2 minutes, then add your cubed apples and potatoes. Sauté for a further 2 minutes, then stir in your chicken stock. Simmer the soup uncovered for 20 minutes, then stir in your cream. Simmer gently for an additional 3–5 minutes, taking care to keep your temperature low so as not to curdle the cream. Using an immersion blender, purée your soup until smooth. Keep warm until serving time.

6 Finally, begin your roasted grapes. Wash your grapes and remove them from the stems, then toss them in a bowl with your olive oil, garlic and rosemary. Spread the grapes in a single layer on a baking sheet, and roast in the oven at 180°C/350°F/Gas 4 for 20 minutes.

7 While the grapes cook, slice your baguette and lay the slices out in a single layer on a baking sheet. Slice your brie cheese and set one slice onto each piece of bread. Bake in the oven for 10 minutes, until bread is toasty and the cheese is melted.

8 Prepare your feast table by burning an incense of myrrh, Solomon's seal root, dried milkweed, goldenrod and grape leaves. Set a small, shallow dish of wine upon your table, in which you have floated aster flowers, and around this place a ring of mugwort boughs. Set a line of candles dividing the table lengthwise, as a symbol of the sun's light straddling the dark and light halves of the solar year.

9 At serving time, set your crostini on a serving tray and drizzle with honey. Carve your stuffed pumpkin into slices for each guest, and present it as a centrepiece for your feast table. Garnish your soup with chopped coriander and sour cream, and set this out with the rest of your feast, reserving the tart tatin for dessert.

Feast of
the Winter Solstice

Feast of the Winter Solstice:
Fire cider pickled eggs;
Lentils and roasted roots with walnut sauce;
Cheesy celeriac mash;
Cranberry gingerbread

One of my favourite personal traditions for the winter solstice is a practice of feeding the earth. Since this holiday, even more than others, calls us to gather together in celebration, I take time on Yule to honour my inhuman family as well. At dusk, I pack a bag to take to the forest – red apples, cakes, honey, butter, birdseed, pinecones, sweet liqueur or wine, red candles and frankincense. I bundle up and head into the night, arriving after a short walk to a tree that I know well. I greet her with kisses and light my frankincense and candles at her feet. I speak to her the story of my year, its dramas and joys, while sipping and offering spirits. I slice the apples, slather the cakes in butter and coat the pinecones in honey and birdseed. When I have nothing more to say of the year behind me, I strike the earth and call everyone to the meal – animals, plants and spirits alike: those I know by name, and those who are still unknown to me. Using wooden or copper tools, I open the earth and bury the buttered cakes, and set the apples and pinecones around the base of the tree. It is important to my practice that this feast be an offering and so I make no requests in

return. Instead, I sing what is in my heart to sing, listen closely for the voice of the *genius loci* and go home to a very different feast, with very different guests.

Although these recipes are designed to be served on the eve of the solstice itself, the wise will begin their preparation much earlier. Winter is the season of food preservation, and our solstice meal makes use of a traditional remedy to highlight this masterful art. Fire cider is a herbal medicine from New England, in which apple cider vinegar is infused with hot spices and honey as a remedy against colds and seasonal maladies. Here, the same recipe is used to preserve protein-packed quail eggs, infusing them with the nutrients of traditional fire cider, bringing bright colours and zesty flavours to the limited winter palate.

While the eggs take at least a week to pickle before serving, the other recipes in this list take time to prepare as well. Move slowly, like winter itself, and use these dishes as meditations on the power of different cooking methods to transform ingredients, elevating even humble roots and dried beans into comfort and indulgence for the longest night of the year.

Serves 4

Prep time for full feast: 2 hours, plus 1 week pickling

Cook time for full feast: 3 hours

FOR THE PICKLED EGGS

* 825ml (28fl oz/3½ cups) apple cider vinegar
* A 7.5cm (3in) piece of ginger, peeled and sliced
* A 5cm (2in) piece of fresh turmeric root, peeled and sliced
* 1 medium jalapeño pepper, cored and sliced
* ½ small white onion, sliced
* 6 cloves garlic, peeled and smashed
* 3 tablespoons chopped fresh rosemary
* 1 tablespoon black peppercorns
* 12 large eggs or 18 quail eggs, hard boiled and peeled

FOR THE ROOTS WITH WALNUT SAUCE

* 6 small beetroots (beets), peeled and halved
* 8 small carrots, peeled and halved
* 175g (6oz) baby (pearl) onions, peeled and halved
* 1 small fennel bulb, cored and cut into 1cm (½in) slices
* 4 tablespoons olive oil
* ½ teaspoon ground cinnamon
* 60g (2oz/½ cup) chopped toasted walnuts
* 4 tablespoons stone-ground mustard
* 2 tablespoons maple syrup
* 2 tablespoons red wine vinegar
* Salt and pepper

FOR THE LENTILS

* 2 bay leaves
* 280g (10oz) dried French green lentils
* 2 tablespoons olive oil
* 1 small leek, halved, rinsed and sliced
* 2 cloves garlic, sliced
* Juice and zest of 1 lemon
* 1 teaspoon ground sumac
* A handful of torn mint leaves
* 3 tablespoons toasted pumpkin seeds
* 4 tablespoons fresh thyme leaves

FOR THE CELERIAC MASH

* One whole celeriac (celery root), peeled and cut into 2.5cm (1in) cubes
* 2 medium potatoes, peeled and cut into 2.5cm (1in) cubes
* 4 tablespoons butter
* 140g (5oz) Gruyère cheese, grated
* ¼ teaspoon grated nutmeg
* 185ml (6fl oz/¾ cup) milk, warm

FOR THE GINGERBREAD

* 225g (8oz/2¼ cups) fresh or frozen cranberries
* 115g (4oz/½ cup) butter, plus extra for greasing
* 280g (10oz/scant 1½ cups) sugar
* 1 tablespoon ground ginger
* 1 teaspoon cinnamon
* ¼ teaspoon grated nutmeg
* A pinch of ground cloves
* 2 tablespoons grated fresh ginger
* 120ml (4fl oz/½ cup) blackstrap molasses
* 60ml (2fl oz/¼ cup) maple syrup
* 2 eggs
* 212g (7½oz/1½ cups) plain (all-purpose) flour
* ½ teaspoon baking powder
* A pinch of salt
* 120ml (4fl oz/½ cup) milk

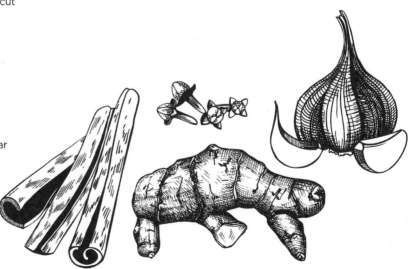

1 Begin by starting your pickles. In a saucepan over medium heat, bring your apple cider vinegar to a simmer along with your ginger, turmeric, jalapeño, onion, garlic, rosemary and peppercorns. Simmer for 2 minutes, then remove the pot from the heat and allow to infuse for 15 minutes. Set your hard-boiled eggs in a clean preserving jar and pour the warm vinegar mixture over the top. Seal and set in a cool, dry place for at least 1 week and refrigerate after opening.

2 On the day of your feast, ideally the winter solstice, begin by making the gingerbread. Preheat your oven to 180°C/350°F/Gas 4 and grease a 23cm (9in) round cake pan. In a small saucepan, combine your cranberries and 60ml (2fl oz/¼ cup) water. Bring to a simmer over medium–low heat and cook until the berries are bubbling and beginning to burst. Remove from the heat and set aside to cool (these will be stirred into your batter shortly and must be cooled to room temperature before adding).

3 In the bowl of a stand mixer, beat together your butter and sugar. Add your dried spices and grated ginger to the butter mixture, then stream in your molasses and maple syrup. Beat in your eggs. In a separate bowl, mix together your flour, baking powder and salt. Slowly add your flour and milk to the butter mixture in alternating batches, finishing with the milk.

4 Pour the batter into your prepared cake pan and tap the pan on the counter to level. Spoon dollops of the cranberry mixture over your batter and swirl it through with a knife, creating ribbons of cranberry through the batter. Bake for 50 minutes, or until a toothpick inserted into the centre of the cake comes out clean. Remove from the oven and allow to cool completely before removing from the pan.

5 Prepare your root vegetables by tossing your peeled and cut beetroot, carrots, pearl onions and fennel with the olive oil and cinnamon. Season with salt and pepper, then lay the vegetables onto a baking sheet in a single layer. Bake at 180°C/350°F/Gas 4 (alongside your gingerbread) for 30 minutes, or until the vegetables are tender when pierced with a fork.

6 While the vegetables roast, prepare your lentils. Put 950ml (32fl oz/4 cups) water in a large pan, add your bay leaves and lentils and bring to a boil over high heat. Cover the pot, lower the heat and leave to simmer for 20–30 minutes, or until the lentils are tender but not mushy. Strain and set aside.

7 Make the walnut sauce by combining your toasted walnuts and mustard in a blender. Pulse until finely ground, then stream in your maple syrup and red wine vinegar. Season with salt and pepper and set aside.

8 To finish off your lentils, heat the olive oil in a sauté pan. Add your leek and garlic and sauté until soft and fragrant. The leeks should be just starting to brown. Add your strained lentils to the pan and cook for 1 minute longer. Remove from the heat and stir in your lemon juice and zest, sumac, mint, pumpkin seeds and thyme leaves. Season with salt and pepper.

9 Finally, prepare your celeriac mash by bringing 2 litres (2 quarts) of salted water to a boil. Add your celeriac and potatoes and cook for 15 minutes, or until tender. Drain the vegetables and add them to a large mixing bowl with the butter, cheese and nutmeg, tossing until they begin to melt. Mash your vegetables with a potato masher or a hand mixer until smooth, mixing until all the butter and cheese are fully incorporated. Stir in your warm milk and season to taste.

10 At dusk on serving night, burn frankincense, evergreens, birch and warm spices as incense. Light white or red candles and scatter caraway seeds on your serving table. Toss your roasted vegetables in the walnut sauce and serve atop your spiced lentils in a large serving tray. Serve alongside your mashed celeriac and pickled eggs, saving the cranberry gingerbread for dessert. Eat by candlelight and savour both food and company as the Earth slips into the darkest night of her solar year.

Feast of Spells

Potions, rites and dinner spells

Feast of Spells

Until now, this book has sought to examine the nature of kitchen witchcraft through various lenses – through history, astrology, planetary magic, and alongside the cycle of seasons. We have examined a number of tools within these settings, each building upon the last, which have revealed new truths and ideas about what constitutes kitchen witchcraft as a theoretical concept. Hopefully, this has invited you to experiment with new ways of thinking about and doing magic, and to explore a number of possible avenues for bringing magic into the kitchen. However, we have yet to look at kitchen witchcraft by itself, as a magical modality in its own right. What does it actually mean to be a "kitchen witch", and what can actually be said about that perspective? Our final chapter seeks to address this question and put to use the various magical tools we have considered so far in our inquisition.

However, it's worthwhile to mention that, while the recipes that follow in this chapter are a useful set of exercises for the aspiring kitchen witch, they do not and cannot represent all of what kitchen witchcraft could be. In many cases, the recipes here represent simplified, stripped-down versions of what I might make at home, and vary significantly from what one might see in my personal practice. This is because the majority of my private work draws from devotional and intimate relationships with spirit – an aspect of my life that is neither easily translatable nor open to public eyes, as is the case for most religious practices. Because this kind of work is so intensely personal, and because readers of this book will likely represent various

traditions and religious beliefs, our final chapter will focus more heavily on planetary magic, sympathetic correspondences and plant sorcery, with devotional work almost entirely omitted. This is where your personal traditions and relationships to spirit will fill in the gaps, and your kitchen witchcraft practice can become fully your own. Moreover, this book seeks not to rewrite traditional magic, but instead to offer experimental pathways into alternative perspectives and methodologies. These recipes are meant to offer additional tools to the witch's practice, and to conjure the question: what does magic look like when it is prepared in the kitchen?

Feast table as sacred space

The recipes within this chapter examine several different applications of kitchen witchcraft, beginning with a concept we encountered in the Feast of the Ancestors – the idea of the feast table as a sacred space or magic circle. In witchcraft, sacred spaces and magic circles are created to perform a variety of functions and to properly structure space for magical acts. They can be used as containers to bind and ensnare powerful divinities and demons; they can be constructed to create the opportune working conditions for carrying out magical work; or they can create a temporary meeting place wherein the numinous can manifest. Their use conjures a temporary, set-apart space which acts symbolically as either a container or a door. In many cases, we use our secular feast tables in a similar fashion – to compel a gathering with those we love, to focus the joyful, nostalgic energy of holidays and festivals, and to create the ideal arena for the festivities to unfold. This mirrors the ancient ideas of feasts presenting an opportunity for gods and men to dine together, and to sit shoulder to shoulder with one another in communion. The chef and the witch are both familiar with this technology – a crafty manipulation of space and ambience as a magical tool, creating a precise context from which to draw forth what we desire – a trick to which any successful host can attest. In both contexts, what is conjured within the circle is both fleeting and sacred, only able to exist within the boundaries of that sacred space.

But more than these superficial similarities in technology, the magic circle and the feast table are both spiritual tools which create a liminal space – a point "between", outside of the ordinary and mundane, acting as a border between the known and unknown wherein special, magical things can occur. In the European canon, these liminal spaces manifest in witchcraft as magic circles, places of power and even fleeting, opportune moments like dusk, dawn, midnight, equinoxes and eclipses. Stories of these places feature heavily in mythology and folklore as well, conjuring images of fairy rings, crossroads and rends in the veil, which are overrun with tricksters, devils and shapeshifters in the mythic imagination. These places and times are regarded as an intrusion of the Other (the divine, the numinous or however you prefer to understand this idea) into mundane reality, with the liminal aspect creating the point of contact – the holy place, date or inscribed circle which exists as a gateway to that which is beyond. When we consider the feast table, which sets apart not only a specific place for feasting but also a specific day or time for engagement, we can see the ease with which this mundane tool, like so many others, can become a magical one as well.

In the case of naturally formed sacred sites, such as holy mountains and cave springs, the Other is said to speak through these places and make itself known to us. In the case of magical sites created or drawn by practitioners – such as magic circles or, for our purposes, feast tables – the Other is drawn forth by the will and craft of the witch, often into a prepared space where both safety and clarity of communication can be ensured. These latter magic circles have been documented as far back in history as Ancient Sumeria, where they were drawn with flour (a curious fact for the kitchen witch) to set apart and purify the ritual space. In the ceremonial magic of the 16th century and beyond, these same markings would have been written in salt or chalk, and would accomplish a similar task by inscribing specific names and seals of power as heavenly reinforcement for the work. In either case, the magic circle represents a carefully curated arena, set apart from the "normal" space of human mundanity so that it may be an effective container for the strange and numinous.

In this chapter, we examine a few possible avenues of working with our feast tables as liminal spaces and magic circles. One of the most straightforward offerings comes in the Feast of Fried Blossoms and Mushrooms, created as a shareable feast for humans and spirits alike. Drawing on our understanding of the ritual feast as meeting place between humans and gods, this recipe features two botanical allies of spirit communication, inspired by the traditional foods of the Fae – fresh flowers and mushrooms. While this recipe leaves our work very open ended, there is another selection which offers a more direct invocation – the Elder and Blackberry Master of the Woods Cake. This invocation is just as nonverbal and symbolic, but both the flavour palette and presentation of this dish are designed to be evocative of a single, feral intelligence – the Master of the Woods personified, through the eye of the kitchen witch, as an otherworldly centrepiece cake. Creating effigies like this as a point of contact with spirit is an ancient and ubiquitous magical technology, familiar to anyone who has worked with statues, icons and altar images before. While our approach here is certainly unconventional, the praxis is familiar, and as a sculptural medium for working our magic, cake is as good a modality as any.

However, there are some other ways we can consider the feast table as a magical, liminal space that may be of more practical use for our work. Within this chapter, we find a recipe for Herbed Yogurt Cheese, which examines the role of the feast table as an altar space – here, an altar to Saturn's aspect as lord of rot and fermentation, which is of particular interest to the kitchen witch. In this example, it is not the ritual feast which embodies the magic circle, but the dish itself. Herbs, ingredients and botanical allies of Saturn are gathered and then allowed to infuse and ferment for several days. If the intention for this recipe is a ritual veneration of Saturn, then it will surely call him forth and embody those fantastic, transformative powers of rot and rebirth in the material sphere. The final product yields an edible invocation, which operates somewhere between a magic circle and an altar image. While this method is certainly suited for work with spirits or planetary intelligences as seen here, we can imagine how this practice might be applied to more secular, practical aims – perhaps creating dishes to embody our intentions, for example.

There is one final entry in this chapter which investigates this technique, though in a slightly different way, through the creation of Ritual Bread Masks. When magic circles and liminal spaces are used to call forth the Other, they are used because they provide a safe boundary and demarcation of "human space" from "Other space", giving us a safe method of return to mundane reality. However, there are methods of invocation which do away with any notions of safety and self, which instead lean deeply into the fusion of the self with the spirit to be invoked. One such technology is the mask, through which the identity of the wearer is obscured and another identity steps forward. Once they are thusly transformed, the witch can evoke the spirit-force of the mask itself, perhaps even engaging in a form of willing possession. In this way, the ritual mask can act as a portal, transporting us both internally and externally when we accept the false face as our own.

Sigilcraft

Other recipes within this chapter consider our investigation from a different perspective, drawing on established occult tools to experiment with kitchen magic. The practice of sigilcraft is one that many witches are likely familiar with, as the creation of talismanic symbols is a necessary, practical skill in many traditions. However, we may consider some new applications of this technology when we experiment with using sigils and magical symbols within a kitchen witchcraft practice. On a very basic level, these images are symbolic representations of the witch's will, designed in such a way that the original intent of the image is only still recognizable by the subconscious mind. For those who have not crafted their own sigils before, various methods abound to produce a similar object – the talismanic glyph – a symbol which is not just a representation of a concept, but a dynamic, operative monograph. As someone whose praxis is greatly informed by chaos magic, my preferred method of sigil creation is the one pioneered in the 1970s by Peter J. Carroll, which builds on the foundational work of artist and magician Austin Osman Spare some decades earlier (in the endless ouroboros that is art and the occult).

In this method, the practitioner begins as they always do – in meditation about the nature of the work ahead. For crafting sigils, distillation of one's intent into a precise statement of desire is absolutely essential, and one should rework and sit with this statement until its tone, wording and expression are fully aligned with the purpose of the spell. The phrasing should neither be too general nor too exact, as either extreme creates roadblocks – too vague a statement is impossible to actualize, and too precise can limit our avenues for manifestation. It is also important to ensure that the statement is confident and self-assured, and that the language used is precise, meaningful and evocative, such that it elicits passionate engagement when read. For example, if someone wanted to create a sigil to quit smoking, the phrase "I want to quit smoking" has its problems – it is very general, the phrasing is not confident, and it gives no details about when or how the practitioner wants to quit smoking. If we chose to rework this intention to be more precise, we might consider as an alternative, "My will is stronger than my addiction to cigarettes." This new sentence is clear, forceful and creates a brief but powerful statement of desire.

MY WILL IS STRONGER THAN MY ADDICTION TO CIGARETTES Fig. 1

MWLSTRNGHDC Fig. 2

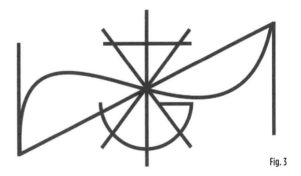

Fig. 3

Once the statement is prepared, the witch is instructed to systematically remove letters from the phrase – a primary abstraction of the desire from the conscious mind. Some methods suggest doing this by removing all repeating letters and vowels from the statement (Fig. 1), but the method you select is largely arbitrary – consider even selecting a planetary number relating to your intention (for our example, Saturn is useful in breaking addictions, so our number for this exercise would be 3) and removing every Xth letter in your statement. Our example combines these methods to limit the amount of letters in the final figure and add an additional layer of significance to the work. When these letters are selected, their shapes are considered (Fig. 2) in determining the form of the final sigil. These lines and curves which formerly made up letters are now considered independently, and are mutated from their original forms in a secondary abstraction – one which does away with the alphabetical form of our desire, shifting instead to an entirely symbolic image. These shapes are then carefully rearranged into the final sigil, which is often worked and reworked until the image is "correct", with each reworking leading to further, subtle abstractions in form.

Finally, the resulting symbol (Fig. 3) is ready to be charged. For Carroll, this occurs in a process called "gnosis", which submits the nonlinear, nonverbal information contained within the symbol to the subconscious mind through a state of deep meditation or ecstatic experience. Popular methods for achieving this form of gnosis are trancework, physical exertion (eg a runner's high), repetitive motion (whirling dervish) or orgasm. The aim of these practices is to achieve a complete suppression of the conscious mind into a "blank" state, however fleeting, during which the practitioner can focus their will and attention upon the sigil. Immediately after the sigil is charged, the sigil paper is burned, buried or otherwise destroyed, and the witch is cautioned to forget the working as best they can – as Spare says, we should "deliberately strive"[8] to forget it. This keeps the symbolic content firmly within the subconscious mind, wherein the will can

bring about its manifestation, unburdened by the attachments of desire. There are certainly variations and amendments that can be made to this basic procedure, as we see with the fascinating but unique approaches to creating hypersigils given by Alan Moore and Aidan Wachter, but this basic framework should be useful in beginning your inquiry of sigil magic.

These sorts of talismanic sigils or other occult iconography are powerful tools in the hands of the witch, creating a symbolic language that slips beneath the linear, rational mind of the ego-self and into the swirling seas of the subconscious. In this chapter, three recipes explore this technology, both directly and indirectly. Most obvious is the Sigil Grissini, which offers a direct, workable praxis for sigil magic given through the lens of kitchen witchcraft. However, there are two other recipes here which examine symbolism in a slightly different way, favouring the employment of existing symbolic structures to give our work its meaning. In the recipe for Protective Chicken Foot Soup, the image of the gnarled and twisted chicken foot is

called upon as an apotropaic mark to turn away or avert that which is detrimental – in this case, physical illness and bad luck. In the recipe for Home-blessing Rosemary Star Bread, we see the use of a repetitive, radiating symbol used as a form of home blessing and protection – borrowing from the long history of these symbols being used to entrap demons and devils before they cross the threshold. These two applications draw on the same use of symbols as dynamic, operative images, but favour historical examples to self-produced ones. These offer a more passive form of magic, since they are less directly tied to the will of the practitioner, but are no less effective, as their historical precedence can attest.

Consecration

Another occult technology featured in this chapter is the vehicle of consecration, where mundane ingredients are transformed into magical tools. In consecration, ordinary objects are given over to a spiritual or magical purpose, sanctified and imbued with a particular role or rulership for our work. These consecrated, talismanic objects passively radiate their virtues, acting as something between a magical ingredient and a self-contained spell. For example, many of the recipes in the Feast of the Heavens chapter recommend specific fumigations and recitations – two common methods of consecration, which here elevate the meal beyond mere mundanity, calling down the virtues of its planetary ruler. Additionally, we see something similar occur at Sunday Mass, when Christians consume the consecrated bread in an act of simulated theophagy. These are just two demonstrations of consecration in action, where the entire meal itself becomes the talisman, and is then consumed in a ritual act which fuses the consecrated object with the very fabric of our bodies.

In our work here as kitchen witches, single ingredients, whole dishes and even entire feasts can receive this magical treatment. Indeed, consecration is likely the most common magical technique you will find presented within this final chapter, as it is an accessible tool with a multitude of possible applications. As we mentioned previously, consecration by smoke and chant are two extremely common avenues, but other symbolic, sympathetic actions may also suit. For example, we can select not just ingredients which align with our intent, but also colours, textures and shapes that evoke the consecrating spirits or energies of our work. One could go as far as to suggest that even the placement of candles, symbols and tablecloths at our ritual feasts could be methods of consecration, by lending further significance and correspondence to our spellwork.

For a fantastic and specific example of consecration in action, consider a love spell from the Book of St. Cyprian: The Sorcerer's Treasure (Hadean Press, 2014)[9], a Portuguese book of magic attributed to St Cyprian of Antioch. In this spell, a woman who wishes to be loved by a man prepares him a meal of consecrated eggs (a beautiful symbol of fertility and sensuality in their own right), which she has beaten and poured down the entire length of her spine before cooking into an omelette, served steaming hot. Here, the ritual of consecration is a symbolic, sensual treatment of the ingredients before preparation, which retain and transfer those energies when they are consumed by the target.

This modality of using layered symbolism and sympathetic correspondence forms the basis for our non-religious exploration of consecration. Many of the recipes in this final chapter rely primarily on fumigation, recitation, plant rulerships and sigils to accomplish this work, though embellishment in your own rituals at home is certainly welcome and encouraged. Each method presented here is slightly different, using different tools and techniques, but all draw from the same central technology of consecration of a tool for creating talismanic ingredients and dishes. For enchanting drinks and cocktails, like old love potions of folklore, the recipes here for Infused Ritual Wine, Cleansing Iced Tea, Bitters and, of course, the two Love Potion cocktails can provide useful schematics for beverage magic of all kinds. These recipes utilize various apothecary techniques, such as tincturing, infusion and syrup making, which yield finished products of differing appearances, flavours and physiological strengths – a useful variety when considering whether you'd like to employ these magics overtly or in secret.

While not a beverage per se, the recipe for Four Thieves Vinaigrette is in this group as well, as it draws upon a familiar method of creating a herbal oxymel, as we also saw in the Fire Cider Pickled Eggs of the Winter Solstice Feast. The other consecration recipes within this chapter draw from the correspondences and energetic relationships between ingredients that we discussed in previous chapters. As a framework for doing magic outside of a theistic or devotional tradition, planetary magic is an extremely useful avenue within the western canon, as the planets are accessible and relatable to all practitioners who wish to work with them. This expands upon our work with planetary rulerships in the Feast of the Heavens, and starts to put those designations to use in practical magic. Consecrated to Jupiter, Mars and the Sun respectively, the recipes for Chocolate, Beetroot and Grapefruit

Celebration Cake, Pine-Baked Polenta Cakes, and Opportunity-conjuring Dandelion and Calendula Scones all provide detailed procedural steps for carrying out a suggested method of consecration to these ruling spheres. These recipes broadly call down the virtues of the planets, creating a finished dish that is consecrated, imbued with power and ready to be put to use in our work. One final offering within this section takes a slightly different approach and seeks to use the benevolent aspects of a planet as a salve against its more abrasive qualities. Here, a Lavender and Potato Galette Against Mercury Retrograde grounds herbs of the high-paced, volatile Mercury into dense, creamy potato (a subterranean nightshade of Saturn, the planet of constancy and dependability) to offset the all-destructive effects of Mercury in his drunken, retrograde state.

Divination

There is another occult sphere in which we may find room to experiment with the tools of kitchen witchcraft. The practice of divination is a central tool in most occult practices, which offers an opportunity to externalize the intuitive process and receive useful, instructive counsel in moments of uncertainty. This is an especially helpful tool for novice occultists who battle with self-doubt and uncertainty as they navigate the first steps of their path. While trusted teachers and educational resources should form the basis of one's early research, divination provides a pathway that builds self-trust, checks our work, and strengthens our prowess in using the intuitive force. In many ways, the divinatory medium can act as a translator between the logical, linear mind of the ego self and the symbolic, subtle mind of the subconscious.

In this chapter, we present two useful recipes for kitchen divination – one traditional, and one less so. Our familiar example comes in the form of the Mugwort and Catnip Divination Tea, which outlines an introductory ritual for tasseomancy, or tea leaf reading. Both of these herbs have beautiful, delicate, twisting leaves, which give clear and easy-to-read shapes in the bottom of a teacup. Additionally, both herbs are regarded for powerfully amplifying intuitive senses, helping us slip deeper into meditation and more effectively translate the symbolism we see. If you've never experimented with tea leaf reading before, there are some tips and tricks within this entry that should help you make your approach. Our second offering comes in the form of the Salem Witch Trials "Witch Cake", which is neither purely of the witch trials nor truly a cake. Instead, this recipe takes its inspiration from a strange form of divination used during the 1692 Salem Witch Trials and expands upon the framework to produce something wholly original. Here, two shortcakes containing a hidden talisman form the basis of our divinatory media, providing a simple, effective yes or no answer.

If you've not already picked up a tarot deck, pendulum, bag of runes or another divinatory medium yourself, we may perhaps be able to experiment with a novel approach here. When we consider the history of divination practices, which span the globe and draw on an incredible variety of materials as tools (consider ovomancy by eggs, turifumy by shapes in smoke, or aleuromancy by flour, as just a few examples of hundreds), we can see that this is not a technology that resides in the medium, but instead in the mediator – in the mind and intuition of a reader who can accurately interpret the signs. Instead of the power to "see" emanating from the deck of cards or crystal ball, divinatory vision is more a matter of discernment, where the reader is able to pluck meaningful patterns from chaos. The divinatory medium has, historically, been what practitioners had on hand – spilled lentils, rooster guts or the passing of clouds in the sky. When we acknowledge that perfecting the art of divination has nothing to do with the tools we use, we're free to tread into more experimental territory.

If we wish to create a kitchen oracle – a simple divinatory tool to use for simple questions of kitchen witchcraft – then we should start by looking for our medium in the pantry. As non-perishable and sturdy options go, dried beans are a cheap, common and durable choice, so we will construct our oracle with nine of them – three black, three white, three red. This might sound silly or overly mundane, but there exists ample historical precedent for humble foods as divinatory mediums – like Allantide apples, Russian divination eggs and even broken wishbones. In our work, black beans will signify "no", the white beans will signify "yes" and the red beans will call for revisiting the question itself and reframing how we think about the situation. To consecrate your kitchen oracle, consider the divinities and energies of your own practice which you associate with kitchen magic. For many,

this could be your ancestral spirits, patron gods and goddesses, or planetary rulers of divination like the Sun or Moon. Perform your consecration when the moon is waxing or full and both Venus and the Sun have no strong negative astrological aspects. To consult, close the eyes and extend the intuition through the hands, making one anonymous selection from your pouch or reliquary. Each question should be asked aloud and will receive one answer. When not in use, your kitchen oracle can be stored in a fabric pouch or felt-lined metal tin (I love to repurpose peppermint tins for these!) and stowed somewhere within the kitchen itself – in pantry cupboards, silverware drawers or tucked into the spice rack.

Sacrifice

Finally, we come to one of the oldest tools of kitchen witchcraft, and some might say of religion in general – offering and sacrifice. While sacrifice is usually performed to curry favour with deities and spirits, we can consider a number of other aims as well: in a feast of high honour, such as a devotional holiday or a funeral celebration; as a scapegoat or *pharmakos* in banishing and cleansing rites; or in bartering for large requests made of one's ephemeral allies. Whatever the case may be, offering and sacrifice occupy one possible avenue for embodying an energetic exchange, where the witch both gives and receives in a meaningful way.

In the very ancient past, sacrificial feasts would be prepared and offered whole, fed to the fire in an all-consuming holocaust, as we see with Jason's sacrifice to Hekate in the *Argonautica*. Here, the witch Medea transmits detailed instructions, in which the sacrifice is made and then immediately abandoned to the goddess:

> *[...] then watch for the time when the night is parted in twain, then bathe in the stream of the tireless river, and alone, apart from others, clad in dusky raiment, dig a rounded pit; and therein slay a ewe, and sacrifice it whole, heaping high the pyre on the very edge of the pit. And propitiate only-begotten Hecate, daughter of Perses, pouring from a goblet the hive-stored labour of bees. And then, when thou hast heedfully sought the grace of the goddess, retreat from the pyre; and let neither the sound of feet drive thee to turn back, nor the baying of hounds, lest haply thou shouldst maim all the rites and thyself fail to return duly to thy comrades.*

APOLLONIUS RHODIUS, ARGONAUTICA,
3RD CENTURY BCE

For the rituals of classical antiquity, these sacrificial objects would have been consecrated before offering, in extended rites which often took weeks, months or years to complete. Sacrificial animals would be looked after and kept quite content, such that they arrived at the altar as calm and "willing" sacrifices. In ancient Greece, the sacrificial blade would be concealed until the instant it is needed, and attendees would writhe and scream in sympathetic pain at the very moment

of death. In the Roman Empire, sacrificial animals would have been gilded and decked in flowers, elevated to a form of near divinity as they approached the moment of no return. At these events, a sacrifice of roast animals might be shared among attending guests first, with only a few of the best portions, along with hair, bones, and other discarded ends, offered to the gods by fire. The irony of offering only the leftovers to their gods was not lost on the ancients, but this banquet was considered to be shared in communion with the gods, with the feast acting as a point of exchange and harmonization between the earthly and divine.

This is not to suggest that vegetarian avenues of sacrificial feast did not exist. Among the ancients, what was valued by men was generally considered to be valued by gods as well, particularly where food offerings were concerned, and so luxury foods like butchered animals were naturally prized – not just for the luxury of the meat, but the sacrifice of a life. However, non-meat offerings were certainly made, especially in the case of complex, artisanal goods like wine, bread, honey and eggs, all of which represent a significant investment of time and resources, thus making them worthy of sacrifice. These rituals may seem simplistic today, but sacrificial feasts have, for most of human history, been sought as a moment of contact with the divine and a reliable avenue for communication with gods and spirits. Just as one might bake cookies for a friend's birthday or a cake for an office party, the sacrificial meal is an offering of effort and attention, communicating not just the value of the exchange, but also the precious relationship between creator and recipient.

While some recipes for sacrificial meals have already been examined in this book, such as the Pharmakos Cakes in Feast of the

Ancestors, it is worthwhile to revisit this concept through a modern witchcraft lens. In our final chapter, we examine just three recipes that utilize this magical tool, as the technology of offering is extremely intuitive and any specific rituals to this effect will always take the shape of one's personal practice and devotional relationships. Nevertheless, these recipes present useful templates for further exploration by considering one traditional animal offering and two vegetarian alternatives. The Sacrificial Quail with Pomegranate Sauce provides the most direct avenue of traditional sacrifice, with a simple, quick-cooking recipe for a delicious whole-animal offering. This small, roasted bird is doused in a spiced, blood-red pomegranate sauce, which can be consumed in traditional feast or offered whole by fire or earth. This is undoubtedly a dramatic, high glamour meal that is best suited to grand, devotional work. For a less formal alternative, the Rosemary, Apple and Cheddar Picnic Pies may suit, as these portable treats are designed for offering and sharing when one is out in nature, or when making a first approach to spirit allies. These treats are no less delicious, but the flavour palette and presentation are unpretentious, making this a nice selection for non-devotional offerings and informal or transactional exchanges with spirits.

Finally, one last recipe gives us an opportunity to look at the technology of sacrifice and offering in a different, more individual way. The instructions given for the Honeyed Berries with Blue Lotus Zabaglione frame this dish as an offering placed before the altar of the body, our bodies, which in traditional witchcraft are considered in some ways to be teachers of occult mystery themselves. In this framework, our physical bodies act as the primary initiator into occult wisdom, by giving us our senses, instincts, psyche and, thus, our most basic identity, which provide sensory tools to navigate the seen and unseen of the world around us. As the body is an indispensable ally and mentor in the magic of the kitchen witch, this recipe presents a ritual of sacrifice to the body, as a means of nourishing and honouring this holy vessel through a sensuous, nutritive offering.

Home-blessing
Rosemary Star Bread

When I move into a new home, I set up blessings and protections on the house and land. In my practice, this is an essential first step, and goes a long way to help me feel settled. This involves a variety of rituals – sigils drawn in holy oil on every window and door, honey-smeared razorblades above every entryway, and a deep, extended fumigation with frankincense to help me start afresh. However, a bit of kitchen witchcraft that could replace many of these rituals is this loaf.

Star breads are visually striking, with their twisting spirals undulating in a hypnotic rhythm. These kinds of patterns are common in the home protection charms of Europe, which complex and repetitive designs to distract meddlesome devils, who are said to be compelled to count these shapes and lose themselves within the pattern. This recipe also calls for two extremely useful herbs, especially for home blessing. The green color of this bread comes from either rocket (arugula) or nettles – whichever is easier to source in your area. Both are boundary-protecting plants of Mars – rocket for its spice, and nettle for its sting. Within the filling of the bread, rosemary is a blessing and saining herb *par excellence*, renowned in several traditions for its use in consecration and purification. These botanical allies combine to produce a talismanic bread, which serves as the perfect charm for any housewarming. While this bread can certainly be eaten and enjoyed (the rosemary hazelnut pesto is to die for!), it could also be hung by the front door, as a protective charm and blessing for the new home.

Makes one 25cm (10in) loaf
Prep time: 40 minutes, plus 1¼ hours proving
Cook time: 20 minutes

FOR THE DOUGH

* 200g (7oz/1 cup) tightly packed rocket (arugula) or fresh nettles
* 120ml (4fl oz/½ cup) milk, warm
* 7g (2¼ teaspoons) active dry yeast
* 1 teaspoon sugar
* 300g (10½oz/2¼ cups) plain (all-purpose) flour, plus extra for dusting
* 60ml (2fl oz/¼ cup) buttermilk
* 1 teaspoon salt
* Cracked black pepper

FOR THE FILLING

* 35g (1¼oz/½ cup) grated Parmesan cheese
* 35g (1¼oz/½ cup) hazelnuts, toasted
* 2 sprigs rosemary, stems removed
* 150g (5¼oz/¾ cup) lightly packed rocket (arugula)
* ¼ teaspoon bay leaf powder
* Zest of 1 orange
* 3 tablespoons olive oil
* 1 egg, beaten

1 Begin by creating the filling for your bread. In a blender or food processor, combine your Parmesan cheese, hazelnuts, rosemary needles, rocket, bay leaf powder, orange zest, and olive oil. Blend until the pesto forms a coarse paste, then remove from the blender and set aside.

2 Next, blanch your rocket (arugula) or nettles for the dough. Get a saucepan of water boiling and plunge the leaves in for 1 minute, then immediately submerge them in ice water. Wring the leaves dry, then add them to a blender with your warm milk. Purée until smooth and evenly incorporated.

3 In a large bowl or the bowl of a stand mixer fitted with a dough hook, combine your warm rocket (arugula) or nettle-infused milk, yeast and sugar. Stir to combine, then allow to stand for 10 minutes or until frothy. Add your flour, buttermilk and salt to the bowl and knead until the dough is smooth and soft, about 8 minutes.

4 Lightly grease another bowl and turn your dough into it. Cover the bowl with a damp tea (dish) towel and set it in a warm place to prove until doubled in size – about 1 hour.

5 When the dough has proved, turn it out onto a floured surface and divide into four equal portions. Roll each portion into a 25cm (10in) round, and set them aside in a stack layered with baking parchment. Take the first piece of dough and set it on a piece of baking parchment. Brush it lightly with the beaten egg. Evenly spread one-third of the pesto mixture across the dough, leaving at least a 1cm (½in) gap at the edges. Repeat this process with the second and third layers, topping the bread off with the fourth and final layer of dough.

6 Trace a 5cm (2in) circle in the centre of the bread and, using a knife, map out 12 even cuts from the edge of your traced circle to the outer edge of the loaf. Use a sharp knife to cut along these radiating lines, and then twist each segment three times, alternating twisting to the left and right. For each pair of segments which turn toward each other, tuck and pinch them together at the top so that they form an even point. You may use a small amount of beaten egg to help the edges adhere.

7 Transfer the loaf to a baking sheet by sliding it on the baking parchment. Cover the loaf once more with a tea towel and allow to prove for an additional 15 minutes. Preheat your oven to 200°C/400°F/Gas 4.

8 When the oven is hot, lightly brush the loaf with beaten egg. Sprinkle the loaf with salt and cracked black pepper and bake for 15–20 minutes, or until golden and fully cooked underneath. When the bread is done, allow to cool on a wire rack before serving.

Pine-baked Polenta Cakes with Arrabiata and Goat's Cheese

This dish was dreamt up while camping near Mount Rainier, during a summer that I spent hopping between national parks along the Pacific coast. Camping is, for me, an ancestral practice – a passion of my father's that was passed on to me over many summers spent hiking and exploring the Catskill mountains. My father, who was always a good cook, was especially skilled with cooking over a campfire, which any experienced camper can attest is no small feat. His creations always went beyond the staples (hotdogs and hamburgers) and really drew upon his culinary creativity to feed a large, hungry family of dozens. Inspired by the innovation he always brought to camp cooking, this dish was born.

As a magical recipe, this selection is very stripped down, requiring no elaborate invocations, sigils or fumigations. Rather, it represents a very passive evocation, where only the intent of the practitioner and the ritual act of feast are used to compel the ingredients to surrender their virtues.

This dish calls for the ingredients of Mars – pine, garlic and chillies – in an effort to evoke some of the planet's more gentle qualities. While Mars is certainly the lesser malefic of the heavens, full of challenging and violent energy, he also embodies some beautiful and useful qualities, such as energy, vitality and a sense of adventure. For an outdoor excursion, there can be no virtues more well-suited for the occasion.

While this recipe is written to be cooked in a home kitchen, it is my hope that the adventurous readers of this book will attempt this selection out in the wilderness as I did. This lends another Martian element to the working, as the recipe would be cooked over an open flame. To adapt this recipe for an outdoor kitchen, you may wrap the cakes, needles and orange peels in kitchen foil, set them under hot coals for 20 minutes, then finish them off on the barbecue. The sauce can also be made in a saucepan over the fire, but you may prefer to make your sauce at home where it will be significantly easier to do so.

Serves 4
Prep time: 30 minutes
Cook time: 40 minutes

* A 500g (1lb 2oz) packet of pre-cooked Italian polenta
* 4 tablespoons olive oil
* Several bunches fresh pine needles, scrubbed clean
* Zest of 1 orange, peeled with a vegetable peeler
* 1 small yellow onion, finely diced
* 4 cloves garlic, minced
* 1 tablespoon crushed chilli (red pepper) flakes
* 1 x 800g (28oz) can chopped tomatoes
* A small bunch of basil, washed and torn
* 110g (4oz/¾ cup) crumbled goat's cheese
* Salt and pepper

1 Preheat your oven to 180°C/350°F/Gas 4 and line a baking sheet with baking parchment or kitchen foil.

2 Begin by slicing your polenta into even 1cm (½in) thick cakes. Brush the cakes lightly with olive oil, then lightly season with salt and pepper.

3 Take half of your pine needles and orange peels – enough to coat the bottom of the baking sheet in a single layer – and sprinkle them into the pan. Place your polenta cakes on top, then cover with the remaining needles and peels. Cover the pan with foil, place in the oven and bake for 20 minutes. Remove the pan from the oven, discard the foil and the top layer of pine needles and bake for an additional 20 minutes, or until the exterior of the cakes is crisp.

4 While the cakes bake, prepare your sauce. Heat your remaining olive oil in a large frying pan (skillet) over medium–high heat. Add your onion and sauté until soft. Add your garlic and chilli flakes and sauté for a further 3 minutes. When the alliums are soft and the chilli flakes are fragrant, add your chopped tomatoes to the pan. Simmer for 30 minutes, or until the sauce has thickened and become less acidic. Stir in your torn basil leaves, season with salt and pepper and keep warm until serving time.

5 Before serving, remove and discard the pine needles and orange peels. To serve, top each polenta cake with a spoonful of fresh arrabiata sauce and sprinkle with crumbled goat's cheese.

Four Thieves Vinaigrette

If you've explored kitchen witchcraft on your own before, you've probably come across recipes for "four thieves vinegar" – a popular and cryptic preparation used in banishing and cleansing magic, derived from a plague-era herbal remedy. As one story goes, this preparation was indeed crafted by four thieves, who used a blend of anti-pestilential herbs infused in vinegar to protect themselves from plague-ridden mites while stealing from the recently dead. Reportedly, the four thieves only surrendered their special recipe when they were discovered and used it to barter against their execution. However, other historians suggest that this may have been a myth, with the name actually deriving from a misspelling of Richard Forthave's surname, who popularized a similar remedy as "Forthave's Vinegar". While the recipe is certainly valuable with or without the legend, there is some debate about what ingredients were traditionally used. No accepted standard for this recipe exists, but modern adaptations have added more common household herbs to the mix, such as garlic, lavender and rosemary, which are not present in earlier versions.

One of the most popular recipes, related by René-Maurice Gattefossé, describes one early iteration of the potion containing three pints of strong white wine vinegar, a handful of each of wormwood, meadowsweet, wild marjoram and sage, fifty cloves, two ounces of campanula roots, two ounces of angelic, rosemary and horehound and three large measures of camphor. The mixture was placed a container for fifteen days, strained and expressed, then bottled. It was used by rubbing it on the hands, ears and temples from time to time when approaching a plague victim.

Today, this same recipe is used in magical work, to ward off energetic and magical pestilence as effectively as literal plague rats. It is used as an anointing preparation and ritual wash and serves as a useful panacea for all manner of protective and cleansing magic. However, the herbs within this blend retain their medicinal virtues as well, and the wise will find that this preparation is just as useful in staving off illness and preventing a cold as it is in magical work. Adapted for flavour and medicinal benefit, this recipe is a playful spin on this classic medieval remedy, bringing it to the feast table in an unconventional way.

Makes 240ml (8fl oz/1 cup) of vinaigrette

Prep time: 5 minutes, plus 2 weeks infusing

* 4 tablespoons dried wormwood
* 4 tablespoons dried meadowsweet
* 4 tablespoons dried lavender flowers
* 4 tablespoons dried rue
* 2 stalks fresh rosemary
* A handful of fresh sage
* 20 whole cloves, crushed
* 5 cloves garlic, minced
* 2 pinches edible (green) camphor crystals (optional)
* 450ml (16fl oz/2 cups) white wine vinegar or apple cider vinegar
* 1 teaspoon Dijon mustard
* 2 tablespoons minced shallot
* 1 teaspoon fresh thyme leaves
* 120ml (4fl oz/½ cup) extra virgin olive oil
* Salt and pepper

I Begin by carefully assembling your wormwood, meadowsweet, lavender, rue, rosemary, sage, cloves, garlic and camphor crystals (if using), then combine them in a preserving jar that's large enough to take the liquid. Pour your vinegar over the top of the herbs and seal the jar. Shake the jar to combine and store in a cool, dark place for 2 weeks, shaking daily.

2 When ready to prepare the vinaigrette, open the jar and strain your vinegar through a fine mesh sieve. Be sure to wring out any liquid from the herbs before discarding. Measure 120ml (4fl oz/½ cup) of vinegar and put the rest back into the jar, to be refrigerated and used within 4–6 months.

3 In a blender or food processor, combine the measured vinegar, mustard, shallot and thyme leaves. Pulse until combined. With the blender or processor running at a low speed, stream in your olive oil, allowing the machine to run until the oil is fully emulsified. Season with salt and pepper and serve immediately for the freshest flavour. Your vinaigrette can be stored in the refrigerator for up to 3 days.

Lavender Potato Galette Against Mercury Retrograde

Mercury retrograde is certainly the most dreaded and maligned of astrological transits, feared and revered as a time when all hell breaks loose on earth. Mercury – the planet of motion, communication and forward momentum – "breaks down", appearing to soar through the heavens in reverse, undoing his work and sending human progress into a tailspin. In retrograde, Mercury brings technological glitches, confusion and relentless impediments to all negotiations, projects and plans. Where previously Mercury had facilitated easy connection with others, here communication breaks down, leading to misunderstandings, arguments and awkward encounters.

As a salve to these harsh effects, many planetary magicians recommend remediation work during Mercury retrograde, in an effort to secure some of the planet's more agreeable virtues before it slips into its drunken, backward state. The recipe found here is a kitchen witch's answer to that question, relying on the botanical allies of right-side Mercury – lavender, dill and marjoram – to steel ourselves against the effects of the planet's backward motion. This dish is best prepared a few days before retrograde properly begins, alongside a fumigation of Mercurial herbs such as frankincense, mastic, elemi,

dill seed, hyssop and lemongrass. Consider offering a portion of this meal to Hermes, the ancient Greek face of Mercury, and reading aloud his Orphic hymn:

Hermes, draw near, and to my prayr incline,
Angel of Jove, and Maia's son divine;
Prefect of contest, ruler of mankind,
With heart almighty, and a prudent mind.
Celestial messenger of various skill,
Whose pow'rful arts could watchful Argus kill.
With winged feet 'tis thine thro' air to course,
O friend of man, and prophet of discourse;
Great life-supporter, to rejoice is thine
In arts gymnastic, and in fraud divine.
With pow'r endu'd all language to explain,
Of care the loos'ner, and the source of gain.
Whose hand contains of blameless peace the rod,
Corucian, blessed, profitable God.
Of various speech, whose aid in works we find,
And in necessities to mortals kind.
Dire weapon of the tongue, which men revere,
Be present, Hermes, and thy suppliant hear;
Assist my works, conclude my life with peace,
Give graceful speech, and memory's increase. [10]

Serves 4–6
Prep time: 25 minutes
Cook time: 25 minutes

* 30g (1oz/2 tablespoons) butter, plus extra for regreasing
* 3 large russet potatoes, peeled and sliced very thinly
* 25g (1oz/¼ cup) grated Asiago cheese (or white Cheddar)
* 2 tablespoons dried lavender flowers, crushed
* 1 teaspoon marjoram
* Salt and pepper
* Fresh dill, to garnish

1 In a 23cm (9in) frying pan (skillet) over medium heat, melt your butter and swirl the pan to coat evenly. Remove the pan from the heat.

2 Beginning in the centre of the pan, lay a double layer of overlapping potato slices, fanning out in a spiral across the pan. Each slice should overlap the one before it by 50 per cent.

3 Toss together your cheese with the lavender and marjoram and sprinkle these across the galette, leaving 1cm (½in) of clearance around the edges. Season with salt and pepper, then repeat the laying process with the rest of your potatoes, until all are used.

4 Cook the galette over a medium heat until the bottom is browning, at least 10 minutes. When the bottom is golden, invert a plate over the pan and carefully, using oven gloves, flip the pan over onto the plate. Add about ½ tablespoon more butter to the pan. Slide the galette back into the pan, raw-side-down, and cook for an additional 15 minutes, or until the potatoes are cooked through and the outside is crispy. Slide the galette onto a plate, season with salt and pepper, and top with a generous garnish of fresh dill fronds. Serve immediately.

Protective Chicken Foot Soup

From ancient Greek mysticism, we receive the concept of *apotropaia* – the idea that objects or figures could avert evil and misfortune by virtue of their own grotesqueness. The word itself means to "turn away" or "ward off", and it was invoked particularly in the case of the averting gods – horrible, chthonic entities which could be called upon for protection and safety, to turn back all forms of evil and misfortune. It is from this concept that we receive images of gargoyles, witch bottles and the evil eye – invoked as fearsome images in their own right, but used to grant protection and safety to the one who wields them. Among these symbols, we also find the chicken, whose eggs and feet have been used to ward off evil in a similar manner since the Hellenistic period. This is the form of apotropaic magic from which this recipe draws its power, using the powerful and grotesque symbol of the chicken's foot to craft a brew that carries forth some of its protective virtues.

In many ways, it can also be said that chicken soup is its own form of apotropaic magic, warding off and turning away illness at the first sign of trouble. Our recipe makes use of several herbs and spices that provide a twofold benefit, lending their powers for both apotropaic magic and medicine. Garlic, caraway and rue are all magical ingredients used in banishing and protection, as well as being medicinal herbs which support the immune system. Even the chicken itself, both breast and bones, contains a number of vitamins and minerals, such as selenium, vitamin C and various antioxidants. Altogether, this dish is a powerful ally against a variety of misfortunes, both magical and medicinal, and should be a useful tool in the hands of the witch who can overlook the dangerous appearance of these ingredients and harness the magic within them.

Serves 6–8
Prep time: 20 minutes
Cook time: 1 hour

* ½ bulb of garlic
* 2 tablespoons olive oil
* 5 chicken feet
* ½ chicken
* 30g (1oz/2 tablespoons) butter
* 1 large yellow onion, diced
* 2 large carrots, peeled and chopped
* 5 bay leaves
* 5 whole cloves
* ½ teaspoon caraway seeds
* 150g (5¼oz/1 cup) pearl (giant) couscous
* 3 tablespoons chopped fresh rue (or 1 tablespoon dried rue)
* 3 tablespoons chopped fresh dill
* Leaves from 2 sprigs of thyme
* Salt and pepper

1 Prepare this dish, if possible, when the moon is waning or new, on a Tuesday at the hour of Mars. Since apotropaic magic is employed by symbol alone, this recipe includes no additional magical steps or procedure, though you are welcome to add your own as always. Make these considerations before you begin.

2 Preheat your oven to 180°C/350°F/Gas 4 and line a baking sheet with baking parchment. Halve your bulb of garlic crosswise and place it on a sheet of kitchen foil. Drizzle both halves with a little olive oil, then seal the foil. On the same baking sheet, place your chicken feet and half chicken and drizzle with the remaining olive oil. Season with salt and pepper and roast alongside the garlic for 35 minutes, or until the chicken is golden and the garlic is browned and soft.

3 When your chicken is ready, melt your butter in a large pan over medium–high heat. When the butter is bubbly, add your onion and carrots and sauté until soft, about 5–8 minutes. Add your roasted garlic, bay leaves, cloves and caraway seeds and stir for an additional 4–5 minutes until the spices are very fragrant. Add your chicken to the pot, followed by the couscous and 2.4 litres (2½ quarts/10 cups) water.

4 Bring the liquid to a boil, then turn the heat down to a low flame and simmer uncovered for 20 minutes, or until the couscous is fully cooked. Turn off the heat, remove the chicken from the pot and shred the meat away from the bones. Return the meat to the pot. If you do not plan to eat the chicken feet, you may remove them at this time.

5 Stir in your fresh herbs and let the soup stand for 5 minutes. Season with salt and pepper, taste and serve immediately.

Ritual Bread Masks

As a magical technology, masks might be one of my favourite ritual tools – and not just because I'm a two-faced Gemini. When you wear a mask in ritual, you embody the ensouling spirit of the object, acting as both medium and mediator for the spirit force of the mask. It is an act of collaboration, in which the human actor gives body to that which is without form, allowing it to enter material reality and walk among us, even if only for a moment. Used as a tool of sorcery in this way, the mask is a uniquely useful ritual object; a tool for mixing ourselves with an Other, to temporarily become something other than what we are so that we may see from a new perspective and access long forgotten senses.

While bread masks are not a common addition to magical ritual, this practice is not without its historical precedent. In Bodnegg, Germany, a local fools guild called the Burnegger Brotfresser (Burnegger Breadeaters) design and bake elaborate bread masks, which are worn for carnival celebrations in early spring. These masks, baked on custom moulds to fit the wearer's face, are bizarre, made even more uncanny by the application of colourful seeds and spices to create eyebrows, lips and other human details. They continue a long and often haunting tradition of crafting carnival masks in Germany, which have been made for these festivals since medieval times. Their traditionally terrifying images are used as a form of apotropaic symbol, employed to drive out and avert evil and misfortune from the community before the coming spring.

For your own rituals, this recipe should be a useful starting place, but will rely upon your own intuition and creative input to be effectively utilized. Bake these masks for your sorcerous rites and devotional celebrations and allow these objects to act as another kind of meeting place, where the edges of our identities begin to blur. What spirits will you call forth from that faceless, formless unknown?

Makes enough dough for 1 mask
Prep time: 45 minutes, plus 1 hour proving
Cook time: 20–30 minutes

* 1 x 7g (2¼ teaspoon) package active dry yeast
* 3 tablespoons extra virgin olive oil, plus extra for greasing
* 550g (1lb 4oz/4 cups) plain (all-purpose) flour, plus extra for dusting
* 1 teaspoon salt (optional)

DECORATIONS (optional)

* 1 egg white, beaten
* Various colourful seeds (poppy, fennel, cumin, anise, dill, flax, etc)

1 Before any baking begins, spend time in meditation about the design you wish to create. Consider how you would like the mask to sit on your face if you intend to wear it, how it should look, and what role it will take within the scope of your ritual. What is this false face meant to evoke and how will you be interacting with this object? All of these are good questions to consider before proceeding. Now is a good time to sketch a basic outline for your design and to decide whether you plan to use any seeds for decoration.

2 In the bowl of a stand mixer, combine all of your ingredients for the dough. If you plan to eat this mask at some point, you may choose to add salt, though this is not necessary for purely ornamental masks. Use the dough hook to knead the dough until it forms a smooth ball, about 8–10 minutes.

3 Lightly grease the inside of another bowl and turn the dough out into it. Cover with a damp tea (dish) towel and set in a warm place to prove until doubled in size – about 1 hour. In the meantime, preheat your oven to 190°C/375°F/Gas 5.

4 When the dough has proved, there is an opportunity available for useful divination. If you are skilled with or wish to experiment with scrying, take a sharp knife or razor blade and slash the surface of your dough, peeling back the skin and revealing the matrix of gluten within. Scrying upon this surface can yield useful information, particularly any instructions for how the mask should be crafted, used or engaged with. Carefully consider what the dough has to say before proceeding.

5 Transfer the dough to a lightly floured sheet of baking parchment. You may now begin to craft the dough into the shape of your mask, rolling, cutting and forming as you see fit. If you want to form the mask into the shape of a face, make a rough bust of your face out of kitchen foil, lightly grease the form with oil and lay the dough over the top. If you are using seed decorations, lightly brush the surface of your dough with the beaten egg whites and adhere the seeds where necessary.

6 If you plan to wear the mask, make two small slits on either side of the mask near where your ears will be. These will be used to thread ribbon, which will hold the mask in place. Fold two strips of kitchen foil, lightly coat them with oil and thread them through the ribbon holes before baking. You may also use foil forms to hold open the dough for the eyes, mouth and nose of your mask if necessary.

7 Transfer the bread, on the baking parchment, to a baking sheet and bake your mask for 20–30 minutes, or until darkened and cooked through. Because these masks are not meant to be eaten, overbaking is less of a concern here, but underbaking will yield a mask that is too soft to hold it's shape. When the mask is baked, let it cool completely before removing any foil forms. Thread a thick, strong ribbon through the holes on either side of the mask, and it will be ready to wear.

8 You may choose to consecrate your mask for its ritual purpose, after which you may leave the mask bare or apply a thin coat of clear varnish to keep the mask from moulding. It is best to keep your mask wrapped up and stored out of sight when not in use, uncovering only when you intend to use it.

Sacrificial Quail with Pomegranate Sauce

Drawing from the technology we discussed at the beginning of this chapter, our sacrificial quail presents an uncomplicated yet richly decadent offering, featuring plants and herbs that were prized in the ancient world as pleasing offerings to the gods – pomegranates, bay leaves and cinnamon. Here, quail was selected as the offering of choice because it is a small but somewhat costly bird, representing a smaller amount of food waste but a higher investment than would be the case for other poultry. This offering is suitable for most occasions, but the presence of pomegranates makes this feast especially appropriate for autumn festivals, symbolic of Persephone's underworld descent.

As an alternative to using meat, vegetarian or vegan chefs might consider the recommendation of Plato, who suggested that those "who will not sacrifice animals, or so much as taste of a cow – they offer fruits or cakes soaked in honey"[11] instead. These alternatives should be of the earth (fruits, vegetables or whole grains for example) and should represent an investment of effort, resulting in a feast worthy of celestial attention. One might consider using a roast pumpkin or squash instead, for which the glaze recorded here would be a most welcome addition.

Serves 1

Prep time: 15 minutes
plus 2 hours marinating

Cook time: 30 minutes

* 1 quail
* 1 shallot, thinly sliced
* 2 tablespoons Worcestershire sauce
* 240ml (8fl oz/1 cup) pomegranate juice
* ½ teaspoon ground cinnamon
* 1 bay leaf
* Salt and pepper

I Begin by washing your quail and patting it dry. In a 1-litre (1-quart) ziplock bag, combine the rest of your ingredients, then add the quail and toss in the marinade to coat. Seal the bag and set the quail in the refrigerator to marinate for at least 2 hours.

2 Preheat your oven to 180°C/350°F/Gas 4 and line a baking sheet with baking parchment. Remove the quail from the marinade and set it on the prepared baking sheet. Roast the bird for 12–18 minutes, or until golden.

3 While the quail is in the oven, tip the marinade into a saucepan set over a medium heat. Bring to a lively simmer and cook to reduce the sauce until it is thick and coats the back of a spoon – about 15–20 minutes. If serving this dish for dinner, carve the quail and serve with the pomegranate sauce on the side, but reserve one breast or leg, along with any bones or leavings, for your sacrificial work. If offering this meal whole, carving is unnecessary, and the sauce can be served over the top of the quail as a deep red glaze.

Sigil Grissini

The creation of sigils and magical symbols is a powerful tool in the hands of the witch. They can act as physical manifestations of our desires, or talismanic images themselves. If you do not have much experience crafting these symbols yourself, this recipe should be a helpful exercise in creating and working with sigils in practical magic. If you're experienced with sigilcraft, perhaps this recipe will call you to consider new applications for this technology.

In this recipe, sigils are created and fixed in simple, easy-working grissini dough, filled and rolled with appropriate plant allies, and charged in the oven as the herbs and aromatics infuse into the bread. These baked sigils can be rolled, stamped, carved or cut out to suit your needs – high-fat grissini dough is very forgiving. For a detailed description of how to craft your own sigils, consult the beginning of this chapter. While the ritual for our sigil grissini can certainly conclude with destroying your symbols in feast, they can also be buried, hung as charms or burned as offerings.

As with any spellwork, begin by forming your statement of intent, and selecting herbs which align with the purpose of your work. Consult the list on the right as a general example, and select your botanical allies wisely.

FLAVOURING HERBS

Select one or more herbs which correspond to your intent. You will need enough to roll your breadsticks in before baking, at least ½ cup

for cleansing & blessing
angelica, bay, cinnamon, hyssop, juniper berry, orange peel, vitex

for protection
cedar, hawthorn berry, rosemary, rose thorn, sesame seed, thyme

for love
cardamom, cracked cubeb berry, lavender, lemon balm, jasmine, orris root powder

for luck & opportunity
allspice, basil, calendula, clove, dried figs, hazelnuts, honey, nutmeg

for banishing & cursing
asafoetida, black salt, cayenne, mace, pine, sumac, wormwood

Makes about 12 grissini
Prep time: 40 minutes, plus 1¼ hours proving
Cook time: 15 minutes

* 1 tablespoon granulated sugar
* 260g (9oz/2 cups) plain (all-purpose) flour, plus extra for dusting if needed
* 185ml (6oz/¾ cup) warm water
* 1 x 7g (2¼ teaspoon) package fast-action/instant active dried yeast
* 2 teaspoons salt
* 6 tablespoons olive oil, plus extra for greasing
* 3 tablespoons flavouring herbs, plus extra for rolling

I In meditation before beginning, consider the aim of your work carefully. Do your best to distil your intention down to a single sentence, using language that is direct and empowering to describe your desires. On a sheet of clean paper, use the instructions from the beginning of this chapter to craft a sigil for your work. Spend time crafting this symbol, reworking several times until you are satisfied, and then set it aside.

2 In the bowl of a stand mixer, combine your sugar, 70g (2½oz/½ cup) of the flour, the warm water and yeast, mixing to combine. Allow to sit for 10 minutes until frothy and bubbly. Add the rest of the flour and all the remaining ingredients, including any herbs you'd like to include in the dough itself. Mix with the dough hook on medium speed until the dough is smooth and shiny. If you do not have an electric mixer, mix with a spoon until combined and then knead by hand for 7–10 minutes. Lightly coat a bowl with olive oil and transfer the dough to it. Allow it to rest covered with a tea (dish) towel in a warm place for 1 hour, or until doubled in size.

3 Preheat your oven to 220°C/425°F/Gas 7 and line two baking sheets with baking parchment. Roll the dough into a flat rectangle 1.5cm (½in) thick. The dough should be fatty enough to roll on an unfloured worktop, but you may use flour if necessary. Using a pizza cutter or a sharp knife, slice 1.5cm (½in) strips of dough crosswise. Roll each strip until they are long and delicate, then roll them in any additional herbs you like. Cut and shape the dough into the symbol that you created in step 1, using water to fuse pieces of dough together. Allow the dough to stand for 15 minutes at room temperature to prove, then bake for 10–15 minutes, rotating halfway through the baking time, until golden brown. Check frequently, as this high-fat dough browns quickly toward the end.

4 For sigils of personal empowerment, attraction and manifestation, eat your bread sigil in ritual. For sigils of banishing or cursing, pin your sigil to the earth with an iron nail and then bury completely. For sigils of home blessing, use red ribbon to hang the sigil in a hidden place within the home. For devotional sigils, use herbs and shapes relevant to your work and burn the sigil in a cauldron as an offering. In any event, burn your original paper sigil and forget your sigil entirely once the work is completed. Start fresh for your next working, never recreating the same sigil twice.

═ Feast of Fried Blossoms and Mushrooms ═

Flowers and mushrooms occupy a strange, liminal corner of plant folklore, in which both are in some way regarded as portals to the Other. Mushrooms embody this readily as they emerge from the ephemeral, chthonic mycelium, like life from nowhere, dazzling us with their ability to arise mysteriously as if from another world. When they grow in circles, these places are said to be direct portals to subtle spheres – called "elf rings" in the British Isles and "hexenringe" (witches' rings) in Germany – through which strange and devious spirits can manifest. Flowers, on the other hand, are said to be the communicating parts of plants, which send their chemical messages out to winged spirits (here, pollinators) in order to survive. Much like the mushroom rings of European folklore, the sweet fragrance of flowers has also long been used to elicit

the presence of spirits and deities, and the offering of fragrant blossoms is often used to initiate such communication. No surprise, then, that both flower heads and mushrooms are both broadly associated with the Fae, some of the most strangely powerful and powerfully strange spirits in the European canon.

Taken together, chthonic mushrooms and ethereal blossoms represent two allies in liminal magic, useful in offerings and celebratory feasts wherever the Otherworld is accessed. This dish is best served on flower holidays, such as May Day or Midsummer, as well as rites of happy transition – births, marriages and housewarmings, for example. Since both flowers and mushrooms are also associated with second sight, this dish would also be welcome at Full Moon feast tables, as a prelude to the night's divinatory rituals.

Serves 4
Prep time: 20 minutes
Cook time: 30 minutes

FOR THE FLOWERS AND MUSHROOMS

* 700ml (24fl oz/3 cups) rapeseed (canola) oil
* 225g (8oz/1 cup) ricotta cheese
* 4 tablespoons grated Parmesan cheese
* 2 tablespoons chopped fresh basil
* 12 squash blossoms
* 100g (3½oz) enoki mushrooms
* 200g (7oz) shimeji (beech) mushrooms
* 200g (7oz) oyster mushrooms
* 12 pansy flowers
* 12 dandelion flower heads
* 12 Queen Anne's lace flower heads
* 50g (1¾oz/½ cup) rice flour
* 45g (6 tablespoons) cornflour (cornstarch)
* 1 teaspoon ground cumin
* 1 teaspoon salt
* 120ml (4fl oz/½ cup) double (heavy) cream or non-dairy substitute

FOR THE AIOLI

* 2 egg yolks
* Zest and juice of 1 lemon
* 2 small cloves garlic, minced
* 1 tablespoon finely diced chives
* 80ml (2½fl oz/⅓ cup) extra virgin olive oil
* 60ml (2fl oz/¼ cup) avocado or rapeseed (canola) oil
* Salt and pepper

I Begin by preparing the aioli dipping sauce. In a blender or food processor, combine the egg yolks, lemon zest and juice, garlic and chives. Pulse until well combined. Mix your oils together, then stream them slowly into the egg mixture while the machine is running. Keep blending until the aioli is homogenous and fully mixed. Season with salt and pepper to taste.

2 Next, heat your oil in a large pan until hot. You can test the temperature by placing a scrap of mushroom stem or the end of a wooden spoon into the oil. If the oil bubbles instantly upon contact, it is ready.

3 While the oil heats, make the filling for your squash blossoms. In a small bowl, stir together your cheeses and basil, season with salt and pepper, and transfer the mixture to a piping bag. Carefully fill each squash blossom with the cheese mixture, being careful not to overflow. Place the filled blossoms onto a plate and set aside.

4 Prepare the mushrooms and the rest of your flowers by patting them dry and trimming away any excess stems or leaves. Each piece should be no larger than one or two bites.

5 When you are ready to fry your mushrooms and flowers, mix together the rice flour, cornflour, cumin and salt in a small bowl. Slowly stir in your cream and mix until no lumps remain. Working quickly, dredge your mushrooms or flowers in the batter, tap or shake any excess batter away, then immediately drop into the frying oil. Take care not to crowd the fryer, as this will lower the temperature of the oil and result in a soggy fry. Cook until the batter is crispy and golden brown, then transfer to a paper-towel-lined plate to drain. Repeat until all the mushrooms and flowers are fried, including the filled squash blossoms.

6 To serve, set a dish of your aioli in the centre of a large serving plate and surround with the fried blossoms and mushrooms. Serve immediately.

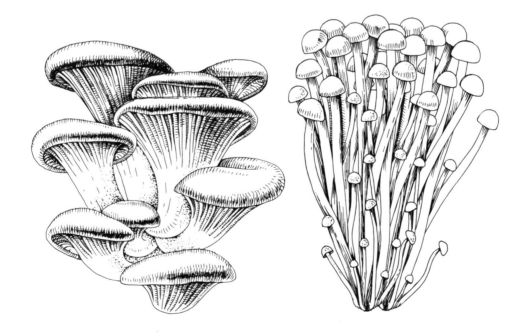

Herbed Yogurt Cheese

As I discussed in Feast of the Heavens, Saturn is the planet of rot and rebirth, ruling a variety of different preparation techniques but especially the art of fermentation. This recipe is an introduction to these arts, beginning with a delicious, natural ferment – rich, creamy yogurt, wrapped and aged in Saturn's edible plant allies to form a fresh and simple homemade cheese. While many cheese recipes will require special equipment and thermometers, this soft, spreadable cheese will only require cheesecloth and time. Prepare this cheese in ritual offering to Saturn, or in celebration of Saturnine sabbats like Saturnalia or the Winter Solstice.

Serves 8–10
Prep time: 45 minutes, plus 48 hours straining and 2 hours chilling

FOR THE CHEESE
* 450g (1lb) full-fat Greek yogurt
* 3 cloves garlic, finely minced
* 3 tablespoons thyme leaves
* 1 teaspoon sea salt
* 2 teaspoons cracked black pepper

FOR THE PETAL WRAP
* 6 fresh pansy flowers (if you're out of pansies, consider other edible Saturnine blossoms – chive flowers, spring garlic, elderflower, plum blossoms or wild blackberry petals)
* 1 tablespoon fresh wood sorrel or chervil
* 1 teaspoon dried or fresh blue cornflower petals (optional)

1 If dedicating this rite to Saturn, begin on Saturday in the early morning. Rise in silence, wash your face and hands, and move quietly to the kitchen in meditation. Upon your hearth altar or oven, burn Saturnine incense of opopanax or myrrh and a single black candle.

2 Prepare your yogurt by pouring off as much excess liquid as you can. In a large bowl, combine your yogurt, minced garlic, all but 1 tablespoon of your thyme leaves, salt and pepper. Stir together using your non-dominant hand (if you are right-handed, use your left) to combine.

3 Prepare your cheesecloth by layering two squares of cloth together, creating a tight mesh. Lay these sheets of cloth over a medium-sized bowl. Make sure the cloth squares are large enough to hold your cheese and leave extra cheesecloth hanging over the edges of the bowl. Spoon your yogurt mixture into the bowl and tap the bowl on the counter to allow the yogurt to settle. Let it rest for 5 minutes, then lift the four corners of your cheesecloth square and tie them together.

4 Place the bound mixture into a plastic 1-litre (1-quart) container or a deep plastic storage container. Slide a wooden spoon beneath the knot of the cheesecloth and suspend your cheese within the container. Your cheese should be hanging freely from the wooden spoon, not making contact with the sides of the container at all. There should be enough room below the cheese to allow the whey to drain, and this can be poured off if need be. Cover with a tea (dish) towel and allow your cheese to firm up in the refrigerator for 48 hours.

5 When the cheese is firm, remove it from the refrigerator and unwrap it from the cheesecloth. Adorn your finished cheese by pressing flowers, wood sorrel, cornflower petals and remaining thyme leaves into its surface, placing the six pansies on the top, bottom and four cardinal directions of your cheese ball. Re-wrap the cheese in fresh cheesecloth, and store for another 2 hours, or until ready to serve. Since yogurt is a natural ferment, this cheese should last for 3–5 days wrapped tightly in the refrigerator.

6 Traditionally, offerings to Saturn were accompanied by incense and blood. This cheese should be buried in a wayside place – crossroads, riverbanks, or abandoned places. In celebration, serve alongside strong red wine, dark breads, walnuts, corn, pickles, olives and other foods of Saturn. For a complete list, consult the chart on page 103.

= Rosemary, Apple and Cheddar Picnic Pies =

My magical practice often sends me wandering – through graveyards, through wilderness or through the night – so it has become important to carry offerings with me when I'm out on such excursions. I pack a bag of things I'll need: harvesting tools, binding twine and a notebook, and a bottle of good drink and a snack to share are never missing. This is because these walks are not solitary adventures, but often present an opportunity to connect with spirits and inhabitants of these places; I make sure not to show up empty handed.

This practice may seem simply courteous, like bringing a bottle of wine to a dinner party, but in the context of kitchen witchcraft, it can have a deeper meaning. If we accept that food is a vehicle for communion among gods and men alike, then there is no more suitable offering for establishing a connection with subtle allies than to share a meal together. Sometimes I return home with a still-heavy backpack, and save my offering treats for myself. Other times, I slip cookies into fox holes, pour wine into tree hollows and break my bread in communion with the subtle and the dead, coming home lighter than when I left. Rarely do these excursions include planned stops, but

instead are guided by the heart, soul and intuitive mind, trusting the hands to know how to offer and when.

Of the recipes I've used for offerings over the years, these are my favourite. Apples and rosemary are traditional offerings to spirits, especially for doing good. There is even something to be said for the magical use of cheese, which features in charms of love and attraction throughout medieval Europe, and which St Hildegard once compared to the miraculous creation of life. We find an echo of this bizarre and divine reference to cheese in the Bible:

Hast thou not poured me out as milk, and curdled me like cheese? Thou hast clothed me with skin and flesh, and knit me together with bones and sinews. Thou gave me life and showed me kindness...

JOB 10:11

In a somewhat less miraculous act of kindness, these picnic pies are a perfect parcel for offering as one wanders through the brambles and graveyards. Trust the body and the intuition to know where they will be received. Be sure to set one or two aside for yourself.

Makes 10 pies
Prep time: 30 minutes
Cook time: 1 hour

* 30g (1oz/2 tablespoons) butter
* 1 large yellow onion, cut into lengthwise slices
* Plain (all-purpose) flour, for dusting
* 1 x 490g (17oz) package frozen puff pastry, thawed
* 3 apples, peeled, cored and sliced
* 225g (8oz) mature (sharp) Cheddar cheese, grated
* Leaves from 2 sprigs of rosemary
* 2 tablespoons milk
* Salt and pepper

I Begin by heating your butter in a frying pan (skillet) over medium–high heat. When the butter is hot, add your onion and toss to coat. Turn the heat down to medium and slowly cook the onion, stirring occasionally until caramelized – at least 30 minutes.

2 Meanwhile, as the onion cooks, assemble your other ingredients. Between two sheets of lightly floured baking parchment, roll out your puff pastry to 5mm (¼in) thick. Using a cookie cutter or tracing with a knife around a stencil, cut out ten 15cm (6in) circles from the pastry. Set these in the refrigerator until ready to use. When the onions are cooked, transfer to a dish to cool to room temperature.

3 Preheat your oven to 180°C/350°F/Gas 4 and line two baking sheets with baking parchment. Remove your puff pastry circles from the refrigerator and lay five onto each prepared sheet. On one half of each circle, lay a single layer of apple slices, followed by a spoonful of caramelized onions, then a layer of grated cheese, a sprinkle of rosemary, and then a final layer of apple slices. Repeat until all of the ingredients are used. Season each with salt and pepper. Fold the other half of each pastry circle over the filling and use a fork to crimp and seal the edges.

4 Brush each pie with a light coating of milk, and sprinkle sea salt and freshly cracked black pepper over the top of each one. Bake for 20–30 minutes, or until the pastry is golden and fully cooked underneath.

Salem Witch Trials
"Witch Cake"

The story of the Salem Witch Trials has, for better or for worse, become an integral part of witch folklore in the United States. It is a story about a true terror of the unknown, the likes of which can turn neighbours against one another in violence – though the involvement of actual witches in Salem is still debated among historians. Despite mounting evidence which points to religious hysteria, ergot poisoning and even widespread PTSD from the French and Indian Wars as possible causes for Salem's 1692 witch panic, these events continue to fascinate us with their deep strangeness, and the possibility that something similar could bubble to the surface within our own communities. Every story of the witch trials points to more questions, leaving us still wondering what actually happened in Salem over 300 years ago.

One of the more curious stories from the Salem Witch Trials was the baking of a "witch cake", the purpose of which was to divine whether or not it was a witch who afflicted the town, or some more natural malady. The instructions for the cake were given by a woman named Mary Sibley, who was later publicly punished for producing the recipe. In the original spell, a rough cake is made from rye flour and the urine of children believed to be bewitched, which is then baked and fed to a dog. If the dog exhibited the same signs of torment and witching, it was taken as a sign that witchcraft was truly at play.

Inspired by the technology of this recipe, our "witch cake" explores one possible application for food as a vehicle for divination, allowing us to reveal information and receive counsel by means of kitchen witchcraft. It employs the aid of three divinatory plants *par excellence* – hazelnuts, vervain and four-leaf clovers. While the latter will certainly be hard to find at the supermarket, four-leaf clovers are an unparalleled ally in divinatory works, and finding two of them for this recipe will be a useful exercise in second sight – being able to "see" or discern our answers from the noise, as a clover with four leaves is spotted within a field. These cakes can be used for divination on any topic or question you wish and will serve as a useful, novel addition to any diviner's bag of tricks.

Makes 2 cakes
Prep time: 30 minutes, plus cooling
Cook time: 30 minutes

* 2 teaspoons vervain, finely ground or powdered
* 1 whole hazelnut
* 140g (5oz/10 tablespoons) unsalted butter
* 60ml (2fl oz/¼ cup) milk or non-dairy substitute
* 260g (9¼oz/2 cups) rye flour
* 70g (2½oz/⅓ cup) brown sugar
* ¾ teaspoon baking powder
* ½ teaspoon salt
* 2 four-leaf clovers (optional)

I This work is best performed when the moon is waxing or full and is without strong negative aspects. On the evening before the cakes are made, sit by candlelight before your altar or a quiet workspace. Burn an incense of black frankincense, storax, hazel leaves, mugwort and yarrow. Set a clean dish upon your altar and use the powdered vervain to draw an X across the dish. Place your hazelnut in the centre of the mark. If lunar divinities are a part of your practice, you may invoke them here, or otherwise read the lunar invocation of your choosing. Knock with your knuckles three times on either side of the dish. Lift the hazelnut into the incense smoke and recite the following:

Remember, hazel, what you revealed in gold, in truth, in treasure hidden beneath the earth,
Commanded by witches who sought to see –
Now, compelled by Selene, you shall do the same for me.

2 Spend time in meditation about the question you wish to ask, and take your time to discern precise phrasing for your question. Before the altar, craft a sigil of your question and rework the design until you are fully satisfied. For a detailed introduction to creating sigils, see page 167. Allow the incense to burn out completely and go to sleep, paying specific attention to any information revealed in dreams.

3 The following day, begin at the hour of the moon. Place your butter in a frying pan or skillet over a medium–low heat and cook until the butter is browning and releasing a nutty fragrance. Transfer the browned butter to a small dish and set in the refrigerator until slightly solidified, about 20 minutes.

4 Preheat your oven to 190°C/375°F/Gas 5. Retrieve the dish of vervain and the hazelnut from your altar. In a small saucepan, combine the milk and vervain powder and set over a low heat until it just comes to a simmer. Remove from the heat and allow to infuse and cool to room temperature.

5 In a medium bowl, mix together your flour, sugar, baking powder and salt. Using your hands or a pastry cutter, work the solidified butter into the flour mixture until it is crumbly and no large lumps of butter remain. Add half of your milk to the flour mixture and work until the dough begins to come together, then add the rest of the milk and mix until a smooth ball of dough forms.

6 Line a baking sheet with baking parchment, and lightly grease a 7.5cm (3in) round cookie cutter. (If you do not have cookie cutters at home, these biscuits can be formed by hand.) Press a 3mm (⅛in) layer of dough into the bottom of the cookie cutter and set one of your four-leaf clovers in the centre. Place your hazelnut on top of the clover and whisper your question into the dough. Seal the biscuit with more dough, pressing into the cookie cutter until the biscuit is 1cm (½in) thick. Inscribe it with the sigil you created, then slide the cookie cutter away from the dough. Repeat this process again exactly, but instead of a second hazelnut, use a ball of cookie dough the same size. When finished, the biscuits should be identical, with the hazelnut fully obscured. Any remaining dough can be wrapped tightly in clingfilm (plastic wrap) and stored in the freezer for up to 2 months to repeat this ritual again.

7 Bake the shortbreads for 18–25 minutes, or until they slide away from the parchment easily and are fully cooked underneath. Let them cool to room temperature. When you are ready to perform the ritual, recite your question aloud, and allow your hands to select one of the cakes. The other cake should be immediately buried, burned, discarded or destroyed, so that there is no possibility of changing your selection. Eat the biscuit you selected and truth will be revealed. If the hazelnut is present, the answer is yes; if it is not, the answer is no.

Chocolate, Beetroot and Grapefruit Celebration Cake

This recipe presents my favourite all-occasion celebration cake, which has never failed to impress a crowd or vanish as quickly as it's set down. It is certainly an exotic offering, drawing on three bold flavours of Jupiter – beetroot, chocolate and grapefruit – to create a treat that is novel and decadently rich. Jupiter, as we discussed in the Feast of the Heavens chapter, is our best planetary ally for all works of success and attainment, and so it is right that we should have his ingredients featured prominently at our celebratory feast tables. If Jupiter also represents displays of grandeur and luxury, then we might consider the chocolate cake itself as a meal of Jupiter, which appears as a centrepiece to any celebration and commands the eager attention of all in attendance.

As always, with the big, expansive energies of Jupiter come big, bold flavours! If you've never experienced a chocolate beetroot cake before, the natural sweetness and earthiness of beets is a perfect complement to dark, bitter chocolate, and will be your new secret weapon for a chocolate cake that is soft and fluffy yet rich as brownies. Benevolent Jupiter might recommend we share the wisdom of this flavour pairing, but consider keeping this recipe your delicious secret!

Serves 8–10
Prep time: 1 hour 10 minutes
Cook time: 45 minutes

FOR THE CAKE

* 225g (8oz) red beetroots (beets), scrubbed with top and root removed
* 200g (7oz) dark chocolate, chopped
* 60ml (2fl oz/¼ cup) strong coffee, hot
* 2 tablespoons rum
* 175g (6oz/¾ cup) unsalted butter, softened, plus extra for greasing
* 130g (4½oz/1 cup) plain (all-purpose) flour
* 4 tablespoons Dutch process cocoa powder
* 1¼ teaspoons baking powder
* 1 teaspoon salt
* 5 eggs, separated
* 200g (7oz/1 cup) sugar

FOR THE GANACHE

* 240ml (8fl oz/1 cup) double (heavy) cream
* 60ml (2fl oz/¼ cup) maple or corn syrup
* Zest and juice of 1 grapefruit (approximately 120ml/4fl oz/ ½ cup juice), plus extra grapefruit zest or candied grapefruit peel to decorate
* 450g (1lb) dark chocolate, chopped
* Salt

I Begin by preparing your ganache. In a small saucepan, warm your cream and maple syrup to a simmer and remove from the heat. Stir in your grapefruit zest. Place your chocolate in a large mixing bowl and pour the hot cream mixture over the top. Allow to stand for 5 minutes, then stir until the chocolate and cream begin to melt together. Add your grapefruit juice and mix until fully combined. Season with salt, and place in the refrigerator until needed.

2 To begin the cake, place your beetroots in a large pan of boiling water and cook until tender – about 40 minutes. When the beetroots are soft, remove them from the pan and let cool to room temperature. Slip off the skins and place them into a blender. Purée until smooth and set aside.

3 Preheat your oven to 170°C/ 325°F/Gas 3 and grease a 23cm (9in) springform pan.

4 In a double boiler or over a bain marie, melt your chocolate. Add the coffee, rum and butter and stir gently until incorporated.

5 In a separate bowl, sift together your flour, cocoa powder, baking powder and salt. Set aside.

6 When all of the butter is melted into the chocolate, remove it from the heat. Quickly whisk in your egg yolks and sugar, followed by the puréed beetroot, and continue whisking until the mixture begins to cool. Set aside.

7 In a stand mixer or using an electric hand mixer, whip your egg whites until stiff peaks form. In alternating batches, fold your egg whites and flour mixture into the chocolate mixture, mixing as little as possible, until all is fully incorporated. Pour the batter into your prepared cake pan and bake for 40 minutes, or until only the very centre of the cake is still slightly tacky, but the edges are set. Remove from the oven and allow to cool fully in the pan before removing.

8 When the cake is cool, remove the ganache from the refrigerator. If it is too firm to spread with a knife, microwave the ganache in 10-second bursts until it reaches the desired consistency. Do not overheat. Once the ganache is spreadable, frost your cake in whatever manner you please. Garnish with grapefruit zest or candied grapefruit peel and serve.

Opportunity-conjuring Dandelion and Calendula Scones

When it comes to using magic to transform our lives, sometimes all that's needed is to open a door. Frequently, we can phrase our intent in an overly specific way that limits how our desires can manifest. When we control how and when our results are delivered, we actually limit the results of our work, and confine the outcomes of our magic. Often the path of least resistance is simply to open up more possible avenues for our desires to manifest, and one of the ways we can do this is by calling forth a bit of luck and opportunity to the situation at hand.

These scones aim to accomplish that, by drawing on a variety of planetary correspondences to conjure a bit of kinetic energy into our lives. While the recipe below is straightforward, the ritual which makes these scones special calls on the blessings of three planetary spheres – the Sun, Mars and Jupiter. Golden flower petals and dried apricots are added to the dough as ingredients of the Sun, connected with success, fame and recognition. These are joined by herbs of Mars, cinnamon and ginger, known to bolster self-confidence and deliver quick magical results. If you follow the ritual, these scones will be consecrated to Jupiter, the great sphere of opportunity, advancement and progression, sealing them as edible talismans for success, abundance and attainment of all we desire.

Makes 12 scones
Prep time: 20 minutes
Cook time: 20 minutes

* 260g (9oz/2 cups) plain (all-purpose) flour, plus extra for dusting
* 50g (1¾oz/¼ cup) granulated sugar, plus extra for sprinkling
* 50g (1¾oz/¼ cup) light brown sugar
* 2 teaspoons baking powder
* Pinch of salt
* 115g (4oz/½ cup) unsalted butter, frozen and grated
* 120ml (4fl oz/½ cup) buttermilk, plus extra for brushing
* 1 egg
* Pinch of ground ginger
* Pinch of ground cinnamon
* Zest of 1 lemon
* 50g (2oz/¼ cup) lightly packed dandelion petals
* 50g (2oz/¼ cup) lightly packed calendula petals
* 75g (2½oz/½ cup) dried apricots, chopped

1 It is best to prepare these on a Thursday, and when the moon is waxing or full. Preheat your oven to 180°C/350°F/Gas 4 and line a baking sheet with baking parchment.

2 In a medium bowl, whisk together your flour, granulated sugar, brown sugar, baking powder and salt. Add the butter and, using your hands or a pastry cutter, work the butter into the flour mixture until it is the consistency of wet sand and no clumps of butter remain.

3 In a small bowl, beat together your buttermilk and egg. Add your ginger, cinnamon and lemon zest and whisk until combined. Pour the buttermilk into the flour mixture and add your petals and chopped apricots as well. Mix to combine just until the dough comes together – it will be a bit sticky, but will hold its shape.

4 Turn the dough out onto a floured surface and roll out to 2.5cm (1in) thick. Using a cookie cutter or a knife, cut out your scones from the dough. You may re-roll any dough scraps to cut out more scones, but not more than once, or the dough will become tough. Place the scones onto the prepared baking sheet, leaving at least 5cm (2in) between them. Brush the tops of the scones with buttermilk, then use a butter knife to inscribe the scones with sigils of Jupiter, or a sigil you've created for opportunities you wish to conjure. Sprinkle the scones with sugar. Bake for 20 minutes, or until the scones come away easily from the parchment paper and are fully cooked underneath. Leave to cool on a wire rack.

5 Before serving, place some charcoal into a heatproof dish and light it. Arrange cloves on top of the coal in an outward-pointing cross. When the cloves begin to burn, pass a scone through the smoke while reciting an invocation to Jupiter, or another deity or intelligence that you feel will be assistive in your work. This scone should be left at the crossroads in offering. Pass the other scones through the smoke. Serve before job interviews, career moves, auditions or before any big steps taken toward your dreams.

Honeyed Berries with Blue Lotus Zabaglione

When most people think about holding space for themselves, they usually think about difficult emotions – holding space to heal from trauma, allowing ourselves to process and giving space for necessary grief. But when was the last time you held space for your joy, or pleasure? To revel in tactile delight, and pass the time with no other objective than to relish the delicious sensation of being alive? In traditional witchcraft, the body is regarded as the gateway to magic and the teacher of feral, non-verbal mystery, through which we are privileged to experience our lives. And as a teacher in the arts of joy and pleasure, the body is an unrivalled professor.

This recipe and ritual are a pathway to this understanding, which seek to honour the body as a teacher in the arts of joy and delight. This feast features a treat of wine, custard and berries that no one could deny, fortified with the aid of a Venusian herb well-regarded for its use in love and pleasure – the blue lotus flower. Blue lotus petals are a mild sedative used widely in ancient Egypt, which can relax our muscles, sharpen focus and help us maintain a state of mindfulness and peace as we sit in a moment of joy. This dish is intended to be an expression of gratitude for the body – the vehicle through which we experience incarnation – and the great capacity that it holds for happiness, rapture and ecstasy. In a world that separates us from an immersive understanding of our bodies and demonizes all but financial forms of decadence, it is important to remember that holding space for our own pleasure is not only an act of intimate self-care, but also of radical defiance.

Serves 2

Prep time: 20 minutes, plus 1 hour chilling

Cook time: 25 minutes

* 120ml (4fl oz/½ cup) double (heavy) cream
* 10g (¼ cup) dried blue lotus petals
* 8 large egg yolks
* 185ml (6fl oz/¾ cup) dry white wine
* 50g (1¾oz/¼ cup) granulated sugar
* ½ teaspoon salt
* 2 tablespoons raw honey
* ½ teaspoon cinnamon
* 125g (4½oz/1 cup) chopped fresh strawberries
* 75g (2½oz/½ cup) red raspberries
* 75g (2½oz/½ cup) white raspberries

I In a small saucepan over medium heat, combine your cream and blue lotus petals. Bring the cream to the barest simmer, with bubbles just appearing at the edge of the pan, then remove from the heat and chill in the refrigerator until cool – at least 1 hour. Strain and return to the refrigerator to chill until needed.

2 In the upper bowl of a double boiler or bain marie, whisk together your egg yolks, white wine, sugar and salt. Use an electric mixer or whisk to beat the egg mixture, scraping the bowl as it gently heats. When the mixture has thickened and forms a ribbon when the whisk is lifted, remove from the heat but continue whisking until the mixture has cooled slightly, about another 2 minutes. Allow to cool completely, then set in the refrigerator to chill for about 30 minutes.

3 In the bowl of a stand mixer or using an electric mixer, whip your blue lotus-infused cream to stiff peaks. Use a rubber spatula to fold the whipped cream into your custard and mix until fully incorporated.

4 Just before serving, warm your raw honey in the microwave until it is loose and runny. Mix the honey with your cinnamon, then toss with your berries in a medium bowl to coat.

5 To serve, spoon a generous helping of zabaglione into a rocks glass or small dish, and serve alongside a heaped spoonful of honeyed berries. If dining alone, enjoy this meal in quiet contemplation, either fully nude or wearing comfortable, loose-fitting clothing that makes one feel beautiful. If enjoying with a partner, this dish can be enjoyed while silently feeding one another, relying only on tactile, non-verbal communication until the meal is complete. In either case, serve this meal to yourself or your beloved with the pure intention of nurturing and honouring the body as teacher, and as a pathway to all of the most beautiful and pleasurable parts of life.

Pressed-violet Offering Cookies

This recipe was developed to celebrate Beltane, the pagan fire festival that occurs at the midpoint between the vernal equinox and the summer solstice. In my practice, Beltane rituals begin by rising early in the morning on 1 May, stealing silently to the forest near my home, and using my left hand to pluck violets before the morning dew has time to dry. I ferry these flowers home and preserve them for the year ahead – some dried in teas and incense, some steeped in syrup and others created into offering cookies to be brought back to the woods in gratitude.

Flowers are the Mercurial, messenger aspect of plants. They are the part of the plant that communicates with the outside world, using chemical signals and colourful patterns to call forth winged spirits (pollinators!) from the ether. It is no surprise, then, that flowers are frequently used in divination and spirit communication for this very purpose. While these violet and lavender shortbreads are perfect for flower festivals, such as Beltane, or as gifts for flower-loving spirits, this recipe can be customized with the right choice of blossoms and flavours to suit any occasion.

Makes 24 cookies
Prep time: 20 minutes, plus chilling
Cook time: 12 minutes

* 175g (6oz/¾ cup) butter, softened
* 175g (6oz/heaped ¾ cup) sugar, plus extra for sprinkling
* 1 egg, plus 1 beaten egg white for brushing
* 1 teaspoon crème de violette or violet syrup
* 1 tablespoon dried lavender flowers, crushed
* 425g (15oz/3 cups) plain (all-purpose) flour
* ½ teaspoon baking powder
* ¼ teaspoon salt
* 4 tablespoons milk or non-dairy substitute
* Fresh violets, or other fresh and edible flowers (cherry blossoms, roses, borage flowers, cornflowers, calendula petals, etc)

1 In the bowl of a stand mixer or in a large mixing bowl, cream together your butter and sugar on medium speed for 3 minutes, or until light and fluffy. Add your egg, crème de violette or violet syrup and dried lavender and mix until combined, scraping the bowl to make sure there are no lumps of butter left behind.

2 In a large bowl, mix together your flour, baking powder and salt. Add the dry ingredients to your butter mixture in small batches, while mixing at a low speed. Add your milk. Stop mixing when the dough just comes together into a soft ball. Turn out your dough onto a sheet of baking parchment or clingfilm (plastic wrap) and shape it into a roll 5–7cm (2–3in) in diameter. Use the parchment or clingfilm to roll the dough tightly, then chill the dough for 30 minutes.

3 Meanwhile, preheat your oven to 180°C/350°F/Gas 4 and line two baking sheets with baking parchment. Wash and pat dry your flowers, removing any leaves or pieces of stem.

4 Remove the dough from the refrigerator and unwrap. On a chopping (cutting) board, slice the dough cylinder into 5mm (¼in) thick slices. Lay the cookies down on your prepared baking sheets and brush each cookie lightly but thoroughly with egg white. Set fresh flowers gently into the centre of each cookie and brush these lightly with egg white as well, then sprinkle with sugar.

5 Bake for 11–12 minutes, or until the edges of the cookies begin to brown, then transfer to a wire rack to cool.

Elder and Blackberry
Master of the Woods Cake

The Master of the Woods is an archetype which appears in various ways within occult mythology, shifting his image throughout history and culture. He is a wild, feral intelligence, who personifies the uninhabitable world-without-us, or the inhuman aspect of nature and reality. The Master of the Woods represents the limit of our human ability to understand the world, as well as the rift in the veil between the rigid world of material reality and the nonlinear sphere of spiritual and psychic phenomena. He is at once a boundary and an invitation, calling us deeper into the subtle world that exists far outside the bubble of human concerns. For these reasons, the Master of the Woods has long been an ally and source of power for witches, particularly in the traditional witchcraft of Europe, where this archetype emerges under various interpretations –

the Devil, the Green Man, the Witchfather, or simply the spirit of the forest.

In an exploration of the feast-table-as-altar, this recipe invokes and invites this feral personality into the home. It makes use of the marginalized and maligned plants of Saturn – blackberry, elder, sassafras – to recreate the forest floor, in the appearance of two powerful Saturnine agents of rot and rebirth – moss and mushrooms. If working with the Master of the Woods is outside the scope of your practice, this recipe can still be executed to produce a delicious cake. However, since this recipe is an invocation, it is worth noting that the intention for the creation of this recipe, and the inclusion of the Master's sacred plants, cannot be removed, and therefore some trace of His presence and imprint will always be present, even if only at the edges of perception.

Serves 8–10

Prep time: 50 minutes

Cook time: 1½ hours, plus cooling the meringue

FOR THE CAKE

* 50g (1¾oz/½ cup) Dutch process cocoa powder, plus extra for dusting
* 60ml (2fl oz/¼ cup) hot coffee
* 120ml (4fl oz/½ cup) root beer, or dandelion and burdock as a substitute
* 300g (10½oz/1½ cups) caster (superfine) sugar
* 80ml (2½fl oz/⅓ cup) olive oil or vegetable oil
* 1 teaspoon vanilla extract
* 1 egg plus 1 egg white
* 200g (7oz/1½ cups) plain (all-purpose) flour
* 1 teaspoon baking powder
* ¾ teaspoon salt

FOR THE FILLING

* 120ml (4fl oz/½ cup) double (heavy) cream
* 4 tablespoons icing (confectioner's) sugar
* 1 tablespoon elderberry powder
* 175g (6oz/1¼ cups) fresh blackberries, mashed
* 70g (2½oz/¼ cup) blackberry jam (jelly)

FOR THE BUTTERCREAM

* 225g (8oz/1 cup) unsalted butter, softened
* 1½ tablespoons powdered sage
* 560g (1¼lb/4 cups) icing (confectioner's) sugar

FOR THE MERINGUE MUSHROOMS

* 3 egg whites
* 100g (3½oz/½ cup) caster (superfine) sugar
* 175g (6oz/1¼ cups) icing (confectioner's) sugar

FOR THE "MOSS"

* 50g (1¾oz/¼ cup plus 2 tablespoons) plain (all-purpose) flour
* 2 tablespoons matcha powder
* 2 tablespoons sugar
* ¼ teaspoon baking powder
* 30g (2oz/2 tablespoons) butter, melted
* 3 tablespoons milk or non-dairy substitute
* 75g (2½oz/¾ cup) pistachios, finely ground
* Edible flowers and berries, to decorate

1 Preheat your oven to 100°C/ 200°F/Gas ½ and line a baking sheet with baking parchment.

2 First, create the meringue mushrooms by placing two of your egg whites in a large bowl. Using a stand mixer or electric mixer, whip the eggs until foamy. Slowly add your caster sugar and whip the meringue until stiff peaks form. Transfer your meringue to a piping bag and pipe 20 tall, conical stems for your mushrooms, and 20 domed mushroom caps. These can be of varying sizes, and some imperfections will make them look more realistic. Place your meringues in the oven and bake for 1 hour, then turn off the oven and allow the meringues to remain inside for another hour.

3 When the meringues are set, remove them from the oven and carefully peel them away from the parchment paper. In a small bowl, use an electric mixer or stand mixer to whisk your remaining egg white until foamy. Add your icing sugar and beat until stiffening – about 5–7 minutes. Transfer the icing to a piping bag and use it to adhere the mushroom stems to the caps. Set the meringue mushrooms aside.

4 Next, begin the cake by preheating your oven to 180°C/350°F/Gas 4. Lightly butter and flour two 23cm (9in) cake pans, and then dust each pan with cocoa powder. In a small bowl, infuse the cocoa powder into the hot coffee for 10 minutes, then stir in the root beer. Set aside.

5 In a separate bowl, beat together the sugar and oil until fluffy. Whisk in your vanilla extract, followed by your egg and egg white, and beat until well combined. Fold your flour, baking powder and salt into the egg mixture, mixing as little as possible. Finally, whisk in your coffee mixture just until combined. The batter will be quite runny.

6 Divide the batter between the prepared cake pans, and bake for 20–25 minutes, or until a skewer inserted into the centre of the cakes comes out clean.

7 While the cake is in the oven, begin the "moss" topping. In a microwave-safe bowl or mug, whisk together your flour, matcha, sugar and baking powder. Stir in the melted butter and milk. Microwave for 90 seconds, then allow your moss cake to stand for 1 minute in the microwave before removing. If the cake is still underdone, return to the microwave for 15–20-second bursts until cooked through. Set aside to cool completely.

8 Next, prepare the buttercream. Using an electric mixer or stand mixer, whip your softened butter until fluffy and aerated. Add your sage powder and begin slowly adding your sugar until fully incorporated. Beat until stiff peaks form, then set aside.

9 Finally, prepare your filling. Using an electric mixer or stand mixer, whip your cream, icing sugar and elderberry powder together until stiff peaks form. Fold in your mashed blackberries, leaving streaks of berry juice through the cream. Set aside.

10 Assemble your cake by placing one cake layer onto your serving plate. Evenly spread your blackberry jam across the cake, followed by an even layer of your elderberry and blackberry filling. Place the second cake layer on top and use a knife or offset spatula to tidy up any filling that escapes the sides of the cake.

11 Next, using your sage buttercream, frost your cake evenly on all sides and over the top. Imperfections will be covered by toppings, so the appearance of the frosting is not so important.

12 When the cake is frosted, retrieve your microwave cake and crumble it into small pieces that look like little bits of moss. In a small bowl, toss these matcha cake crumbs with the ground pistachios, and dust the top and sides of the cake in the "moss" mixture.

13 Finally, retrieve your meringue mushrooms. Dust the tops of the mushrooms with cocoa powder and set them atop your cake. Finish decorating with forest fruits and edible flowers and serve.

Bitters: A lucky blend, an attraction blend and a protection blend

Tinctures are an incredibly useful tool in the hands of the witch or herbalist. Relying upon an alcohol solvent that can extract vitamins, minerals, essential oils and, most importantly, alkaloids from our plants, this preparation can produce some of the strongest and most fast-acting medicines that we can make at home. Outside of a medicinal context, the same method can be used to extract a more complete profile of flavours and fragrances than can be removed through infusion alone. For this reason, tinctures have found their home in culinary arts as well, as bitters and extracts used to flavour cocktails, cakes and pastries.

As a magical recipe, these bitters can be taken on-the-go to affect your desired intent, based on what the blend consists of and how it is consecrated. Below are three recipes for common magical concerns and my recommended procedure for making bitters at home. Feel free to experiment with these and to develop your own recipes for other kinds of magic once you feel comfortable with the technique. While tinctures and bitters never truly "expire" as alcohol is a preservative, they will begin to lose their strength and flavour after one year, so it is best to use them as quickly as possible – and better yet, to brew a few bottles as gifts!

Makes 300+ doses
Prep time: 10 minutes, plus 2–4 weeks steeping

FOR THE LUCKY BLEND
* 1 tablespoon whole cloves
* 2 tablespoons chamomile flowers
* 1 cinnamon stick
* 1 tablespoon bayberry root
* A small bunch of fresh basil, stems removed
* 350ml (12fl oz/1½ cups) neutral grain spirit (at least 150 proof)

FOR THE ATTRACTION BLEND
* 1 vanilla pod (bean), sliced
* 1 teaspoon cubeb berry
* 5 whole fresh roses
* 1 tablespoon damiana
* 3 whole star anise seeds, lightly toasted
* 350ml (12fl oz/1½ cups) neutral grain spirit (at least 150 proof)

FOR THE PROTECTION BLEND
* 1 tablespoon wormwood
* 2 tablespoons juniper berries
* A sprig of fresh peppermint or 1 teaspoon dried peppermint
* 2 tablespoons motherwort
* A bunch of fresh thyme
* 350ml (12fl oz/1½ cups) neutral grain spirit (at least 150 proof)

1 For any of these blends, first spend time in meditation on the intention for making these bitters. Consider the nature of your specific desire, how you plan to interact with these herbs and what you hope to achieve. Craft a sigil of this intention and trace it onto a bay leaf or piece of unbleached paper using food-safe ink.

2 Before beginning, consider proper astrological timing and, using astrological days, hours and aspects, select the best time to begin. As a suggestion, consider crafting the lucky blend under Jupiter, the attraction blend under Venus and the protection blend under Mars or Saturn.

3 At the proper hour, carefully measure your herbs. If you are using dense roots, barks or berries, consider grinding these finely in a spice grinder or mortar and pestle. Fill a preserving jar with your plants, ensuring that the top 1cm (½in) of the jar is left empty. Slip the leaf or paper with your sigil into the centre of the jar. Fill the jar to the brim with your neutral grain spirit and seal tightly.

Store the jar in a cool, dark place for at least 2 weeks and up to 1 month, turning and shaking the jar every few days.

4 When the bitters are sufficiently infused, strain the blend through a fine mesh sieve and press any remaining tincture from the herbs before discarding. Store the finished bitters in dark glass bottles with dropper caps, keeping any extra stored in airtight jars hidden in the back of the cupboard or pantry. Make sure any bottles or jars are sufficiently labelled. Bitters can be taken 5–10 drops at a time, either on the tongue or stirred into a glass of water, tea or whatever else you like. If you prefer an external application, apply a few drops of the bitters to your wrists or temples and massage into the skin.

Infused Ritual Wine

This recipe and ritual is intended to be used as a template, which can be personalized to your tastes and traditions at home. Depending on your practice and preferences, the herbs here can be adjusted or swapped for those which are more suited to your work. This particular blend of herbs was chosen to represent the seven planetary spheres – bay for the sun, blue lotus for the moon, lemongrass for Mercury, cinnamon for Mars, roses and damiana for Venus, juniper berry for Jupiter and black elderberry for Saturn. However, these seven herbs are also known for being potent and magical in their own right. In the Bible, lemongrass and cinnamon are given as two of the main ingredients in creating the holy anointing oil. Blue lotus and damiana are mild sedatives, used extensively in trance, meditation and visualization. Roses and liquorice are both attractive aromatics, suitable as offerings or assistive in calling spirits and blessings to the practitioner. Bay is a remarkable plant of prophecy and success, and elder unlocks the door to spirits and subtle worlds. As an offering or a ritual tool in itself, this wine is sure to be potent and effective.

While this recipe is just a guideline, it yields an infused wine that can serve as a useful, consecrated standard. Return to this recipe over and over and experiment with altering the ingredients to your tastes and ritual goals. However, it is this author's recommendation that you prepare this brew as instructed at least once, to experience for yourself the way the flavours and effects of these herbs manifest in the finished product, and make your adjustments based on your experience.

Serves 4–6

Prep time: 5 minutes, plus 1 lunar cycle infusing

Cook time: 20 minutes

* A 75cl bottle red wine
* 1 bay leaf
* 2 dried blue lotus flowers
* 1 stalk fresh lemongrass
* 6 dried roses
* 2 tablespoons damiana
* 1 cinnamon stick
* 2 tablespoons juniper berry
* 2 tablespoons elderberry
* A quartz point that has been charged under the full moon

I At the day and hour of the sun (see page 100), or on the eve of the full moon, set a large saucepan over a low flame and gently heat your wine to a simmer. Take your bay leaf and inscribe it using food-safe ink with sigils of your craft, or of the ritual for which you are brewing the wine.

2 Add the bay leaf to your wine first, calling in the prophetic and clarity-giving aspects of the sun. Next add your lotus blossoms, calling in the dreamy, regenerative energies of the moon. Follow this with your lemongrass, which should be beaten with the back of a knife to release its fragrance. This calls in the manifestation power of Mercury, the magician.

3 Follow these with your roses and damiana, for the peace and pleasure of Venus. If you have not worked with damiana or blue lotus before, you can expect a mild sedative feeling, similar to drinking a few glasses of wine. These plants are also known aphrodisiacs, in keeping with Venusian virtue. Follow these with cinnamon, calling in the warm, protective aspects of Mars.

4 Finally, add your juniper and elderberries, for Jupiter and Saturn, respectively. These berries may give your wine a deeper, darker hue and a subtle sweetness. Simmer gently for 20 minutes, and once your wine has infused, strain the wine through a fine sieve and pour into a clean wine bottle. Add your charged quartz crystal to the bottle and seal with a cork for one lunar cycle. If you do not have quartz on hand, other crystals may suffice, but be mindful that some crystals are water soluble and should never be used in food or drink preparation, such as malachite, selenite, desert rose or calcite. If you're at all unsure what kind of crystal you have, do not use it.

5 This wine will be intensely aromatic, spicy, and will assist with entering meditative and trance states during ritual. It should be refrigerated when not in use and consumed within 1 month of brewing.

Love Potions:
One to secure a new love;
One to strengthen an old love

I imagine that when most people think of kitchen witchcraft, this is the kind of work they imagine – a capable, working knowledge of herbs and the ability to distil and concentrate their effects in a way that creates transformative change in our lives. While herbs are certainly a central aspect to kitchen witchcraft, their properties need to be identified, awakened and utilized by the witch if their effects are to be harnessed at all. The recipes here explore the technology of herbcraft through the lens of one of witchcraft's most storied and legendary concoctions – the love potion.

However, the examples of traditional love potions recorded in grimoires are often less than romantic, and sometimes even sinister. In the 18th-century book of French magic *Le Petit Albert*, the author recommends a potion of one's own blood, combined with the hearts of doves, sparrows and swallowtails – all traditional birds of Venus, used in magic to call down her favour. In the *Picatrix*, a number of disturbing love potions are mentioned, variously calling for measures of leopard blood, gazelle brains, human sweat, lapis lazuli powder and a litany of other exotic ingredients and grotesqueries. There are also a number of love potions described during the European middle ages which feature deadly, psychedelic poisons, such as henbane and datura, that are capable of rendering victims immobilized, confused and helpless, leading some historians to suggest that these potions were likely concocted in bad faith, to force a target into marriage through violence and scandal. Regardless of their specifics, these spells all had some basic

mechanics in common – the consecrated potion was to be administered in secret to an unwitting target, delivered directly by the hand of the person who wished to be loved. Our recipes here draw their inspiration from this technology and seek to re-examine the love potion with ingredients that are more accessible, ethical and safe to ingest than those utilized by witches past.

The herbs selected here have been carefully chosen for what they bring to the conversation of love, and what kinds of magical work they are traditionally used for. The potion to secure a new love features the herbs of first romance, corresponding to attraction, flirtation and discovery. Here, in lieu of songbird hearts and human blood, we find traditional herbs of Venus – roses, myrtle and fruit blossoms – infused in a deep-red cherry reduction to produce a narcotically fragrant elixir. For the potion to strengthen an old love, we encounter the herbs of constancy and devotion, which facilitate communication, intimacy and groundedness. However, this blend is not without its romantic flair, as fennel and rosemary are two well-regarded aphrodisiacs. The rest of the herbs in this recipe are used in magic to focus the passions, returning the gaze toward the relationship instead of allowing eyes to wander. In either case, these potions are intended to encourage, not compel, the passions of your companion, and can be administered in a traditional, discreet fashion, or enjoyed willingly by both parties – for what could be more romantic than permitting yourself to be bewitched, heart and soul?

Makes 1 potion
Prep time: 15 minutes, plus cooling
Cook time: 1 hour

FOR THE POTION TO SECURE A NEW LOVE

* 450ml (16fl oz/2 cups) fresh cherry juice
* 3 myrtle leaves
* 1 fresh rose
* 2 fresh apple or cherry blossoms
* 1 sprig fresh lemon balm
* 6 hazelnuts
* 1 tablespoon raw honey (optional)

FOR THE POTION TO STRENGTHEN AN OLD LOVE

* 450ml (16fl oz/2 cups) orange juice
* 1 sprig fresh rosemary
* 3 bay leaves
* 1 tablespoon deer's tongue
* 1 tablespoon poppy seeds
* 1 tablespoon raspberry leaf
* 1 sprig fennel fronds
* 1 tablespoon raw honey (optional)

I To prepare either potion, begin on a Friday at the hour of Venus, at a time when the moon is waxing or full and when Venus has no strong negative aspects. Do everything in your power to immerse yourself in the nature of the work – play happy music that makes you think of love, get dressed up to cook in an outfit that makes you feel worthy of love, or even scrub down your cooking tools in an infusion of rose petals and myrtle leaves – a true Venusian brew.

2 When ready to begin, add the fruit juice to your saucepan and set over a medium flame.

Simmer until the liquid is reduced to 120ml (4fl oz/½ cup) – about 1 hour. Use a mortar and pestle to grind the rest of your botanicals together, releasing their fragrance and relishing the variety of perfumes that arise.

3 When the juice is done, place your ground herbs in a 180ml (6oz) preserving jar along with the raw honey. Pour the hot reduction over the herbs and allow to steep until cooled to room temperature. Consecrate as you wish. Strain the potion and serve as a cocktail mixed with wine, gin, Champagne or your spirit of choice.

Mugwort and Catnip Divination Tea Ritual

Online and in bookshops, useful guides for tea leaf reading abound. Otherwise called "tasseomancy", this practice often utilizes herbs with a double-focus in mind, relying upon them as a brew to enhance our divinatory senses, and also as a tool of divination themselves. For this reason, tea leaf reading is a suitable medium for exploring kitchen witchcraft in that it allows us to examine the role of herbs in magic two ways with one practice. Here, the botanical allies of mugwort and catnip are considered, both for their use as gentle, trance-inducing sedatives, and herbs of divination outright.

If you've never encountered or ingested these herbs before, you can expect them to produce a subtle calming effect, similar to a strong cup of chamomile tea. Nevertheless, for readers who regularly take medication or have existing health concerns, running any new herbs past your doctor is always the best practice. On the palate, mugwort can be quite bitter, but catnip is a plant of the mint family, which has a delicate, refreshing flavour that softens mugwort's edge. For those sensitive to bitter tastes, a spoonful of honey or sugar will go a long way here, as drinking the tea should be a calming, pleasurable experience and the final brew should be adjusted to your tastes. For those who are new to tea leaf reading, the ritual instructions below provide a useful structure for experimenting with this artform yourself. Every witch will find their strengths within a particular divinatory modality, but it's always good to stretch our skills and try our hand at something new once in a while!

Makes 1 cup of tea
Prep time: 2 minutes, plus steeping
Cook time: 5 minutes

* 2 tablespoons dried catnip leaves and flowers
* 2 tablespoons dried mugwort leaves
* 1 teaspoon honey (optional)

I Begin by heating 240ml (8fl oz/ 1 cup) water to a boil. As the water warms, prepare your altar space or another meditative workspace by lighting a candle (plain, any colour you wish) and burning an incense of divinatory herbs, such as hazel leaves, yarrow, storax, black copal, poppy seeds or damiana. You may also choose to burn any remaining mugwort or catnip leaves you have on hand, as the effects of these herbs can be experienced by breathing their smoke as well. If you have any other rituals you normally use to prepare for divination, you may include these here too. If you plan to use any other divination tools, such as tarot decks or pendulums, make sure these are close at hand.

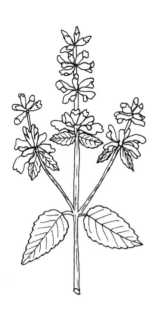

2 Place your dried catnip and mugwort into a tasseomancy cup or regular teacup, and set it on top of a saucer or plate. Set this cup in front of your candle and remove all other light from your space, especially artificial light. When the water is boiling, bring it into your ritual space and pour it over the herbs in your teacup. Sit in meditation while the herbs steep for a full 15 minutes and use this time to focus on drawing forth the intuitive mind and intuitive senses.

3 When the tea is fully steeped, sip the tea slowly while staring into the candle flame. Maintain a gentle, soft focus on the candle, and a gentle, soft focus in your mind on the question you'd like to consider. As you drink, feel the herbs produce their subtle, calming effects as focus and visualization become easier. When there is only the last tablespoon or so of tea remaining in the cup, ask your question aloud, then invert the cup onto the saucer with an audible, finalizing tap.

4 Spend another minute here, paused in gratitude for the answer you will receive, and for the plants as assistants in this work. When you are ready, flip over the cup and examine the leaves left there for your answer.

5 If you are not using a tasseomancy cup or symbol guide to assist you, lean into your intuitive senses and follow your mind's free association with the shapes in the cup, discerning what images they remind you of and what those symbols signify for you. When you are interpreting symbols here, consider both the image's manifest and latent content – what it appears to be, and also why it manifests the way that it does. For example, if you recognize the shape of a wine glass, consider its appearance. Is the glass full or empty? Is it upright or overturned? What feelings or thoughts come to mind when you encounter this symbol and what could it mean in the context of your question? Next, consider why this answer might appear as a wine glass and not a different sort of vessel – a mug, a water glass or a Champagne flute? What is unique about the symbol of a wine glass that would be missing from these other images? What does this unique symbol signify that others could not? These considerations are simple tools, but they may help in discerning the answer you receive.

Cleansing Iced Tea

In modern occultism, the word "cleansing" is used to refer to a very broad swath of magical work. Cleansing rites are often recommended as a panacea, meant to remove and cure all that which is "negative" in our lives and restore the "good vibes" we desire. Many of these broad cleansing rituals rely on the presence of specific ingredients – salt, white sage, rosemary – to do the bulk of our magical heavy lifting, without much attention paid to the specifics of what is being removed and how. If you've experimented with quick-fix cleansing rituals like these and found them to be a bit lukewarm, it makes sense – magic requires certain measures of discernment and intentionality to be effective. However, grounding our work with a deeper knowledge of plant magic and medicine, as well as a more mindful approach to how we target our work, may provide another useful framework for thinking about cleansing magic and how we might engage with it in a more intentional way.

This recipe seeks to cleanse us of stress, anxiety and the subtle effects of these concerns upon the body, by using herbs that provide a twofold benefit through both their magical and medicinal properties. This recipe is meant to help us remove tension and distractions, restore mental clarity, soften anxiety and strip away stagnancy from our minds and bodies. It features two natural and flavourful anti-anxiety herbs, lavender and peppermint, along with herbs that lower inflammation (clover), relieve muscle pain (rosemary, marshmallow), bolster the immune system (lemon) and support the body's detox pathways (dandelion root, fennel seed). Unsurprisingly, many of these herbs are also noted for their use in cleansing magic, with hyssop, lemon, peppermint and rosemary being some of the most popular choices in that regard. The resulting brew has a clean, herbaceous flavour, which stimulates the palate and refreshes the senses – a necessary respite from the restless pace of our lives, conjuring a moment of serenity in which we can truly release our troubles and be cleansed of them.

Makes 4–6 servings
Prep time: 10 minutes, plus chilling
Cook time: 10 minutes

* 1 tablespoon fennel seeds
* 1 tablespoon dandelion root
* 1 tablespoon marshmallow root
* 1 tablespoon crushed peppermint leaves
* 1 tablespoon dried hyssop
* 1 teaspoon dried lavender flowers
* ½ lemon, sliced, seeds removed
* 1 stalk fresh rosemary
* 6–10 fresh heads of red or white clover (optional)
* Honey or sugar, to taste (optional)

I If timing this work to lunar cycles, cleansing magic is best performed when the moon is waning or new. In a medium saucepan, heat 1.4 litres (48fl oz/6 cups) water to a gentle simmer. In a muslin (cheesecloth), combine the fennel seeds, dandelion root, marshmallow root, peppermint, hyssop and lavender. Make sure the bag is sealed tightly so that no herbs may escape.

2 Place the tea bag, along with the lemon slices, fresh rosemary, clover blossoms and honey or sugar, if using, into a heatproof jug (pitcher) with at least 1.4 litres (48fl oz/6 cups) volume. When the water is at a strong simmer, remove from the heat and pour it into the pitcher. Breathe in the fragrance of the infusing herbs and allow to cool to room temperature.

3 Place the tea in the refrigerator and chill for 2 hours. When ready to serve, remove the bag from the tea and wring it dry over the jug. Remove the lemon slices and discard. Add ice to a glass and pour the tea over top, adjusting sweetness if necessary.

4 You should enjoy this drink in a quiet place, free from distractions, where you can allow yourself to stop for a few moments. As you drink, sip slowly and stay with the sensations of your body, noticing how your body responds to the flavours, temperature and herbs of the tea. Take note of any changes that occur in your mental or emotional state and remain in a place of quiet meditation until the drink is complete, allowing yourself to stop and sit with the experience. Any remaining tea can be stored in the refrigerator for up to 3 days.

Chamomile

Field thyme

Big plantain

Roschip

Chamomile

Field thyme

References and Further Reading

REFERENCES:

[1] Ovid, translated by James George Frazer, *Fasti* (William Heinemann Ltd: 1931)

[2] Aristophanes, translated by Eugene O'Neill Jr., *Plutus* (Random House: 1938), line 595

[3] Maslama ibn Ahmad al-Majriti, translated by John Michael Greer and Christopher Warnock, *The Picatrix* (Adocentyn Press: 2010), pp. 266

[4] Alexander Carmichael, *Carmina Gadelica*, first published 1900

[5] Nicholas Culpeper, *The Complete Herbal*, first published 1652

[6] John Michael Greer and Christopher Warnock, *The Picatrix* (Adocentyn Press: 2010)

[7] Orpheus, translated by Thomas Taylor, *The Hymns of Orpheus* (University of Pennsylvania Press: 1999)

[8] Austin Osman Spare, *The Book of Pleasure (Self-Love): The Psychology of Ecstasy* (Theophania Publishing: 1913)

[9] Saint Cyprian of Antioch, *Book of St. Cyprian: The Sorcerer's Treasure* (Hadean Press: 2014)

[10] Orpheus, translated by Thomas Taylor, *The Hymns of Orpheus* (University of Pennsylvania Press: 1999)

[11] Plato, translated by Benjamin Jowett, *The Laws* (Oxford University Press, 1888)

FURTHER READING:

Albertus Parvus, translated by Tarl Warwick, *Petit Albert* (Ouroboros Press: 2013)

Corinne Boyer, *Plants of the Devil* (Three Hands Press: 2017)

Daniel A. Schulke, *Thirteen Pathways of Occult Herbalism* (Three Hands Press: 2013)

Gwion Raven, *The Magick of Food: Rituals, Offerings, and Why We Eat Together* (Llewellyn: 2020)

Hans Dieter Betz, *The Greek Magical Papyrii in Translation* (The University of Chicago Press: 1986)

Harold Roth, *The Witching Herbs: 13 Essential Plants and Herbs for Your Magical Garden* (Weiser Books: 2017)

Hildegard Von Bingen, translated by Bruce W. Hozeski, *Hildegard's Healing Plants From Her Medieval Classic Physica* (Beacon Press: 2001)

Jean Chevalier and Alain Gheerbrant, translated by John Buchanan-Brown, *The Penguin Dictionary of Symbols* (Penguin Random House: 1997)

Johan George Hohman, edited by Daniel Harms, *The Long-Lost Friend: A 19th Century American Grimoire* (Llewellyn Publishing: 2012)

Peter Grey, *Apocalyptic Witchcraft* (Scarlet Imprint: 2013)

Index

Acknowledgements

❋ Endless love and admiration for my mother, Nada Powers, who has been telling me for decades that I will be a famous author someday. You have been the most passionate supporter of this book since day one, and have kept me focused, determined, and with my eye on the prize at every step. I hope you see how much of you there is in the finished product.

❋ Eternal gratitude to Bee Hollywood and Dakota St. Clare, who grant me the honour of working alongside them at Catland Books, and whose support of my work during the process of writing this book will never be forgotten. Your dedication to our shop and community inspires me every day.

❋ Endless admiration for Frances F Denny, Brita Olsen and Joey Popovich of the photography team, who were willing to immerse themselves in the world of the Witch's Feast and lend their brilliant creative vision to this project. Cooking and shooting together as a team was both the greatest challenge of my career and the most fun I've had in decades, and I could never have done it without you.

❋ Special thanks to the entire team at Watkins, who believed in this project and made this dream possible. I am especially grateful to my editor, Ella Chappell, who took a chance on this book and, with the patience of a saint, nurtured it into something greater and more beautiful than I ever could have hoped.

❋ And finally, I send my deepest gratitude and respect to two of my mentors, Sarah Sutherland and Damon Stang, who believed in me, generously shared their wisdom, and inspired me with their passionate love of food and magic – all priceless gifts which I can never hope to repay.